A Place to Call Home

A Place to Call Home

*Immigrant Exclusion and Urban Belonging
in New York, Paris, and Barcelona*

Ernesto Castañeda

Stanford University Press
Stanford, California

Stanford University Press
Stanford, California

Printed in the United States of America on acid-free, archival-quality paper

Library of Congress Cataloging-in-Publication Data
Names: Castañeda, Ernesto, author.
Title: A place to call home : immigrant exclusion and urban belonging in New York, Paris, and Barcelona / Ernesto Castañeda.
Description: Stanford, California : Stanford University Press, 2018. | Includes bibliographical references and index.
Identifiers: LCCN 2017050477 (print) | LCCN 2017055064 (ebook) | ISBN 9781503605770 (electronic) | ISBN 9781503604780 (cloth : alk. paper) | ISBN 9781503605763 (pbk. : alk. paper)
Subjects: LCSH: Immigrants—New York (State)—New York—Social conditions. | Immigrants—France—Paris—Social conditions. | Immigrants—Spain—Barcelona—Social conditions. | Social integration—New York (State)—New York. | Social integration—France—Paris. | Social integration—Spain—Barcelona. | New York (N.Y.)—Emigration and immigration—Social aspects. | Paris (France)—Emigration and immigration—Social aspects. | Barcelona (Spain)—Emigration and immigration—Social aspects.
Classification: LCC JV7048 (ebook) | LCC JV7048 .C37 2018 (print) | DDC 305.9/06912—dc23
LC record available at https://lccn.loc.gov/2017050477

Typeset by Thompson Type in 9.75/15 Sabon

Cover design: Rob Ehle

Cover photograph: Street scene at the Arc de Triomphe, Paris, taken by the author.

*I dedicate this book to all the people
looking for a place to call home*

Contents

Preface

WHEN I LEFT MY HOME IN MEXICO CITY IN 1999 to attend the University of California, Berkeley, I was excited about the opportunity to attend college abroad. The environment was welcoming, and my transition was smooth, but I had not realized how much I would have to adapt. The language barrier was one of the most obvious challenges. Although I had received a good score on my TOEFL (Test of English as a Foreign Language) and I could follow readings and lectures well, I was skeptical about the writing conventions of academic English and had some trouble conversing with my American friends. I found it frustrating being unable to convey complex ideas in English as easily as I could in Spanish.

Mexicans and other Latinos in the San Francisco Bay Area helped me feel understood. I met several immigrants from a region in central Mexico called Los Altos de Jalisco, who worked in the city of Berkeley. Many of them worked long hours in cafés and restaurants and sent most of their disposable income to their families in Mexico. I also discovered that many were undocumented and therefore could not travel back to Mexico to see their loved ones.

Most of them wanted to learn English; some even asked me to teach them. They assumed that learning English was a purely technical process that anybody who knew the language could teach. In their eyes, this process was similar to learning how to use an espresso machine, an electronic cash register, or another piece of equipment they had learned to master after moving to the United States. As a nonnative speaker, I did not see myself as qualified to teach English, so I recommended they look for classes at local nonprofits, including the University. They tried, but it was hard to find English courses that were ongoing and affordable. Furthermore, they worked more than ten hours per day and often at two different jobs. When they described their work schedules to me, I realized why taking English classes was impossible for most of them. Unable to refer them to classes, I became a type of cultural broker, teaching them a few words and phrases whenever I saw them.

The Mexican workers I had come to know had no time to organize, attend meetings, or even to meet socially, beyond playing soccer sporadically. By comparison, as a student, I was active in several student clubs and organizations, and I even founded three student groups. These differences in class, roles, legal status, and social positioning were glaringly apparent, and I saw how these differences influenced the pace at which newcomers integrate into their new cities of residence.

These men and women were confined to low-paying jobs where their co-workers and managers also spoke Spanish. As a result, some had been in Berkeley for many years, yet they spoke rudimentary English or only a few basic phrases. Furthermore, they mainly socialized outside of work with other first-generation immigrants from Mexico. Not speaking English affects migrants' integration into their new cities. They wanted to learn English and enjoy the benefits this would award them.

Anti-immigrant activists often criticize immigrants for not speaking English. To the uninformed, limited English proficiency may appear as a sign that immigrants do not want to integrate. Although it is true that many immigrants lack English proficiency, that assumption is false. There are contextual and structural reasons why some immigrants take a long time to learn the local language.

Understanding the Immigrant Experience

There are a variety of immigrant stories. First- and later-generation immigrants measure the American Dream using different standards. Many adult migrants toil for years to provide an education for their children who, in turn, clamor for social justice and aspire to become middle class. When living for two years on a Latino-themed floor in a dormitory at Berkeley, I met many Latino students who migrated as children or were born in the United States to immigrant parents. They helped me learn about their lives and struggles in the United States. In everyday conversations, some expressed the grievances that their parents could not verbalize when working in the fields or in manual labor. These children of migrants were getting a college education at one of the best universities in the world. They had the opportunity to organize events to highlight their cultural heritage, the injustices faced by their communities, and to voice their political concerns. They often volunteered in programs to help more Latinos attend college. Although we followed different paths and had different linguistic and socioeconomic advantages, we bonded over our shared interests in current events in Latin America and the successes of Latinos and their contributions to the United States.

I came to know my way around the Bay Area and made many friends from extremely diverse backgrounds. In 2003, I moved from Berkeley to New York City to begin a PhD program at Columbia University. When I arrived in New York, I did not know anyone, nor did I know my way around the city. Fortunately, the university provided me with a new community, and after a year or so, I felt at home. Soon I was participating in several graduate student associations and organizing meetings for a group of Mexican graduate students and professionals living in the city.

Although international graduate students may begin to feel at ease living in New York within just a year or two, this is generally not the case for immigrants who work in nonprofessional jobs. As I discovered, it may take them years or even decades to begin to feel like a New Yorker, a process directly related to the problems of language and assimilation already mentioned. For many Mexican immigrants in New York, there is little time to do anything other than work and commute. Socialization is often limited to interactions with people at work and contact with people in their hometown.

I grew up reading about the French Revolution and the Enlightenment. At Berkeley, I minored in French to gain access to another cultural world, just as learning English and studying abroad had allowed me to experience American culture. With the support of two fellowships, I lived in Paris for a year conducting full-time research for this book. Moving to Paris can be a uniquely pleasant experience for some, but it can be quite different for an unemployed immigrant from the global south. Fortunately, I had resources and tools to complete the research I had in mind.

My experiences in having a goal, moving, adapting, and purposely moving again are very common for Americans who frequently move within the United States for educational and employment reasons. Labor immigrants also share this mobility. Yet legal, cultural, and structural barriers vary by level of education, class, and nationality.

This book addresses how various demographic, political, and social arrangements make newcomers feel at home. As I will show, subjective feelings of belonging are as important as objective measures of integration to understand the political and social behavior of immigrants and their descendants. Newcomers are subject to processes of both inclusion and exclusion. However, it is interesting to find out in their narratives what experiences influence immigrants the most as they try to find a place to call home.

Acknowledgments

FINANCIAL SUPPORT TO CARRY OUT MUCH OF THIS PROJECT was provided by the Paul F. Lazarsfeld Fellowship of the Department of Sociology at Columbia University. Columbia's Graduate School of Arts and Sciences provided support for fieldwork abroad during each summer from 2004 to 2009. The Alliance Program's Mobility Grant provided funds to visit Professor Patrick Weil at University of Paris Panthéon-Sorbonne during the fall of 2007. The Mobility Exchange Fellowship of the Alliance Program allowed me to be a visiting scholar at the Institute d'Études Politiques de Paris (Sciences-Po) during the academic year of 2007-2008.

Nicolas Gourvitch, Manuel Guardiola, Xavier Chartres, and Antonio Snyder provided me with temporary housing in Paris as I struggled to secure housing; I thank Abed Alame and the Malattos for trusting me and renting a place in Paris to me. Amy Hsin and Francesc Ortega were gracious hosts during one of my visits to Barcelona and then in Canet de Mar. Anna Ortubia swapped apartments with me, which allowed me to spend time in Madrid. This in turn allowed me to better understand the uniqueness of Barcelona within the Iberian Peninsula. The family of Abdul excelled at the art of hospitality in both Paris and Algeria.

Besides housing and research funds, every publication is the result of a collective effort. I want to thank Patrick Weil, Alexis Spire, Nancy Green, and Pierre Ives Saunier with whom I met and had intellectual discussions in famous Parisian cafés. Patrick Simon and Nancy Foner's invitation to present my work at INED allowed me to do follow-up research in Paris in 2009. The

University of Texas at El Paso provided support to do follow-up fieldwork in Barcelona during the summer of 2011. Research funds from American University allowed me to go back to the three cities in 2017.

Through the years, I have benefited from doing short fieldwork stints in shared sites with skilled ethnographers such as Robert Smith, Leslie Martino, Adrian Franco, Alexandra Murphy, Christian Muench, Bettina Salvioni, Pau Serra del Pozo, Curtis Smith, and Alexandra Delano. They have a way with people, and they make fieldwork an informative, interactive, and social activity.

I also thank the close reading and feedback on previous versions from colleagues at Columbia University; the CUNY Graduate Center's Immigration Working Group; the faculty, fellows, and associates of the International Development and Globalization Interdisciplinary (IGERT) program directed by Joseph Stiglitz at Columbia University; the members of NYLON, a research network based at NYU's Institute for Public Knowledge and the London School of Economics. Tom DiPrete, Ho-Dae Chong, Amanda Czerniawski, Daniel Fridman, Jennifer Jennings, Marissa King, Emine Onculer, Matt Salganik, Delia Baldassarri, David Madden, Randa Serhan, Harel Shapira, Cecelia Walsh-Russo and many others at Columbia provided feedback on the original proposal. At NYU, Hillary Angelo, Melissa Aronczyk, Claudio Benzecry, Ruth Braunstein, Daniel Aldana Cohen, Will Davies, Emma Jackson, Hannah Jones, Jane Jones, Andreas Koller, Monica Krauze, Owen Whooley, Michael McQuarrie, Tey Meadow, Ashley Mears, Laura Norén, Erin O'Connor, Matthew Powers, Anna Skarpelis, Jonathan VanAntwerpen, Grace Yukich, among many others, read draft chapters and related papers. Among the larger sociological community, I thank Chris Bail, Frank Bean, David Cook-Martin, Joanna Dreby, David Fitzgerald, Rene Flores, Norma Fuentes, Roberto Gonzalez, Ray Hutchison, Tomás Jiménez, Jennifer Lena, Nicole Marwell, Cecilia Menjívar, Silvia Pedraza, Victor Rios, Chris Tilly, Van Tran, Jonathan Wynn, Viviana Zelizer and many other friends and colleagues who have provided feedback and support through the years. I stand on the work and example of many academics who have laid the groundwork and provided the analytical and theoretical tools for me to be able to do this work. Science is a collective endeavor, and I am humbled to be part of this community.

Priscilla Ferguson and Angela Aidala provided support and advice during the early writing. Emmanuelle Saada was very patient discussing with me the nuances and particularities of the French and North African cases.

Debra Minkoff and Karen Barkey provided constructive criticism of an early version. Richard Alba and Cathy L. Schneider provided feedback on early chapter drafts. The late Aristide Zolberg and Michael B. Katz read an earlier, and much longer, version of the whole manuscript and provided useful advice and supporting words. Eduardo Bonilla-Silva provided feedback on the introduction and the New York chapter. Ali Chaudhary provided feedback on the introduction. Robert Brenneman provided feedback on the chapter on religion. I owe many insights to multiple anonymous reviewers; their patience and engagement made this book stronger. All errors and stubborn claims remain my own.

I want to thank those who trusted me even before I could provide a clear synopsis of my research. Special thanks to Craig Calhoun, Richard Sennett, and Robert Courtney Smith for their support throughout the years. Chuck Tilly was an exceptionally brilliant, cheerful, and generous coadvisor. Gil Eyal's advising, feedback, intellectual challenges, and suggestions have taken my work to another level from what it would be without his support and intellectual input. I have learned much from him, and from many other researchers in New York City. Thanks to all for bearing with my early drafts.

I especially thank my interviewees, who engaged with me in countless hours of discussion. Their generosity in sharing with me their experiences of suffering and social marginalization made this work possible, and I am afraid that I will never be able to repay them or improve their situation. As is often the case when one does fieldwork for a long time and in multiple locations, I have learned much more about their lives, challenges, and victories than I am able to write about here.

I thank all my research assistants and students at the School of Public Affairs of Baruch College, City University of New York, University of Texas at El Paso, and American University for their questions, hard work, and for sharing with me their family stories of immigration and belonging. Richard Dugan, Jonathan Klassen, Annie Rhodes, Heather Rosoff, Maura Fennelly, Kelley O'hana, Casey Chiappetta, Marcela Maxfield, Margaret Pinette, and many others helped make the prose more readable. I thank all the members of my writing group in Texas. Thanks to all my colleagues at American University and in particular to my Washington writing group: Nicole Angotti, Michael Bader, Taryn Morrissey, Randa Serhan, Kirsten Stoebenau, and Rachel Sullivan Robinson, who helped see this project come to fruition.

Joe Heyman, Howard Campbell, Gina Nuñez, Eva Moya, Oralia Loza, Laura Guerrero and many others in Texas provided support and advice. I thank Alexandra Delano, Miriam Ticktin, and Bastian Vollmer as well as the Zolberg Institute for Migration and Mobility at the New School for Social Research, the Center on Migration, Policy & Society at the University of Oxford, along with American University, for providing support, time, and library access to write this book. I thank Kate Wahl, Frances Malcolm, Marcela Maxfield, and Olivia Bartz for believing in this project and giving it a home at Stanford University Press.

This book would not have been possible without the support of my parents, Ma. Elena Tinoco and Ernesto Castañeda Sr., my sisters Mónica and Claudia and their families, my wife Lesley Buck, and the inspiration and energy brought by my sons Ernesto and Alexander.

A Place to Call Home

1 Context of Reception, Individual Experience, and Urban Belonging

HAVE YOU EVER FELT OUT OF PLACE, LIKE A COMPLETE STRANGER? Have you ever moved to a new city where you do not know anyone? Have you ever lacked a place to call your own? Now imagine all of this and that you are from a country with a different language and customs. When you move to a new country, you must constantly question what locals consider appropriate social interaction. Moving to a new country requires checking your assumptions. You need to be fast on your feet and learn to adapt quickly to a new set of situations considered mundane by locals. As an individual abroad, you have to learn to decode the unwritten rules, norms, and assumptions that are second nature to natives, so ingrained they have become hard to explain. To integrate, you must first explicitly understand your own social norms and the culture that you carry.

Like a chameleon, a successful immigrant has to adapt quickly to a changing environment and play the insider/outsider role as demanded by each situation. This is not an easy task, especially when busy with work and raising a family. Furthermore, migrants deal with constant uncertainty about their economic prospects and about whether the federal government will kick them out or allow them to stay in their new place of residence (Castañeda 2013a; Gonzales 2015; Dreby 2015). Developing a sense of belonging may initially appear as an individual experience and decision, but social, political, legal, and economic conditions shape this process.

Would the same person have similar experiences integrating in different cities? Integration is experienced individually but within the cultural context of the country of origin and their new country. Although resettlement always

1

presents challenges, local dynamics can make it easier, or more difficult, to belong. Cities can either mitigate or exacerbate the process of integration. This book discusses how social processes in different cities have an impact on immigrant inclusion and sense of belonging. It uses a comparative mixed-methods approach to show how immigrants with similar backgrounds and socioeconomic statuses fare very differently in three global cities due to different micro and macro factors. This book shows the interconnections between individual dispositions and historical forces while inhabiting a new city. Employment rates, political participation, the ability to engage in cultural practices, legal status, and interactions with individuals from diverse backgrounds all combine to integrate immigrants. For newcomers, the feeling of belonging is an indicator of policies and practices striving to create a welcoming environment that maximizes immigrant contributions to their new cities.

Immigrant Integration

Migration is the more general term that denotes geographical movement. Migration entails both emigration, leaving your place of birth, and immigration, arriving into a new area. Calling people migrants acknowledges that relocation may be permanent or temporary, that they can move to multiple locations through life, and that people often engage in transnational activities like remitting and keeping in touch with their hometowns. Calling individuals "immigrants" puts the emphasis on newcomers settling down in a particular place. Researchers are also concerned with the second and third immigrant generations, who are most often born in the new place of residence and are citizens; yet, as descendants of immigrants, they may go through processes that categorize them as members of a different race or ethnicity (Castañeda 2018).

The emphasis of this book is on immigrants living in a new city that may eventually feel like home. Immigration scholars use different terms to refer to the process by which immigrants keep ethnic differences or get absorbed into a new place of residence. I use the term *integration* to describe the ability of newcomers and their offspring to interact on mostly fair and equal terms with established city residents. This is a normative goal rather than a description of reality because it presumes equal opportunities and outcomes, given equal merit and effort, in spite of one's culture, religion, or place of birth. In other words, integration means upward social mobility, no residential segregation, intermarriage, and the potential for equal participation in politics and public activities. Unlike assimilation, integration does not imply losing the culture of the country of origin but actually being able to sustain it while also adapting to a new city. This term is also similar to the concept of incorporation—the inclusion of an excluded group into the political structures of a society (Bohrt and Itzigsohn 2015; Bean et al. 2012; Gerstle and Mollenkopf 2001; Aranda 2008). The possibility of integration is important to understanding immigrants' feelings of belonging in the cities where they live.

The term *assimilation* stresses the need for immigrants to become similar or indistinguishable from natives. The term *acculturation* implies the adoption of the mainstream culture and the erasure of the emigrant culture. This is what the Americanization project was in America for decades. Assimilation and acculturation have become negative terms in contemporary social science because they have historically been part of coercive, ethnocentric, or patronizing frameworks. For the same reasons, outside academic theoretical debates, assimilation and acculturation to the majority culture continue to be the desired objective of nativists. Chosen assimilation is not a bad thing when it is a chosen option or happens naturally through time (Alba and Nee 2003), but some immigrants resent it when they have to erase who they are after moving across political borders.

Multiculturalism is an alternative conceptual and political model that celebrates cultural diversity and provides a way to discuss economic and civic equality without presuming a need for cultural homogeneity. In practice, multiculturalism means cohabitation while respecting cultural differences. Still, theorists who posit multiculturalism as a normative goal often overlook the fact that people may see some cultural practices as incompatible with each other or that immigrants may not feel at home despite having adopted the culture of the majority.

Cosmopolitanism is understood by some authors as a noncommunitarian, practical, global citizenship that goes above local particularisms, nationalisms, or identity politics (Vertovec and Cohen 2002). For many, cosmopolitanism is an ideal, an aspiration for the future, a liberal project (Nyers 2016; Balibar 2004); for others, cosmopolitanism is a voluntary and humanistic disposition (Appiah 2006). Immigrants may live what some see as a "practical" or "migrant" cosmopolitanism but often without full rights (Nail 2015). Yet a cosmopolitan identity has usually been accessible only to highly educated elites working in international fields (Calhoun 2002).

The extensive literature on multiculturalism, cosmopolitanism, and immigrant integration shows that it is difficult to settle the theoretical debates between top-down integration and multicultural policies in a purely philosophical manner. We can address the shortcomings of both assimilationist and cosmopolitan approaches by comparing objective markers of exclusion (Koopmans 2009; Waldrauch and Hofinger 1997; MIPEX 2014; Pineau, Waters, and al. 2016; Jackson and Doerschler 2012), while also focusing on subjective meanings and cultural differences between hosts and immigrants. Disgruntled natives are highly vocal, but empirical work is needed to understand how immigrants experience these models in reality.

Contribution and Approach

New York, Paris, and Barcelona are famous for their wealth, monumental architecture, and tourist attractions. These cities also depend on the cheap labor of millions of immigrants, and yet city branding campaigns often omit them. Immigrants are invisible populations that make these cities function. Their lives, struggles, and experiences go unrecognized in many social arenas. Furthermore, the experiences of these migrants in different cities are rarely compared.

Classic work in historical/comparative sociology (Moore 1966; Skocpol 1979; Tilly 1984) shows how placing local issues in a historical and comparative perspective provides information about what is unique about each case and what processes are common across cases. This book considers the subjective experiences of immigrants and then places them in larger socioeconomic and political contexts. It addresses the interactions among laws, stereotypes, and subjective feelings of belonging. It argues that beyond immigration laws and philosophies, social interactions and cultural practices determine integration. This does not mean that government policies are unimportant but that immigrants' subjective perceptions of integration, their experience of belonging, and their cultural practices also matter. This simultaneous approach of material and experiential factors is rarely undertaken to compare immigrant integration in different contexts. Analyzing institutional and individual perspectives simultaneously and comparatively is highly time consuming, but it is good to test and generate immigration theory. Interviewing immigrants throughout metropolitan areas tells us how immigrants see their place in the city. Evidence comes from ethnographic work, as well as interviews with sometimes hard-to-reach populations in migrant sending and receiving communities. This book offers a window into the challenges that international migrants encounter when they leave their homes and adapt to life in a new city.

Pundits, opinion leaders, and anti-immigrant activists and politicians frequently present immigrant culture as fundamentally incompatible with that of the receiving society (Houllebecq 2015; Huntington 2004, 1996; Buchanan 2006; Caldwell 2009; Coulter 2015; Schult 2017). On the other hand, sociologists writing about immigration often emphasize socioeconomic structures, immigration policies, discrimination, and institutional racism as inhibitors of complete immigrant integration. This book describes structural limitations while taking immigrants' experiences into account. The goal is to explain objective structural integration as well as immigrants' feelings of belonging. "Belonging" refers to the sense of feeling "at home" while conducting routine activities like working, socializing, and raising a family with or without the granting of legal citizenship by the state. Being part of a city occurs regardless of legal status, as Galvez writes of Mexican immigrants in New York and their public religious practices:

> While much writing on immigration assumes that citizenship is a condition that begins after the bestowal of the juridical attributes of belonging . . . Mexican immigrants are engaging in political, activist activities which enhance their sense of well-being . . . even while their juridical status remains unchanged . . . Mexican immigrants' involvement in such activities . . . may not register on formal surveys of political activities, [but] it is no less important and real for the people involved. Indeed, it is their engagement and willingness to stand up for themselves and other members of the community they have created that will have the biggest impact on their quality of life in the United States. (Gálvez 2009: 7)

Galvez's work on citizenship brings up all the domains in which people participate in city life despite their lack of residence permits or legal citizenship. Some scholars use the concept of cultural citizenship to refer to participation in urban public issues despite national legal citizenship (Coll 2010). Urban theorists and advocates talk about a "right to the city"; scholars sometimes use the term *urban citizenship* to refer to this participation in city life (Gebhardt 2016; Smith and McQuarrie 2012; Però 2007; Castañeda 2012c). To avoid confusion about legal rights and protections, in this book I use the term *urban belonging*; although others use the term to discuss various related phenomena (Crul, Scheider, and Lelie 2012; Centner 2012), I define it as a subjective feeling of belonging that responds to real social integration that includes economic, political, and institutional integration.

Finding a place to call home may sound mundane and unimportant, but it gets to the crux of the immigrant integration question. Dutch sociologist Jan Willem Duyvendak has done pioneering work on homemaking and immigrant integration in cities (Duyvendak 2011; Duyvendak, Geschiere, and Tonkens 2016). Italian sociologist Paolo Boccagni describes the different emotional and social connotations of "home" in the context of migration and the importance of studying it (Boccagni 2016). Feeling at home is the opposite of feeling excluded or like an outsider.

The Challenge of Difference

Polemicists argue that Latinos are inassimilable because of their religion and because there are concentrations of Spanish speakers in certain areas; similar claims are made about Islam and Arabic in Europe (Huntington 2004; Caldwell 2009). Yet these authors base their arguments on general assumptions and impressions; they know very little about the process of migration and the actual cultural practices of migrants.

Ethnographers document everyday practices, collective traditions, and beliefs (Jiménez 2010; R. C. Smith 2006; Mooney 2009). In contrast, journalists, policy makers, government officials, politicians, and lawyers—those who most often discuss immigration policy in the media—tend to present analyses that overemphasize laws and the state as the main determinants of immigration and incorporation, thus exaggerating the power of the state in managing migration. The state[1] clearly matters because (a) it promulgates immigration laws that create or dispel illegality (Ngai 2004; De Genova 2004) and (b) it treats newcomers in ways that foster or inhibit pathways for social interaction and behavior across its entire population. Furthermore, the challenge of integrating immigrants results from the tension between the idea of homogenous "nation-states" and the universal right of human mobility, both recognized by the member states of the United Nations. Politicians may scapegoat migrants to air economic grievances and advance partisan political disagreements in other areas (Castañeda 2006; Shapira 2013). Often, anti-immigrant speeches and campaigns have more to do with position taking in local political dynamics than with the actual immigrants. Outspoken anti-immigrant voices affect belonging. Yet, established city residents play an important role in integrating immigrants. Therefore, immigrants themselves are the best judges of whether a particular city is predominantly hostile or welcoming.

Comparative Immigrant Integration Research

Previous research compares immigration, citizenship, and social mobility in different places (Hoerder and Moch 1996; Portes and Rumbaut 2001; Reitz 2003; Lucassen 2005; Calavita 2005; Kasinitz et al. 2008; Pedraza-Bailey 1985). Others compare political integration (Alba and Foner 2009; Gerstle and Mollenkopf 2001). Some research has been done on how unsanctioned residents gain access to and participate in the public sphere of the receiving country or on how immigrant groups behave politically when their members lack voting rights or make cultural claims (Koopmans et al. 2005). This book contributes to the growing research that compares policies and contexts of migration and immigrants' belonging across cities in the United States and Europe (Bean et al. 2012; Ersanilli and Koopmans 2011; Alba and Foner 2015; Adida, Laitin, and Valfort 2016; Berry et al. 2006; Abdelhady 2011; Foner et al. 2014).

In rich democracies, the extent, nature, and function of the welfare state varies within different state–society arrangements, historical legacies, and prevalent ideologies. Much has been written attempting to explain the relationships among the welfare state, citizenship theory, and immigration policy (Sainsbury 2012; Fox 2012). Most of these studies stay at the normative, legal, or theoretical level, and, although interesting and important on their own, they fail to connect the macro and the micro by not describing how these citizenship regimes, policies, and regulations translate on the ground. Studies that attempt to reconstruct the elements that bridge the policies of the state and everyday practices include works focusing on the daily practices of governing and regulating citizens and aliens (Somers 2008); the social history of the passport (Torpey 2000); the history of policing foreigners in Paris (Rosenberg 2006); as well as the role of policy makers (Weil 2003), bureaucrats (Spire 2005), and social workers (Fox 2012) separating "worthy" from "unworthy" immigrants, who should be deported and kept outside. Some compare different models or philosophies of integration or criticize this approach (Bertossi, Duyvendak, and Scholten 2015; Alba and Foner 2014). However, there are relatively few studies that link the lived experience of immigrants with government services and policies in cities in different countries. This work starts to sketch what this bridge could look like.

Social Context

Research shows how the context of reception shapes immigrant integration and social mobility. By "the context of reception," immigration scholars mean the place-associated factors that may foster or hinder the integration or successful settlement of recent immigrants. The context of reception and the tolerance of minority cultural practices impact integration outcomes. The context of reception shapes (a) the objective conditions that allow for immigrant integration into their new societies and for opportunities for upward social mobility in the long-term and (b) the subjective feeling of belonging experienced by immigrants in their new cities. Other important factors include asylum and immigration laws, government programs to aid newcomers, employment opportunities, the tolerance of natives toward immigrants, and the density of nongovernmental agencies assisting newcomers (Alba and Foner 2015; Castañeda 2012c; Menjívar 2000; Stepick and Dutton Stepick 2009; Pedraza-Bailey 1985).

A classic example of the effect of the context of reception and administrative treatment is the discrepancy between the experiences of Cuban and Mexican immigrants in the United States. Until 2017, Cubans were immediately welcomed by refugee service organizations; provided with residency papers, work permits, and financial support; and mentored by a strong Cuban community. In contrast, Mexicans, often not viewed as refugees, are denied work visas, and after arrival in the United States, they have to figure out the logistical and economic details of settlement alone or with the help of their social networks (Portes and Rumbaut 2006; Portes and Stepick 1993; Pedraza-Bailey 1985; Pedraza and Rumbaut 1996; Flores-Yeffal 2018). Although many of the first waves of Cuban immigrants arrived with capital and high education levels, the later waves did not necessarily do the same. However, they still benefited from a welcoming context paved by previous waves. Today, Cuban Americans tend to have higher educational levels, higher business ownership rates, and a louder political voice in the United States than Mexican Americans, due to a large degree to the different legal and social treatments and contextual framings that both groups receive. This differential treatment is based on geopolitical reasons rather than "immigrant quality." For decades, Castro's Cuba was seen as an enemy regime, and Mexico as a close US economic partner. Cuban exiles and defectors were offered political asylum until January 12, 2017, but those coming from Mexico are rarely recognized as exiting Mexico for political reasons and governmental failings. Thus, the social context of exit and reception has important implications for the prospects of immigrant groups (Massey 2018; Pedraza 2007).

Experiencing the City as an International Migrant

How does it feel to experience a city for the first time? Are there differences in this experience caused by different types of migration, such as moving from a rural location to an urban area in a different country? How do changes in socialization patterns affect this experience? These are frequent themes of classic sociology, as are the relative anonymity and isolation created in urban life that develops into a blasé attitude and social ennui (Simmel 1971, 1908). Yet they are often set aside, deemed as antiquated and inappropriate in contemporary empirical research. However, these are powerful concepts that help create an understanding of the social psychology of the immigration and integration experience.

This book makes a theoretical contribution by showing how objective conditions and subjective understandings before and after migration affect integration outcomes and the overall well-being of individuals of certain categorical groups (Latinos and North Africans). Objective conditions set the backdrop in which actors operate, whereas personal expectations and inclinations shape how individuals understand their social actions. Therefore, to understand the migration experience and integration outcomes, we have to study agency and structure, political economy, and meaning making simultaneously. I did this by obtaining first-person narratives, mapping their social context by reviewing secondary sources, and observing social actions coming from the individualized embodiment of culture and structure.

Finding a home in a city regardless of legal status is parallel to the experience of early inhabitants of some European cities. Max Weber writes about medieval European cities as the destinations of craftspeople, traveling merchants, fugitive slaves, veteran soldiers, former serfs, criminals, and landless peasants. In these cities, they lived outside the control of feudal lords, kings, and religious authorities. There is an old German phrase, *Stadtluft macht frei nach Jahr und Tag*—"city air makes you free after a year and a day." It refers to the legal principle that a person who lived in the city for more than a year without a lord or employer claiming his or her return to the previous place of residency was free of that previous bond (Sennett 1994: 151). The word *citizen* was originally used to designate the residents of a city, meaning those who, through their daily economic activity, established local residence without the explicit permission of any external authority (Weber 1958; Castañeda 2012c; Castles and Davidson 2000). After the consolidation of the nation-state model, moving across political boundaries has become harder for immigrants arriving in cities today. Even when they remain a year and one day, they are not "free" from the bondage to the state in their country of origin or from the surveillance apparatus of the receiving state. Even today's so-called sanctuary cities offer little protection against federal immigration agencies in the context of generalized deportation campaigns.

Why Select These Cities and Groups?

The United States, Spain, and France all have similar percentages of foreign-born residents: 13.21 percent, 12.13 percent, and 11.72 percent, respectively (OECD 2015). The cities discussed are among the highest magnets for migrants in their respective countries. New York's population is about 37 percent foreign born, Paris's is 20 percent, and Barcelona's is 18 percent (Foner 2013; US Census Bureau 2010; Ajuntament de Barcelona 2017; INSEE 2012).

Although some discourses emphasize the immigrant history of the United States, people tend to underemphasize the immigrant histories of France and Spain, although all three countries have a long history of migration and intercultural exchange (Calavita 2005; Hoerder and Moch 1996). Spain became a major destination for people from Europe, Latin America, Asia, and Africa at the end of the twentieth century and before the economic crisis of 2007. But in fact, the history and national identity of Spain has been clearly marked by centuries of Muslim reign and multicultural cohabitation (Gaïd 2008), as well as by the French invasion of 1808 (Carpentier, Pérez Galdós, and Blanco White 2008) that produced a true melting pot. Spain has large numbers of immigrants from other European countries, to the point where nowadays many small towns with significant British and German populations have elected mayors and city council members of these nationalities (EFE 2009).

Both France and Spain were colonial rulers of Morocco. Therefore, a colonial past has meant bidirectional influence and population flows in all the circuits studied in this book. Shepard defines *decolonization* as when the question of colonialism ends and the immigration question begins (Shepard 2006: 4). Despite apparent differences, the United States, France, and Spain are all countries of immigration, with around one-tenth of their residents being foreign born. However, they differ widely in the ways they frame the expectations, demands, opportunities, and avenues of political voice given to immigrant groups.

Because of economic opportunities, New York, Paris, and Barcelona are among the main cities of destination for migrants in their respective countries. Each flow has inspired an interesting and important body of academic literature, but, unfortunately, the findings and theories proposed for each migratory circuit have not been systematically compared. Comparative work and theory testing across time and place are key for theory building (Castañeda, Morales, and Ochoa 2014; Demetriou 2012; Skocpol 1979; Tilly 1984).

The comparative design of this research shows the effects of different processes, policies, and social arrangements on immigrant incorporation. Like Mexicans and Latinos in general in the United States, Muslims from North Africa are currently the most visible immigrant group in France. As some immigrants themselves say, "North Africans are the Mexicans of France" (Dendoune 2007). In 2006, Spain also had a large number of North African residents—over half a million Moroccans, 40,000 Algerians, and 1,300 Tunisians—as well as Latinos—over 376,000 Ecuadorians, 225,500 Colombians, 60,000 Dominicans, 40,000 Cubans, and 10,000 Mexicans, among others (Rius Sant 2007). Although there are Muslims in New York and Latinos in Paris, they are relatively few in number, and both groups tend to be middle class and relatively socially integrated (Pew Research Center 2007; Bail 2014).

For decades, Latinos have been the largest immigrant and minority group in the United States. Similarly, Algerians have been and are now along with Moroccans and Tunisians, the largest immigrant group in France. These groups represent large immigrant populations who have been in these cities for generations, thereby creating ethnic groups. Both North Africans and Latin Americans are present in large numbers in Spain and in Barcelona in particular (INE 2007), which makes it an ideal city to analyze and compare with New York and Paris. By looking at Barcelona, one can see how much depends on the receiving society and on the context of immigration, as well as on the subjective feelings of belonging, cultural similarity, and relative deprivation of the different immigrant groups (Loch 2009). For example, I found that in Barcelona Latinos expected rapid integration and were disappointed when faced with cultural differences. In contrast, Moroccans did not expect a rapid integration; thus, they were more satisfied with what they found: employment opportunities, a certain amount of upward social mobility, and opportunities for cultural and religious expression. This urban

Table 1.1. Similarities and differences between some national pairs.

	Mexico	United States	Mexico	Spain	Morocco	Spain	Algeria	France
Distance	Proximate		Distant		Proximate		Proximate	
History of migration	Territorial war; a century of migration		Former colony; recent migration		Former colony; recent migration		Former colony; a century of migration	
Majority religion	Catholic	Protestant	Catholic	Catholic	Muslim	Catholic	Muslim	Catholic
Language	Spanish, indigenous	English, Spanish	Spanish, indigenous	Spanish, Catalan, Basque	Arabic, Berber, French	Spanish, Catalan, Basque	Arabic, Berber, French	French

belonging then both shaped and was shaped by daily interactions with other Barcelona residents.

Although geographical proximity explains some migratory patterns, history, and geopolitical forces are more important. For example, many immigrants in France come from current and former colonies. The same is true in Spain, and most recent waves of immigrants to the United States come from areas deeply affected by US military or economic interventions (Mexico, Puerto Rico, the Philippines, Cuba, Vietnam, the Dominican Republic, Central America, Afghanistan, Iraq, and so on). Most Mexican immigrants live in the US Southwest, which used to be part of Mexico. The ways that colonial and national history are understood in the official histories of migrant-receiving countries and migrant-sending countries are often very different. How these differences are either understood and addressed, or ignored in the national public sphere of the receiving country, as well as in the transnational sphere of international relations and diplomacy, plays a significant role in providing further fuel for political, moral, and symbolic contention among newcomers, minorities, and the majority group within the receiving country. A closer look at the histories of these locations provides further evidence for the relevance of these comparisons. Table 1.1 exhibits several important features of comparison between some of the transnational sets studied.

Data and Methods

This book presents a three-city, multiple-group study, in which the key dependent variable is immigrant structural integration, both self-reported and measured. The independent variable is the context of reception, broadly defined. The research design used transnational lenses to show how the immigrants' place of origin shapes immigrant expectations abroad. Multisited ethnography was used to understand immigrants' types of adaptation into the new cities they inhabit. Evidence comes from interviews, surveys, and years of fieldwork in New York, Paris, and Barcelona, as well as in migrant-sending communities in Mexico, Algeria, and Morocco. Fieldwork in sending countries started in 2003 in the Mixteca region in central Mexico, the place of origin for many immigrants in New York. In 2007 and 2008 I compared this migrant flow to that from North Africa to Paris and Barcelona by also doing fieldwork in Algeria and Morocco. However, because of space considerations, this book focuses on New York, Paris, and Barcelona.

I have conducted fieldwork and participant observation within the Hispanic community in New York intermittently since 2003, both while living in the city for seven years and then during frequent ethnographic revisits (Burawoy 2003) since moving away. I conducted ethnographic observation in Paris and Barcelona during the academic year of 2007–2008, as well as brief revisits to Paris in 2009, Barcelona in 2011, and both cities in 2017.

Most interviewees came from the largest immigrant and ethnic groups in each city. Interviewees were mainly Algerian, Moroccan, and Tunisian, as well as Mexican in Paris and Mexican and Moroccan in Spain. Most interviewees in New York had origins in Latin America and the Caribbean. I speak English, Spanish, and French and hired Arabic-speaking assistants for interviews with Arabic speakers.

It is problematic to use traditional random sampling strategies to recruit stigmatized groups and undocumented immigrants (Düvell, Triandafyllidou, and Vollmer 2010). Case studies often recruit mainly through immigrant organizations and generalize from those to the whole population, but most immigrants are not members of immigrant or ethnic associations. Thus, I avoided interviewing immigrants recruited mainly through organizations. I focus on belonging to metropolitan areas, not just to particular neighborhoods with immigrant concentration. Thus, I interviewed people from ethnic enclaves as well as people who lived in metropolitan areas that are not thought of as "immigrant neighborhoods" (Castañeda 2012b).

Close to a hundred students—enrolled in a course I taught at Baruch College of the City University of New York during three consecutive semesters (spring 2009 to spring 2010)—opted to carry out ethnosurveys (Massey and Zenteno 2000) and in-depth interviews with immigrants, after at least five weeks of training on interviewing techniques, safety, and human subjects research ethics. To ease fears that respondents would be traced back to their addresses, many participants were approached in public places, and no identifying information was collected from interviewees. Most student interviewers were bilingual and of immigrant origin themselves. Whenever preferred by the respondent, the interview was conducted in Spanish. Interviewers and interviewees having similar ethnic backgrounds and the ability to communicate in Spanish often increased trust and data reliability. Therefore, it was easier for respondents to talk about their undocumented status and struggles. Unlike the decennial census, we also gathered data on migrant generation, housing, and immigration status. Two research assistants and I conducted interviews in Paris; one assistant was a French citizen born in Algeria, and the other was of Mexican origin. Two Mexican assistants helped me with interviews in Barcelona. I conducted all field revisits alone.

I interacted with Mexicans in the three cities; I interviewed over 100 Mexicans in New York and over thirty in Paris and Barcelona each. I interviewed sixty-five North Africans in Paris, fifty-four in Barcelona, and a handful in New York. I also interviewed other immigrants, mainly Latin Americans: 315 in New York, forty-three in Barcelona, and twenty-two in Paris. Overall, close to 700 people answered my standardized questionnaire (see Appendix). Dozens of informal conversations provided additional information. The purpose was not to create large probability samples but to conduct ethnographic observations and to elicit self-assessments about integration and belonging from different types of immigrants, and to compare them with objective measures and institutional contexts in the tradition of historical-comparative sociology.

The mode age for interviewees was thirty-three. The gender distribution reflected the proportion in the immigrant population. No Moroccan women were interviewed in Barcelona in 2008, but I interviewed a dozen in 2017. In 2008, it was relatively rare for Moroccan women to participate widely in the labor market and public spheres, but more families have been reunited and formed in the last decade, as the second generation comes of age. The Paris sample is majority male despite the population being balanced. Interviewees include members of the first, 1.5, second, and third immigrant generations.

Face-to-face confidential ethnosurveys, with both closed and open-ended questions (Massey and Zenteno 2000; Massey 1987) were written in English and translated into Spanish and French. Respondents were Algerians, Moroccans, and Tunisians in Paris, and Moroccans in Spain. Respondents in New

York were Hispanics, mainly with origins in Latin America and the Carib-bean. These groups represent large immigrant populations who have been in these cities for generations creating ethnic groups through their US-born off-spring, who are often seen as ethnic or visible minorities.

The number of ethnosurveys varied as a function of the different resources and size of the surveying team. The largest waves were in Paris (2007–2008; $N = 65$), Barcelona (2007–2008; $N = 33$), and New York City (2009–2010; $N = 364$). In these specific periods, students, assistants, and I interviewed 364 Hispanic New Yorkers, among them 129 Dominican, ninety-five Mexican, sixty-six Puerto Rican, and sixty-four Cuban, Central American, and South American respondents. Original interviewees in Paris included six Kabyle Algerians, twenty-four non-Kabyle Algerians, twenty Moroccans, and fifteen Tunisians. In Barcelona, thirty-three Moroccans and thirty Latinos were in-terviewed. The religion of the Maghrebins surveyed in Paris varied: fifty-eight Muslims, one Jew, three atheists, and two other. In Barcelona, Moroccans' religion also varied: three reported being Christian, three refused to answer, and twenty-seven self-identified as Muslim. The religious affiliation of Latinos in New York also varied, although the majority were Catholic. More informa-tion on data gathering, basic demographics, and comparative analyses can be found in previous publications (Castañeda, Morales, and Ochoa 2014). In addition to the numbers already given, in 2011 and 2017 I interviewed and interacted with dozens of Mexicans in Barcelona. In 2017, I focused on inter-viewing Moroccan women in Barcelona.

Additionally, in 2009 I surveyed 121 Mexican professionals living abroad through an online survey. Respondents were recruited through email listservs of alumni from Mexican universities, online groups on social media, and snowball sampling. The sample was not meant to be probabilistic; the purpose was to oversample a hard-to-reach Mexican population abroad and to include Mexican professionals, who are often not discussed in general immigra-tion studies.

A drawback of taking a transnational lens is that it often limits the im-migrants studied in a destination to one or a few nationalities. I tried to study immigrants' interethnic relationships and realities in the cities of destination beyond a theoretical ethnic community. However, for narrative reasons, in the book I primarily compare Latinos, mainly Mexican immigrants, in New York (R. C. Smith 2006b) with Moroccan, Algerian, and Tunisian immigrants in Paris (Sayad 2004; Silverstein 2004; Amrani and Beaud 2004) and Mexican and Moroccan immigrants in Barcelona (Portes, Aparicio, and Haller 2016). But, to provide a more comprehensive picture, I also discuss the experiences of other immigrants.

The bulk of the data backing up my claims comes from ethnographic work, from interviews with individuals of immigrant origin, and from conversations with community leaders as well as with immigrants not active in ethnic associational life. I attended dozens of immigrant organizations' events. More specifically, I collected data by lengthy participant observation, including spending countless hours talking to immigrants in these three cities and accompanying them through everyday activities such as going to soccer games, religious services, or grocery stores in their neighborhoods. Insights come from talking to as many immigrants as possible as well as from an embodied understanding, through accumulating miles walking in the city as a flâneur, an outsider observer (Brown and Shortell 2015; Castañeda, Beck, and Lachica 2015). Fieldwork and interviews were conducted in New York (2003–2010) and in Paris and Barcelona (2007–2008), with revisits to the three cities since then, most recently in May 2017.

Factors Affecting Immigrant Integration

The sense of belonging in social, cultural, political, and economic fields is determined by the interaction between the immigrants and the context of reception. The context of reception includes the everyday attitudes of natives, formal and informal markets, residential segregation patterns, local and central state institutions, and avenues for political voice through political organizations (both those that previously existed and those that immigrants created). Thus, the explanatory model is one of multiple causes along a number of dimensions. Well-known institutional features described in the literature provide different contexts in each of these three cities, as summarized in Table 1.2.

In Chapter 6, I discuss the impact the contextual factors in Table 1.2 have on immigrant belonging. The argument is that it is not enough to want to integrate if the context does not allow for it. Nonetheless, as the next section explains, objective conditions do not solely predetermine a subjective sense of urban belonging.

Findings on Subjective Belonging

The Parisian metropolitan area is a social field where changes to habits, cultural practices, and worldview are less often understood as voluntary but are

Table 1.2. Contexts of reception.

Dimension	New York	Paris	Barcelona
Model of integration	Laissez-faire	Immigrants are expected to completely assimilate with little organizational support to do so.	Immigrants are expected to learn Catalan language and culture. Natives are accepting of immigrant cultures.
Cross-cultural context	Multicultural	Monocultural	Multicultural
Religious tolerance (versus secularism)	High	Low	Medium
Federalism (local autonomy versus centralization)	High	Low	Medium
Legitimacy for making claims on an ethnic basis	High	Low	High
Legitimacy of minority religious and cultural practices in public	High	Low	Medium
Approximate population within city limits	8.5 million[a]	2.2 million[b]	1.6 million[c]
Approximate population in metropolitan area	14 million[a,d]	10.6 million[e]	5.5 million[f]
Percentage foreign born	37%[a]	20%[e]	18%[c]

[a] 2016 Population Estimate (US Census 2017a).
[b] 2014 population Paris (Department 75) (INSEE 2017a).
[c] Ajuntament de Barcelona, 2017.
[d] New York-Jersey City-White Plains, NY-NJ Metro Division (US Census 2017b).
[e] Unité Urbaine (INSEE 2017b).
[f] Barcelona Metropolitan Area (Institut d'Estadística de Catalunya 2017).

instead felt to be imperative for acceptance into society. Immigrants in France feel extreme pressure to speak in "unaccented French" and are highly aware of the stigma surrounding Islam, including the wearing of headscarves. Many immigrants internalize their differences as inadequacies and thus experience the negation of their religion as a form of "symbolic violence"—the presumption that French cultural ways are better than those of the immigrants (Bourdieu 1996 [1989], 1991). Algerian, other North African immigrants, and their offspring often reported a strong feeling of alienation and sense of exclusion *despite* citizenship or legal status (Sayad 2006, 2004). Many experience these symbolic exclusions, often over several generations. Part of the dissatisfaction of second and later generation French citizens of Maghrebi origin is the feeling that some pieces of their identity traits are dismissed, minimized, or disrespected. This is due in part to the expectations, values, and beliefs of human equality of mainstream French society, contrasted by discrimination in the labor force and intolerance of public religious displays. Furthermore, contemporary French culture discourages political and social organization around race or ethnicity (Favell 2016).

A longstanding emigrant-sending country, Spain did not become a country of immigration until around the 1970s and took off during the "prodigious decade" from 1998 to 2008 (Portes, Aparicio, and Haller 2016). Its government and society are still adjusting to this new reality (Rius Sant 2007). Barcelona has a shorter tradition of international immigration than Paris or New York. Immigration to Barcelona intensified in the 1990s and early 2000s, an époque of large economic expansion that ended with the economic crisis of 2007 (Castañeda 2012a). Barcelona has inclusive policies at the governmental level, and immigrants have shown their willingness to integrate. Barcelona is not without xenophobia or opportunistic politicians, but immigrants feel at home thanks to multicultural policies in support of Catalan and immigrant cultures, a series of amnesties, and frequent social interactions between natives and newcomers.

The experiences of Latino immigrants in New York lie between those of Barcelona and Paris. Before migrating, migrants often overestimate the economic success they would achieve in the United States (Castañeda 2013a), but they also expect a level of discrimination and cultural difference greater than that which they actually experience. The low number of work visas and residency permits creates legal uncertainty and fear, yet the large numbers of jobs available and the space for cultural expression and nostalgia result in a de facto citizenship despite the lack of de jure citizenship for many immigrants. Although the majority of first- and subsequent generation Latinos in the United States are legal citizens or residents, their prospects for highly paid white-collar employment are negatively impacted to a degree by the profile and stereotypes created by the low education levels of most first-generation immigrants. As in Paris and Barcelona, most new immigrants in New York tend to be at the very base of the social pyramid. America's well-known history of discrimination and inequality based on skin color, facial features, and order of arrival places them at the bottom. As I will show, immigrants themselves and their offspring often internalize these prejudices and see their national origin and immigration status as justified reasons for their low socioeconomic status. The segmented assimilation (Portes and Zhou 2003) of immigrants and their children into a low class strata makes their children classify themselves—or be classified—as aggrieved minorities. Yet, this segmented assimilation could even be interpreted as a symbol of overall integration and a feeling of belonging, *despite* the economic stagnation of some later generation Latinos, because it takes a particularly American form. As Robert Smith (2014) argues, Mexican youth assimilation into black culture may provide a pragmatic manner to acculturate into America as a youth and experience higher mobility as adults.

The aim of this book, though, is neither to prove nor disprove *segmented assimilation theory* or *neoassimilationism,* two influential camps in the contemporary sociology of migration (Portes 2007; Alba and Nee 2003; Bohrt and Itzigsohn 2015; Portes, Aparicio, and Haller 2016; Bean et al. 2012; Bean, Brown, and Bachmeier 2015; Telles and Ortiz 2008). Instead, this book takes a big-picture look at a number of contextual factors and large social dynamics while taking a procedural approach to integration by looking at the everyday understandings of migration by immigrants themselves. The approach is more Weberian, looking at large social change patterns and the *verstehen*—the meaning making of particular actors. This approach is also similar to Znaniecki's "humanistic coefficient" approach (Castañeda 2017) and compatible with phenomenological approaches that take structural issues into account simultaneously. Giddens's structuration theory and Bourdieu's concepts of capital habitus and field inspire the dual attention to agency and structure.

I hope that after reading this book, readers will have a better understanding of how a particular context of reception will have an impact on the "objective" possibilities of integration based on legal and labor market realities, as well as a "subjective" feeling of belonging. This homemaking and sense of being at home is what I refer to as *urban belonging.* This feeling is ultimately individual, so it will depend on personal biographical trajectories and intersectionality. Yet some critics focus too much on identity issues as if identity was purely a personal decision, fashion, or taste. Historical legacies, social boundaries, and national origin will largely affect the probability for an individual assigned to a categorical group to feel—or not—this urban belonging. I contribute a sociological understanding of immigrant integration from the point of view of the migrants themselves in a way that incorporates structural factors as well as social-psychological understandings. Although, clearly, what the natives think, and do, about immigrants matters; the host society does not completely determine immigrant self-worth and sense of belonging. Immigrants have agency in creating a home (Coll 2010), and their emigration, family, and community experiences also shape their self-understanding (Fernandez-Kelly 2008) and urban belonging.

2 New York

Jobs but No Papers

DANIEL, A MEXICAN IMMIGRANT WITH WHOM I DEVELOPED a friendship and kept in touch with for a dozen years, retells his story of family chain migration that brought him to New York:

It was not my plan to end up living in the Big Apple. My father was born in a small town in the state of Puebla, Mexico. In 1953, he was part of the last waves of migrant workers to come to the US under the Bracero program. He enrolled as an agricultural worker, with the intention of learning more about the new agricultural machines and techniques used in this country. In the early 1970s, he came to New York City because it was the destination of family and friends from his hometown in the Mixteca. Yet, my father used to tell me how hard it was to find tortillas at that time. He told me that he felt so happy every time he met another Mexican. Most of the Spanish-speaking people in the East Village, where he used to live, were from Puerto Rico. Soon after, one of his brothers joined him in New York. After a few years, my dad went back to Mexico. Then my older brothers moved to New York in the late 70s and early 80s, and by the time I was born, almost all of them were living and working in New York. Since I was four years old, my parents and I used to come every two or three years to visit them, but there was never the intention, or at least I never thought, that I would end up living in the Big Apple. However, by the time I finished high school, three of my older brothers went to Mexico. They had the idea of bringing all of us to the US. They convinced my parents to do so, and as a minor, I had to come along. After moving to New York, I enrolled in classes of English as a second language (ESL) classes in the CUNY system.

I was the only Mexican taking them, and I made friends especially from Asia. (Daniel, thirty-six, New York, 2014)

Daniel recounts how his move to New York took place within a family decision-making process set in a larger social context that included social ties connecting Puebla and New York. Today, Daniel knows how to navigate through the New York metropolitan area; he has learned English and has made many friends of different ethnic, class, and religious backgrounds. He graduated from Columbia University. He is a New Yorker in all regards but on paper. He has been waiting for his green card for over a decade. His student visa has now expired, and he could not find a business willing to sponsor his working visa during the economic crisis of 2008. He was a couple of years too old to benefit from Obama's Deferred Action for Childhood Arrivals (DACA) program, so he is currently unable to work in the formal economy. He started a couple of businesses. Nonetheless, he cannot plan for the long term, and he is constantly worried about the risk of deportation.

Juana,[1] a restaurant owner, told me, "I am not a legal citizen, but I feel I am American. I have lived here [in the Bronx] for twenty-two years. My son was born here," as she pointed in the direction of her teenage son who was at the restaurant counter helping her. Juana continued, "I have not gone back since I left. I do not know what is happening in my hometown of Puebla, Mexico, anymore. I now feel that my place is here" (August 2009). This conversation took place in what looked like a typical Italian-American small pizza joint, but along with pizza slices, this one also featured an extensive Mexican food menu. Although Juana displayed all the signs of being culturally Mexican, she felt like a New Yorker, and she saw no intrinsic contradiction in this. She and her son are bilingual and bicultural. She cannot vote because she is not a citizen, and her son is a citizen but too young to vote; nonetheless, one of the restaurant walls, otherwise empty, prominently displayed a picture of President Obama celebrating his election. Although not yet eligible to vote, they deeply care about American politics. Despite her undocumented status, Juana felt a belonging to New York City over any other place; I call this urban belonging.

When I told her that I was from Mexico City, Juana said she remembered visiting it when she was young but that she did not like the busy and crowded feeling of the Mexican capital, or its potential for robbery and violence. She told me how much safer she felt in the Bronx and in New York City overall.

In contrast to her sleepy hometown, she said there were many more economic opportunities in New York. I asked her how the economic crisis was affecting her restaurant. She said that although the number of customers had decreased, she would keep at it and weather the storm. *"No hay de otra,"* she said, which translates to "There is no other option." This was not the first time she had to overcome major challenges. Juana then said, "Even with the crisis, people keep coming to the restaurant looking for jobs, telling me they arrived two or three weeks ago from Mexico." I asked if they could find work in that economic climate. "Yes, they will get jobs as dishwashers for four dollars an hour. This is very little money but still more than they could earn in the Mixteca region of Mexico, so they keep coming but less than before," she concluded.

The woman's son wore a T-shirt of an American heavy metal band. His experiences in high school and the perceptions that his teachers and peers have of Mexicans will influence his path. Whether he finishes high school and attends college will determine whether he integrates into the American middle class or into its underclass.

These experiences of urban belonging and legal exclusion are common for the thousands of Mexicans and Latinos who live, study, and work in New York City. They speak Spanish and engage in cultural celebrations and public events. They feel attached to New York neighborhoods; they work to pay their expenses and send money to family in their places of origin. Although often socially invisible to other New Yorkers, they experience urban belonging and are assimilating culturally while maintaining their traditional cultural practices. However, many are in a legal limbo that has a negative impact on their further integration into New York because it is harder to plan for the future. Thus, they often hedge their bets between the city they reside in and their place of origin, for example by building houses in Mexico and delaying buying real estate in the United States.

History of Migration

National Context

Unlike Spain and France, in the sixteenth century the United States was not a colonial power but a series of European colonies.[2] What is now the United States became densely populated only in the last couple of centuries. As in other parts of the New World, colonizers and the diseases they unknowingly brought with them killed much of the indigenous population living on the

Eastern shore. The armed newcomers displaced most of those who survived. As a result, the European settlers quickly ended up outnumbering the natives. Therefore, the United States of America is indeed a country of immigrants, and the country has portrayed itself as such, especially following the 1960s (Zolberg 2006; Gabaccia 2010). John F. Kennedy popularized the vision and phrase of *A Nation of Immigrants* in his book of that title (Kennedy 1959). This reconceptualization as both the home of waves of immigrants and a nation with its proper culture and political goals constitutes an "American paradox" in the celebration of an immigrant past and the frequent demonization of contemporary immigration (Pedraza 1996).

According to Aristide Zolberg (2006), the United States is a "nation by design" because immigration policies have been used as nation-building tools based on national and racial preferences. Recurrent nativist movements have not been rare, precisely because despite its ethnic and cultural diversity, the United States has been very successful in creating a common national identity. There is ample room for immigrant groups and subcultures to exist in the American social landscape without really threatening the future of the United States as a state and a political union. Despite this great achievement, nativist groups and official histories have long tried to give closure to the era of immigration and to stop defining the United States as a country of immigrants. Zolberg notes that the United States declared itself as no longer a country of immigrants as early as 1930 (2006: 9). Anti-immigrant activists now talk about how their immigrant ancestors came to this country "legally," but this is anachronistic because legal migration is a relatively new concept, and it was indeed easier to immigrate to the United States in previous centuries. The post–civil rights, politically correct argument of those against immigration is claiming to accept the United States as a diverse country whose residents are the descendants of immigrants and slaves but one that is now closed to contemporary immigrants for economic, cultural, or religious reasons. This narrative justifies the emphasis on "securing the border" (Nevins 2010).

History of Migration to New York

In a 1897 case (*In re Rodriguez*), U.S. courts declared Mexicans to be white for naturalization purposes (FitzGerald and Cook-Martín 2014). Thus, the US Census Bureau has tried not to racialize Hispanics/Latinos; instead it treats them as an "ethnicity" whose members can belong to different "races" (see

Castañeda 2018). Therefore, "Hispanic" and "Latino" are officially a multi-racial pan-ethnic group (Okamoto 2003; Mora 2014). These labels assume a common culture and language among people from many different nation-states and immigrant generations (Espiritu 1992). Immigrants often had limited contact with conationals from outside their region of origin before migrating. For example, many of the immigrants from the Mixteca region I studied had very few interactions with people from other parts of Mexico before moving to the United States. Therefore, recently arrived immigrants tend to primarily identify with people from their own place of origin, then with those from the same country, and only later with a larger Latino "community."

For decades the term *Hispanic* most often referred to a person of Mexican origin living in the southwest (Guzman 1971), but as Mexicans have moved to new destinations, including New York, the term has widened to include Mexicans and other Latin American groups, which are now almost everywhere in the United States (Massey 2008). The US Census Bureau estimates based on the American Community Survey that there were 57.5 million Hispanics in the United States as of July 1, 2016, and over 36 million of them are of Mexican descent. The majority of Hispanics are US-born. Despite common perceptions, the majority of the foreign born are in the United States legally. The US Census estimates that around 17.8 percent of the overall United States identifies as Hispanic.

Hispanics in New York were often thought of as predominantly Puerto Rican, but in the last decade Dominicans and Mexicans have each become as numerous as Puerto Ricans. People from the Dominican Republic living in New York are, for the most part, documented—although many recent arrivals are not. Many Mexicans in New York benefited from the Immigration Reform and Control Act (IRCA) amnesty in 1986 and are now legal residents (R. C. Smith 2006). However, subsequent Mexican arrivals are likely to be undocumented, as is the case for many Central and South American arrivals in the last thirty years (Lobo and Salvo 2013; Bergad 2013; R. C. Smith 2006; Jones-Correa 1998; Lacomba 2016).

Mexicans live in New York because there is demand for their labor in both extremes of the labor market—from delivery boys to traders with experience in Latin American markets. Mexicans in New York come from all social classes, and many have relatively high levels of education (Suro 2005), including hundreds of Mexican professionals and students enrolled in institutions of higher education. They come from various parts of Mexico, though a majority come from the Mixteca region, which connects the states of Puebla, Guerrero, and Oaxaca; the next largest sources are Mexico City and the State of Mexico (R. C. Smith 2006; Massey, Rugh, and Pren 2010, Smith 2013). Many Mexicans in New York have indigenous roots, and their first languages are Mixtec, Zapotec, Mayan, or Nahuatl.

It is impossible to enumerate all Mexican-origin residents in the New York metropolitan area at any given time. This is due to new immigration, return migration, and migration of Mexicans within the United States, as well as overcrowded housing, long working hours, undocumented status, and the desire to stay under the radar (Nuño 2013). According to the latest decennial census, there were 319,263 Mexican-origin individuals living in New York City (US Census 2010). If one includes all five New York City boroughs, plus Long Island and northeastern New Jersey, the count nearly doubles to 607,503 people (Bergad 2013). There is evidence that some migrants went back to Mexico after the financial crisis of 2007 (Parrado 2012; Massey 2012; Passel, Cohn, and Gonzalez-Barrera 2012). Still, some estimated the number of Mexicans in New York to be over 750,000 in 2008 (Hellman 2008). According to the Mexican Consulate, there are around 1.2 million Mexicans in New York City (Semple 2010). This last estimate is partly based on applications for *matrículas consulares*, or consular identification cards (Massey, Rugh, and Pren 2010; Suro 2005) and the population served by the Mexican consulate in New York City. Regardless of the actual current size of this population, Mexicans are one of the fastest-growing groups in New York City, mainly due to a high birth rate (Bernstein 2007; Nuño 2013; R. C. Smith 2006). Thus, Mexicans are projected to become the largest Hispanic group in the city by 2025, surpassing Puerto Ricans, Dominicans, and South Americans (Bergad 2013; Lobo and Salvo 2013). According to the 2010 US Census, 28.6 percent of New York City's population is Hispanic. In 2014, the New York–Newark–Jersey City metro area had close to 5 million Hispanic residents, the second largest concentration of Hispanics in the country, second only to the Los Angeles metropolitan area.

East Harlem, also called "Spanish Harlem" or "El Barrio," is a neighborhood that has served as an arriving path for multiple waves of immigrants; southern Italians in the 1930s were able to recreate many of their social and religious practices on these streets (Orsi 2002), as did Puerto Ricans after the 1940s (Bourgois 2003, 55–65; Dávila 2004). Lately, Mexican, Central American, and West African immigrants have arrived to East Harlem. In the early

2000s, El Barrio seemed like the center of the Mexican community in New York. In 2014, the number of Mexican inhabitants and businesses continued to grow. Some landlords report preferring Mexican renters because they say they pay the rent on time, do not want to cause any trouble, and show a "do-it-yourself" attitude when it comes to dealing with emergencies and apartment repairs (Thompson 2007; Fuentes 2007). Despite the many outward signs in Spanish Harlem pointing to a large Mexican community, this is a very diverse neighborhood (Castañeda, Beck, and Lachica 2015), and Mexicans are widespread throughout the New York metropolitan area (Bergad 2013).

The Migration Process and Experience

When I asked over a hundred Mexicans in New York why they had migrated specifically to New York, the most common answer was because of family members who were already living there (family reunification and social networks, as discussed in the literature). In a very common response from the 1.5 and second-generation Mexicans, Vanessa, twenty-seven, said, "My father knew people here in Staten Island, New York; therefore, here is where we decided to reside." Jessica, twenty-five, said that it was because her parents had always heard that New York City had the most opportunities and the best education. She said that her family lived in Texas for a year, but it was too hard for her parents to find a job, so they moved to New York. Joseph, thirty-four, also went to Texas first and stayed with family but ultimately moved to New York. Gerardo, thirty-six, said, "There were fewer immigration officials here at the time." The latter two examples show that not all migration is direct; people may move to different places between and within countries (Besserer 2004).

New York was attractive to middle-class interviewees because of the size of its business, cultural, and diplomatic sectors. L. C., who was born in Thessaloniki, Greece, says she first moved to New York because her father was a Mexican diplomat transferred to work at the UN headquarters in New York. Jorge, a forty-seven-year-old songwriter from Mexico City, said he moved to New York because he is a fan of John Lennon who used to live in the city. Christina, twenty-five, said that it was because of "hearsay, New York is the place to be, the City of Dreams."

I also asked, "Do you think your life is better as a result of living in the United States?" Ninety percent of respondents answered yes while highlighting employment and education opportunities. Some elaborated on this, claiming, as Mario, a forty-one-year-old man from Puebla, said, "It is much easier to make a living here than in Mexico." Gerardo, thirty-six, born in Mexico City, said "Mexico didn't offer me the same opportunities as New York." Roberta, forty-two, said, "I am fulfilling my dreams of becoming a nurse." Jinet, twenty-six, a hairstylist who came from Mexico at fifteen, said, "Yes, I have been able to work and sustain myself here."

Nonetheless, it is not all rosy. Many interviewees point to the bittersweet life after migration. Is life better as a result of living in the United States? Ignacio, a thirty-six-year-old busboy from Chilpancingo, Guerrero, answered, "Yes and no; yes, I can afford to raise family and live comfortably. No, because I am far away from my extended family, and I miss Mexico and the open space." Misael, a thirty-seven-year-old waiter from Acapulco, Guerrero, said, "In some ways yes and in others, no. It has been mostly for my children, and their education." Jorge, the songwriter said, "Yes, it is better economically but not emotionally." Javier, thirty-three, a cook and student from Chiapas, said, "It's a struggle, but yes, it is better. Everything is easily accessible, and there are opportunities everywhere." Mazola, an eighteen-year-old woman, says, "At least I'm surviving." Many pointed to the opportunities but also to the rush, stress, and constant hustle to survive and get ahead in New York City.

New York is not the panacea that many imagined. Many also miscalculated the cost of living in the city and the emotional toll of living apart from their families in Mexico (Castañeda and Buck 2011; Castañeda 2013a; Martinez 2016). Many interviewees became disillusioned with the contrast between their expectations before migration and the rough immigration realities. For Jose, a thirty-two-year-old cook, it is not better because "New York means more work." For Carlos, a twenty-seven-year-old man from Guanajuato, life in New York "seems tougher." For Jorge, a twenty-nine-year-old construction worker, life in New York will be better "when I get my legal papers."

Social Integration: New Yorkers' Openness to Multiculturalism

> *There is a lot of opportunity here, and I like the mixture of people in NYC.*
> **Ricky, a second-generation youth from the Bronx**

Most often, locals and immigrants find it possible to cohabit peacefully and productively. This happens most successfully in large, diverse cities such as

New York, but it can be more difficult in smaller suburban and semiurban communities such as the Hamptons, in Long Island, New York, where locals are less accustomed to the presence of the latest wave of newcomers (Dolgon 2005; Castañeda and Beck 2018). Natives and newcomers may engage in contentious politics, with each side defending its prerogative to exist within a given cultural domain.

There is a social distance between natives and immigrants—especially those newly arriving and those from stigmatized groups—but this distance is often overcome by the third generation, and ethnicity is overtaken by other characteristics such as class, gender, and education as a predictor of success (Kasinitz, Mollenkopf, and Waters 2004; Kasinitz et al. 2008). Furthermore, propinquity at work and school allows for many acquaintances across categorical groups (Castañeda 2018). Nevertheless, it is true that many new immigrant Latinos do not want to be noticed because they lack papers. Fearing deportation, they prefer to live in relative anonymity and not to draw attention to themselves (Hellman 2008; Thompson 2007).

The everyday pressure to conform to a mainstream culture in the United States is less intense than it is in France, but, although most undocumented Latinos are able to find employment, their access to social services, quality housing, and leisure time is rather limited. Their lack of documents and the resulting low wages, difficult working conditions, and dearth of benefits create economic and legal marginality (Castañeda 2013a).

In cultural terms, as in large American cities with considerable immigrant populations, in New York, incorporation is mostly left to the immigrant (Bloemraad 2006b) and is, to a great extent, voluntarily striven for given the attractiveness of American popular culture. Incorporation is sped up due to the global presence of American television, movies, and music industry. A culture of migration, social remittances, and transnational spheres that provide a certain superficial familiarity with the United States before migration aids the process (McMurray 2001; Quinones 2001).

In view of its history of tolerance of religious and ethnic communities, the political culture of the United States provides a political voice to immigrants; first through voluntary associations, such as hometown associations (Waldinger 2015), local community organizations, or local boards, and then through elected office and political appointments (Kasinitz, Mollenkopf, and Waters 2004). Access to public officials is not perfect, but it can channel energy through certain political avenues (Marwell 2007). As generations of politicians and spokespeople have shown, in the United States it is possible to have caucuses, representatives, and organizations such as the National Association for the Advancement of Colored People (NAACP) or the Mexican American Legal Defense and Educational Fund (MALDEF) to speak on behalf of minorities and immigrants. Lately, the Hispanic media and the Catholic Church have become important supporters of undocumented immigrants' rights and have supported their campaigns and marches for legalization (Fitzgerald 2009b).

In the United States, migrants, including undocumented ones, act as de facto citizens in the sense that they contribute to the host country through their labor, social security contributions,[3] sales and income taxes, consumption, food, music, and culture, as well as political actors. Hence, despite the legal and economic vulnerability of many, Mexicans are part of the newest New Yorkers. At the same time, New York City allows immigrants to maintain ties to their native country. Those immigrants then become more at home and more American. Juana and her son had lived in the Bronx for only two years and already felt like New Yorkers. They know their neighbors, and they work, communicate, and play soccer with others. It is this tolerance for diversity that makes people from different backgrounds want to come together (Foner 2013; Kasinitz et al. 2008; Sassen 2001).

Institutional Integration

Entering the United States outside of official ports of entry has been a centuries-long practice. In fact, entering through Ellis Island or Angel Island in California was a simple administrative procedure that prevented only a small percentage of Europeans from entering the United States, and most of the sorting was done preboarding by the shipping companies transporting the immigrants (Daniels 2004). In contrast, being allowed to pass through official customs entry points as an immigrant, seasonal worker, or even as a working-class tourist today is harder than ever, especially when coming from developing countries with a recent tradition of being immigrant-sending countries. Xenophobic campaigns to paint undocumented migrants as lawbreakers are easy to accomplish in any place and time and they often help political entrepreneurs get into office, but they leave symbolic scars on newcomers and hosts.

Today, the United States has a love-hate relationship with Mexican foreign-born residents. On the one hand, it has become quite acceptable to complain about illegal immigration and criminal elements coming from Mexico and calls to protect the border (Castañeda 2014), as exemplified by the anti-immigrant speeches of Donald Trump and others. Mexican immigrant bashing can be partly due to scapegoating, xenophobia, and political opportunism. It can also be due to the ingrained sense of the importance for the respect of the rule of law, paired with the lack of familiarity with both historical and contemporary immigration realities (for example, how hard it is for Mexican workers to come legally to the United States today and how comparatively easy it was for European groups to immigrate before 1924). Subsequent changes in immigration law have used either racist or numerical quotas limiting the number of people who can immigrate legally from Mexico, China, India, or the Philippines without family members who are US citizens.

On the other hand, on average, American citizens are quite tolerant in their everyday interactions with individuals who have different origins, accents, and levels of education. Alexis de Tocqueville famously contrasted this democratic demeanor to the strong emphasis put on social status and aristocratic background in old France. Given its history as a settler colony, the United States has mastered the ability to create political unions, even if contentious, out of people from different religious and ethnic backgrounds, as inscribed in the motto *E Pluribus Unum*. The plural point of departure acknowledges important cultural differences and is thus compatible with the practice of multiculturalism and the political integration of immigrants. Unity is created not only by gradual assimilation and religious tolerance but also by the belief in core ideals of equality and democracy. Therefore, US cities are open to immigrants both socially and institutionally.

Exclusionary legal and speech acts can occur along with processes that foster inclusion. Individuals can both express anti-immigrant policy preferences and have close relationships with individual migrants (Lou Dobbs, Jeb Bush, Donald Trump, and many others actually are married to immigrants). Rhetorically, nativists make the argument that they are only against "illegal" immigrants, but because they are unwilling to give them amnesty or create a way for them to become documented, they are, in effect, against the most visible immigrant groups who carry on the stigma of having undocumented members in their families and communities (Castañeda 2018). Claims about human rights and equality in principle are often overshadowed by historical inequality along categorical lines, structural racism, openly racist and nativist discourses, the inactions of liberal citizens, as well as by what Eduardo Bonilla-Silva (2006) calls racism without openly racist attitudes.

Integration Models and Context of Reception

Without being as explicit about it as Canada or England are, the United States has a multicultural citizenship regime. This de facto multicultural liberal system coexists alongside a de jure system that leads to some immigrant detentions and the expulsion of some immigrants, causing major traumatic effects for their families and communities (Castañeda and Buck 2011, 2014). Yet the United States has a "liberal citizenship regime" (Peled 1992). Immigrants are permitted to keep their cultural practices, and integration occurs gradually through generations; ethnicity does not preclude citizenship (Brubaker 2004). Generations of Americans have been transformed by the legacy of the civil rights movement. Although not as open about it as Canada (Bloemraad 2006b), the United States values multiculturalism (Lacorne 2003), even if this model has faced criticism from conservatives.

Yet justifying anti-immigrant views under the guise of respect for the rule of law has become widespread. Beyond xenophobic reasons, a new wave of nativism at the national level has appeared mainly due to political opportunism, ideological struggles, economic insecurity, and different designs for the future of America (Castañeda 2006, Shapira 2013).

Some argue that these nativist anti-immigrant attacks create a process of reactive formation among immigrants (Portes 2007), meaning that because they have been singled out as different, Latinos and others (regardless of their nationality or legal status) may actually seek to further differentiate themselves from the mainstream society. Some point to a downward assimilation of dark-skinned Puerto Ricans and Dominicans who may be racialized and join an African American underclass (Portes and Zhou 2003; R. C. Smith 2006; Dávila 2004; Fuentes 2007). Immigrants from Puerto Rico and the Dominican Republic have faced a racialization that pushes them into a dichotomy between "black" and "white" that is much less nuanced than it is in their homelands (Levitt 2001).

The long-term impact of the racialization of Mexicans, as well as Central and South Americans, in New York remains to be seen. If we want a promising future for these New Yorkers, avenues for education, legalization, and higher-paying jobs must be opened (R. C. Smith 2006). Success and integration depend on local neighborhood and school contexts as well as on access to residency papers. Furthermore, acculturation into black urban culture during youth may not necessarily mean downward mobility in the long term, as is assumed by the segmented assimilation theory, but it may constitute another way into the American mainstream (Smith 2014).

Federalism and State–Immigrant Relations

The U.S. federal system allows for immigrant mobilization and incorporation to happen at the local level. Activity at the neighborhood, town, city, county, and state level is the bedrock for relevant national coalitions to eventually emerge. Hispanic politicos can start their career in a state far from Washington, D.C., and still have an impact in national politics whether or not they run for national office. Although Washington, D.C., is important in setting national immigration guidelines, more recently states, counties, and even cities have increasingly attempted to regulate immigration by passing laws in regard to employment, housing rentals, and local policing agreements with immigration authorities. Given the multilayer patterns of state–society relations, immigrants also interact in many different ways with federal authorities and with local authorities, sometimes pitting one against the other. The federal government is in charge of immigration law, and, until recently, state and local officials did not deal with immigration enforcement. Recently, many police departments have become deputized immigration agents, and misdemeanors, such as jaywalking or receiving a traffic ticket can result in deportation (Golash-Boza 2015). Such cooperation varies state by state and particularly with the so-called 287 g agreements that legally delegate immigration enforcement to local authorities (Armenta 2015). Anti-immigrant actors support programs like these after what they see as the inaction or limited capacity of the federal Immigration and Custom Enforcement agency (ICE) to capture and deport every individual who lacks documents.

In contrast, many police departments and officials prefer to rely on the cooperation of immigrants as community members who would willingly approach the police for protection, to report crimes, and to cooperate in investigations. New York City has mostly maintained this avenue of cooperation with immigrants.

New York prides itself on being a city of immigrants from all corners of the world, as symbolized by the Statue of Liberty and the Ellis Island museum. City governments most often cater to this reality. City Hall is happy to celebrate its historical welcoming of immigrants, and has an Office of

Immigrant Affairs. Fittingly, in 2008 then Mayor Michael Bloomberg signed Executive Order 120 mandating that services and paperwork be conducted in any language through translators and translations of official documents. In 2015, Mayor de Blasio launched a city ID, partly to document undocumented New Yorkers.

New York City is a sanctuary city; it effectively grants amnesty in everyday life to most immigrants, yet racial profiling exists and has a greater impact on those with stereotypical indigenous, black, or Arab features than on those with white and Asian phenotypes. Some Mexican immigrants have also complained about poor police treatment, and 23 percent of Mexican immigrants interviewed had negative views of the police. This partly derives from the mistrust that migrants have of the police in Mexico. Jose, a twenty-eight-year-old waiter from Mexico City, said he does not trust the police. But Mario, a twenty-year-old waiter also from Mexico City, said, "Police here are better than where I'm from." Still, Ricky, a twenty-two-year-old, second-generation man born in the Bronx to Mexican parents and who works in an office supply store, said, "Cops always pay extra attention to young minorities." Ignacio, thirty-six, a kitchen helper from Chilpancingo, believes that police "discriminate against Latinos, especially Mexicans." Guadalupe, a twenty-five-year-old woman who arrived in New York at age sixteen, said, "They are racist. No one will tell me otherwise. They don't even let you talk if you need help. I would never even look at them in the eyes." Vanessa, a twenty-seven-year-old student who came to New York as a child, said, "It's ridiculous, racial profiling; it's racist and stupid." G., a construction worker from Mexico, said, "I try to avoid them. Sometimes they harass us for no reason." Isabel, a forty-seven-year-old hairstylist, said, "I have never been personally mistreated, but I have a lot of friends who have." Yolanda, a forty-two-year-old woman working in the service industry, said, "I have had numerous run-ins with them over the years; I don't like them." Eddie, a thirty-eight-year-old carpenter, said, "They look at minorities as if they were criminals, and half of them are minorities themselves." Maria, a thirty-three-year-old hairdresser, said, "They protect us, but I am scared because of my background. They are hard on Mexicans." Cesar, a twenty-six-year-old Puerto Rican born in New York, said, "They discriminate and are hard on us all the time. I have been arrested because I looked like someone else, even though I had been working all day." "They are good but harsh," said Dona, a thirty-year-old woman, who sells food in the streets of East Harlem. She complained of the many times the police have forced her to move her cart, or when the police have taken the food she was selling because she does not have a permit. Thus, sometimes there are tensions between policing goals and informal economic activities like selling ice cream or tamales on small moving carts.

Political Integration

Avenues for Political Voice along Ethnic Lines

Since the institutionalization of the civil rights movement in the United States, it is acceptable, if not expected, that groups will organize politically and socially around ethnic, cultural, and even racial lines. The inclusion of spokespeople in the political system diffuses many groups' collective claims and may actually moderate the claims of other disadvantaged groups while fostering patron–client relations between elected politicians and their various ethnic communities (Marwell 2007; Dávila 2004). Unfortunately, this began happening at the same time that cities lost much of their fiscal base, due to "white flight" and neoliberalism (Wacquant 2008), which made winning political offices in cities a relatively "hollow prize" (Katz 2008: 85).

Nonetheless, as Michael B. Katz (2008) pointed out, the symbolic victory of gaining ethnic representation at the government level also reduced symbolic boundaries between blacks and whites, thus decreasing grassroots contentiousness by incorporating some of the leadership into the state. Politicians of ethnic origin may also become city-, state-, or even nationwide representatives as part of multiethnic, multiclass coalitions that use inclusive universalistic discourse (for example, Fiorello LaGuardia, Antonio Villaraigosa, Barack Obama). Therefore, the American system is a priori open to representativeness, cultural difference, and equality once groups and individuals are able to overcome, by themselves, their initial exclusion and economic difficulties, as has occurred historically with Catholics, Jews, "white ethnics," and to some degree African Americans (Alba 2009).

The United States has come a long way in creating a model and establishing real-life accommodations to make room for African Americans, as well as for Latinos, Filipinos, and other minorities, providing them with consigned avenues through which to voice their political claims. This has resulted in a large co-opting of radical groups and demands, along with the incorporation of minorities into urban and national politics. Thus, immigrant political integration and participation is a result of previous struggles, victories, and setbacks.

Paths and Contexts of Immigrant Political Participation and Contention

The life chances of Latinos are still behind those of whites (Massey 2007). Yet tolerance of differences and avenues for meritocratic advancement open some doors for minority individuals. Mexican and other Latino leaders with a national and international profile serve as models of achievement to immigrant leaders in New York and inspire hopes for their own future inclusion. The election of El Pasoan Carlos Menchaca to New York's City Council in 2013 broke this glass ceiling for the New York Mexican American community. I witnessed early discussions among community leaders on whether to back Menchaca and volunteer for his campaign. I was present at a meeting of community leaders where they discussed the issue and then agreed that they should not see his youth or sexual orientation as issues and that he should be supported as a member of the Mexican community. He was elected, and he has been vocal about the concerns and needs of the Mexican community, as well as those of his other constituents.

A prime example of Latino political institutionalization is the National Association of Latino Elected and Appointed Officials (NALEO), which is "committed to promoting the advancement and policymaking success of Latino elected and appointed officials." According to NALEO (2007), there were 3,743 Latino elected officials in 1996 and 5,129 in 2007, with twenty-four Latinos in the US House of Representatives in 2008 and three in the Senate. By January of 2010, there were 5,739 Latinos serving in elected office nationwide (NALEO 2010). Most of these numbers had increased by 2014 (NALEO 2015). Yet it was not until 2017 that a Mexican American woman became a federal senator: Catherine Cortez Masto, a third-generation immigrant from Nevada. This shows the discourse and possibility of representation amid few actual examples and real underrepresentation. Nonetheless, immigrants in New York are better represented than those in Paris and Barcelona. (See Table 2.1.)

Collective Voice and Social Movements

Puerto Ricans used to be concentrated in El Barrio (East Harlem), Bushwick, and in other neighborhoods where they had considerable political influence (Dávila 2004; Marwell 2007). Many have moved out to other neighborhoods, states, and the suburbs. Dominicans are concentrated in certain neighborhoods in northern Manhattan, specifically in Washington Heights, and are also very well organized politically (Kasinitz, Mollenkopf, and Waters 2004).

Table 2.1. Latino politicians in the United States.

Office level	1996	2007	2010	2014
Federal representatives and senators	17	26	24	31
Statewide officials (including governor)	6	6	7	9
State legislators	156	238	245	294
County officials	358	512	563	547
Municipal officials	1,295	1,640	1,707	1,766
Judicial/law enforcement officials	546	685	874	878
School board/education officials	1,240	1,847	2,071	2,322
Special district officials	125	175	248	237
Total	3,743	5,129	5,739	6,124

Mexicans in New York City are currently seen as the group "coming of age" (R. C. Smith 2006b) and still lack political influence equal to that of Puerto Ricans or Dominicans; unlike these groups, Mexicans are not concentrated in particular neighborhoods but dispersed throughout the New York metropolitan area (Castañeda, Beck, and Lachica 2015).

Although undocumented Latino immigrants prefer to keep a low profile to avoid problems, enduring poor working conditions in exchange for an expected better future, the children of immigrants are often vocal, active, and politicized.

There have been some important instances of collective action, especially in reaction to the Sensenbrenner law proposal, which would have further criminalized undocumented migrants and people providing help or religious services to them (Pulido 2007). Marches against this law on May 1, 2006, in New York and around the country resulted in a record number of participants in the immigrant rights marches. Aspiring New York City and statewide politicians made an appearance in those and following May 1 marches and rallies; they meet with Latinos during campaign time to secure the future votes of those who they believe will one day become citizens. To many, these marches marked a renewal of the immigrant rights movement and Latinos becoming an important voting bloc; however, it also created a backlash from white nationalists.

Welfare Provision: Access to Government Services

According to the national myth, which carries on in the libertarian tradition of the frontiersmen and the cowboys, the United States is a country of rugged individualism. Yet another traditional view, which goes back to de Tocqueville, is that Americans are known for their civil associations and ethnic mutual aid societies (Moya 2005), as well as philanthropic and religious groups that provide relief to the poor (Katz 1996). The United States is a de facto welfare state because significant sums of money are spent on social services, entitlements, and other provisions (Baldwin 2009). Nonetheless, among rich countries, the United States has relatively low welfare expenditures and less emphasis placed on decreasing inequality than most Western European countries. This has increasingly been the case since Reaganomics and neoliberal economic and fiscal tenets have become popular among policy makers, pundits, and public opinion (Davies 2017). Economic inequality has risen sharply in the last thirty years, and entitlement programs and services are often the first things to be cut in times of economic crisis (Volscho and Kelly 2012).

However, as Ira Katznelson (2005) documented, there was a time when large social welfare, employment, and housing programs helped the children and grandchildren of European immigrants. After the Great Depression, important government aid programs, such as the GI Bill, access to subsidized home mortgages, and construction subsidies for the burgeoning suburbs and housing subdivisions helped working-class ethnic whites raise their standard of living and enter the middle class (Gans 2017; Coontz 1997). In fact, the history of the interventionist welfare state goes back even further to the turn of the twentieth century, when reformist politicians, social activists, social workers, and social scientists aimed to intervene on behalf of poor immigrants who dwelled in tenements living in extreme poverty (Ward 1989).

Recent decades, however, have seen a major decrease in the public and private support of social welfare and in collective efforts to help individuals who are supported by the state. This has deeply impacted African Americans, Puerto Ricans, and immigrants who arrived recently, with the important exceptions of political refugees from "enemy regimes." But in recent years, the support for refugee resettlement has dwindled, and even the policy giving asylum to Cubans has ended.

Not only has effective welfare support for new immigrants decreased, but services such as health care have also become less accessible for many undocumented immigrants nationwide. In New York City, however, everyone, regardless of immigration status, has access to medical services and other social services. Nonetheless, the high cost of living and the low salaries of nonunionized service sector jobs make it difficult to save and secure a path to the middle class (Thompson 2007).

Although welfare policies have changed over time, there are certain historical constants in the country's position that explain these changes. As social historian Michael B. Katz writes,

> Relief, or welfare, rarely has had a humane, effective alleviation of suffering as its primary goal. Anxieties about social order and discipline, worries about labor supply, resentment of taxes, and political ambition all have fueled relief policy. In fact, political ambition has driven the supporters of relief as well as its critics, for American urban politics has always been about "the distribution of goods and services." Ward politicians used outdoor relief to cement loyalty. Local manufacturers depended on it to sustain their workforce during slack seasons. (Katz 1996: 37).

Access to welfare programs in New York is both temporary and conditional and is sometimes tied to political support and patron–client relations, but it does work as an avenue for immigrant incorporation (Marwell 2007). The United States has a long history of providing national and local services to specific immigrant populations. These programs are amplified in some localities due to patronage politics, acting as an avenue for the political incorporation of immigrants.

Permanent residents and legal immigrants have access to most public services in New York. Undocumented migrants can attend public schools and pay local tuition at the City University of New York, a victory won by immigrant student activists, including Angelo Cabrera. But, it would be false to say that Mexican immigrants in New York move to the city to abuse welfare programs. On the contrary, many Mexican immigrants prefer not to use the welfare programs which they or their citizen children are eligible for, in case they may be blamed or deported for using them incorrectly. For example, Liza, who was born in California but was raised in Chihuahua, moved back to the United States and found that she qualified for a number of welfare programs, given her income. She did not apply for a while because she felt stigmatized for not speaking English. When she applied later on, her citizenship was questioned by the authorities. Researchers have found similar underuse of social programs by immigrants in other parts of the country (Schmalzbauer 2014). As Jennifer Van Hook and Frank Bean demonstrate, Mexican immigrants have lower welfare dependency rates than both native and other immigrant groups, even when controlling for immigrant status and other variables (Van Hook and Bean 2009).

When Mexicans in New York were asked, "Have you ever been helped by the government?" answers often included enrollment in public schools and financial aid but little beyond this. Undocumented immigrants have very little access to government programs and services besides public education. Citizens have access to more programs but these programs are also limited.

Economic Integration

> With enough work here, you can do anything. My family is able to have a better lifestyle [after migrating]. They know that if they work hard enough, they would be able to have a decent time when they are old. That would have never been possible in my country.
>
> **M., twenty-three-year-old Mexican man who arrived in New York at the age of seven**

A popular perception spread by political speeches is that most Mexicans are undocumented. Many Latinos and brown-skinned individuals are framed as "Mexican" in a racializing manner. Yet the majority of Latinos in New York are citizens, legal residents, or visa holders and can work legally. As my interviewees often say, "*Venimos aquí a trabajar*" ("We came here to work"), and, despite sporadic, symbolic, but terrorizing raids and deportations, for the most part they are able to do so (Thompson 2007). Even the undocumented Latinos living in New York, who cannot vote, have what I call "economic integration," because most are employed. It seems that being able to work, even when the jobs are low paying, undesirable, or low status, helps first-generation Mexicans maintain a better integration with their host society (Fox 2004) than that of unemployed French of Maghrebi-origin as discussed in future chapters.

In contemporary America some citizens are citizens de jure but have no access to jobs or security (Somers 2008), whereas there are other residents who have access to jobs but not to voting rights or juridical security to protect them from being deported. Many nonimmigrant American citizens, who enjoy both employment and political rights, are either oblivious to this reality or directly benefit from the cheap labor of these disenfranchised groups with partial rights.

Subjective feelings of inclusion, economic incorporation, and upward mobility are distributed in different ways depending on individual habitus and trajectories. Labor market participation is crucial to understanding urban belonging and manifests in different outlooks and trajectories. I identify three main groups.

The first category is made up of *the content*: successful immigrants who either have achieved upward social mobility or are happy with their status, especially in relation to their life and economic standing prior to migration or to the status of their parents. Miguel, a twenty-two-year-old Dominican who lived in Bushwick, Brooklyn, reflected on his eight years in Brooklyn, "I would say we live more comfortably here than we did in the Dominican Republic. We live in a nice apartment building here in Bushwick. There aren't any problems with heating, electricity, or running water. There really isn't anything for us to complain about [sounding really sure]. I would say we have everything we need" (speaking in the spring of 2010). Miguel feels accomplished and rather happy with his experiences and outcomes. This group of content immigrants includes the first-generation immigrants, who compare their new lives to worse economic or political conditions in their countries of birth, as well as immigrants who have achieved social mobility and professional success. H. C., a thirty-two-year-old ophthalmic assistant who came with her parents to New York as a seven-year-old girl, said, "I'd been given opportunities in this country that I know for a fact I would not have received had I remained in Honduras. I am now bilingual and working on my third language. The quality of life and the resources that are made available to me in the USA are tremendous compared to what my country of birth had to offer."

The second category comprises *the struggling*: immigrants who are still at an early phase of immigration and their final place and assessment of the immigrant experience is still to be determined. This group compares the amount of leisure time back home to the demands of long hours of low-paid work in their new places of destination:

> I have two years living in Washington Heights, and life is worse here than over there [Dominican Republic]. Here, I don't have time for anything. See, I am twenty-one years old, and I have no time for anything. It is all work and more work, lots of stress. No, I do not have many friends; the only people I know is the people I work with; two of them are from the same hometown as mine. I sometimes see them, but there is not much time for that. (Juana, twenty-one-year-old Dominican, New York, spring 2010)

One interviewee went to college, despite her status as undocumented, and graduated; because she cannot get a job in the formal economy for somebody with her qualifications, she currently tutors high school students and helps them prepare to take college entrance exams. Others describe their struggle to make ends meet given their low wages and the high cost of living of the New York metropolitan area. Juanita, an undocumented single mother, mentioned working seven days a week, "I wake up at 3 am to make the churros, then sell them, then babysit and clean neighbor homes." Many others also underlined their heavy workloads, long schedules, and low pay.

The third category is the *underclassed*: those immigrants who have become downwardly mobile, both socially and economically (in terms of income or in professional or symbolic status), and those who are the children of immigrants who have been racialized and have faced what Portes and Zhou (2003) call "downward assimilation" or "assimilation into the rainbow underclass." Legal status plays a big role in determining opportunities, social mobility, and wages. They reject their low position in the labor market and drop out of the formal economy altogether. Philippe Bourgois describes the lives of some Puerto Ricans who did not make it in the legal economy either because they lacked the cultural capital or because they felt that the menial jobs given to them minimized their personal worth and earned them no social respect. Bourgois' informants found a new place and source of respect in the informal economy by selling crack in a New York neighborhood in East Harlem. As he stressed, these drug dealers have previously held numerous jobs in the legal economy, yet they "had deeply negative personal experiences in the minimum wage labor market due to abusive, exploitative, and often racist bosses or supervisors. They see the illegal underground economy as not only offering superior wages, but also a more dignified workplace" (Bourgois 1989).

Latinos in New York are in all of these three situations. We asked, "What do you think about your social position in the United States; your place in American society? Do you have room to move up in society?" Among the content we have Monique, a forty-year-old Mexican American born in Southern California now working in human resources in New York, who said, "I am a middle-class American, proud of my heritage and grateful to live in the US where I can combine both heritages and bring the best forward." Talking about the intersection of ethnicity and class, Milly, a thirty-six-year-old secretary from Atlixclo, Puebla, said, "If I can get a good job and earn good money, buy a house and a nice car—my skin color won't matter as much. Being a minority is not as bad as being a poor minority." Kelvin, a sixteen-year-old second-generation Mexican, was one of the few to believe in meritocracy: "If I work hard, I'll make it." Eddie, a thirty-eight-year-old carpenter, said, "Anyone can become what they want here; you have to work very hard though." J. R., a twenty-year-old stock boy born in New York to a Colombian mother and Mexican father, felt he "would have a better position once I have my degree." Ricardo, a sixty-one-year-old maintenance worker from Guadalajara, Mexico, said, "I am content." Jorge, a thirty-one-year-old man from Puebla, said, "I am a chef. That makes me proud."

In contrast, many see their situation in a less rosy way, often because of the lack of papers. Selina, a twenty-eight-year-old woman, answered about her social position, "How can an illegal think about social positions?" Evelyn, a twenty-six-year-old Dreamer, said, "I have no rights; illegals don't have rights." Maria, a thirty-three-year-old hairdresser from Tepalcingo, Puebla, said she was "not sure where I fit" within US society. Jeannette, a twenty-two-year-old bookkeeper born in Queens to Dominican and Mexican parents, said, "I don't think I fit into our society and its concerns, and this is why I don't vote." Jasmine, a thirty-year-old hotel house cleaner from Guadalajara, said, "I don't think I will move up a lot." Yolanda, a forty-two-year-old service worker from Chinantla, Puebla, said, "I am not involved in society at large," and saw her social status as "very marginal." Olivia, a twenty-three-year-old hairstylist, said her status "won't improve unless I am able to become a resident." Jorge, a forty-seven-year-old factory supervisor who played the guitar and sang at bars and restaurants, said, "I have no papers; I am working class." Jinet, a twenty-six-year-old hair stylist, said, "Hard to move up because of my papers." For Ignacio, a thirty-six-year-old Mexican busboy, "Being illegal keeps me from being a member of society." Jose, a thirty-two-year-old cook, considers his status "low, no social status in the US." Carlos, a twenty-seven-year-old migrant worker from Guanajuato, qualified his social status as "low; the bottom rung." Pablo, a twenty-three-year-old unemployed Mexican immigrant, said, "They consider me a criminal all the time." Some still have hope for the future. Maria, a forty-eight-year-old laundromat attendant from Tehuacán, Puebla, said, "I want my children to be successful. I don't care much about my status at this point." Dona, the thirty-year-old Mexican street food vendor, said, "I'm poor but with dreams."

Interviewees were asked about their biggest concerns about the future. For Daniel, a twenty-year-old Puerto Rican man born in East Harlem, it was "finishing school and getting a degree." For Milly, a thirty-six-year-old secretary from Atlixclo, Puebla, it is, "getting my degree and finding a place of my own." J. V., a thirty-year-old Mexican man who had lived in New York for fifteen years, said his concerns were "family and job security. I want to own a house someday." Ignacio said his main concern is "making sure my kids have a better chance for success than I did, opportunity."

Many of these interviews happened soon after the economic crisis of 2008. Margarita, a forty-two-year-old housekeeper from Puebla, was worried about "the situation of the economic crisis and that I will get laid off." Jose, a twenty-eight-year-old waiter from Mexico City who arrived in New York at age twenty, was concerned about "getting old poor." Daniel, a twenty-eight-year-old restaurant worker from Oaxaca, Mexico, was concerned about "getting old and not enjoying the fruit of my hard work in Mexico." Amparo, a fifty-one-year-old manicurist from the city of Puebla who has worked in New York for over thirty-two years, dreams of "making enough money to return to Mexico and that my son lives a good life." Edwin, a taxi driver hopes to make "enough money to move to Ecuador." For Mario, a twenty-five-year-old pharmacist from Santiago, his main concern was "finishing my house in the Dominican Republic." Gildardo, a thirty-six-year-old Mexican storeowner, hoped to "make enough money to send my kids to college." The plans for Bradley, a twenty-three-year-old college student born in Harlem of Puerto Rican and Haitian parents, were "finishing school and making enough money to get out of Harlem. I am most worried about finding a good job, especially in this economy. I don't want to stay in sales all my life; I want to eventually have a career in public relations."

In the shorter term, a common concern is "making a lot of money to send home," said Miguel, a twenty-eight-year-old Mexican waiter who has been working in New York for three years. Another common concern is family reunification. For Fabiola, a thirty-one-year-old server from the port of Veracruz, her main concerns are "my daughter and my parents. I'm worried about living here while she is little." She has not seen her young daughter in five years. Jinet, twenty-six, is worried about "not being able to go home or to bring my child here." Joaquin, a forty-two-year-old Dominican truck driver, hoped to "be able to bring my older kids from the DR so that they can get an education and also work here so they can support themselves." Leandro, a twenty-one-year-old Dominican studying at CUNY with a student visa, looked forward to "becoming a permanent resident." Jen, a thirty-one-year-old Dominican legal assistant who arrived in New York at age twelve, said her "biggest concern for the near future is being unable to cover law school expenses when I start attending classes."

Jorge, a twenty-nine-year-old construction worker from Puebla, feared "being deported." Jessica, a twenty-five-year-old college student and tutor from Mexico with an expired tourist visa, was concerned about "being caught by the immigration services [ICE]." Encarnación, a twenty-six-year-old housekeeper, also feared deportation. Gavino is a twenty-two-year-old head chef who moved to New York from Mexico at age seventeen; his number one hope for the future is"getting my green card." The same goes for Juan, a twenty-six-year-old Ecuadorian busboy who arrived in New York at sixteen. Olivia, the hairstylist, also worried about "being able to stay here." Joseph, a thirty-four-year-old waiter from Puebla, wishes to "get papers so I can go back and visit my sick mother." Guadalupe, twenty-five, was concerned about "not being able to obtain the proper papers for the future and provide a better life to my daughter. I am in the process of having my papers fixed. I want to obtain a professional job and earn the money I should."

Some immigrants still believe in the American Dream, some have achieved it, others are trying, and others live at bottom of New York society.

Conclusion: The New New Yorkers

When asked, "Do you consider yourself more of a New Yorker or Dominican?" Rafael, a thirty-five-year-old Dominican working in wholesale store inventories, stressed the impact of the social context on his identity: "It really comes down to where I am at the time you ask me. Because I am in New York right now, I feel like I am a true New Yorker; but every time I go back to the DR, I feel Dominican." This brief exchange shows that to feel ethnic, to live in an immigrant enclave such as Washington Heights, and to keep strong ties and identification with the country of origin—in other words, to be transnational—does not necessarily mean that the person cannot also feel like "a true New Yorker." Compared to other contexts, New York allows for this binationality. Especially for Dominicans in New York, the immigration transition is eased by a large, concentrated, and dense community in neighborhoods full of ethnic businesses and organizations.

Many Mexicans in New York work in the service sector, but many are also highly accomplished professionals, artists, and business owners. A fifty-year-old Mexican man, married to an American-born wife, and who owns an architecture firm in New York said,

My wife and daughter are here, also my firm. Belonging is something so subjective. It does not matter where we are; as long as we are safe, we are "home."

As this example shows, financial success along with physical safety and cohabitation facilitate urban belonging. Immigrants in New York are able to get
jobs and integrate socially, which helps them quickly identify as New Yorkers.
The well-being of some others is negatively affected by the lack of papers and
safety nets and the high cost of living, but it is aided by the liberty to keep
religious and cultural practices alive while simultaneously integrating to New
York and American society.

3 Paris
Few Cultural Rights

DUE TO AN EGALITARIAN PRINCIPLE, in France there are few official publicly available datasets on poverty, well-being, or health outcomes by race, ethnicity, religion, place of birth, or immigrant generation; hence, the importance of gathering original data to assess immigrant integration. Soon after I moved to Paris to conduct research for this book, I talked for three hours with a Berber from Tunisia in a café in Belleville, a neighborhood in eastern Paris. He told me that he did not feel *chez lui* (at home) in France and that his home is in Tunis, where he wants to retire and spend the rest of his life. Despite living in France for more than seven years, speaking French, and working as a baker, he said that he was constantly reminded of his immigrant origin and that he did not feel welcome. He claimed that due to discrimination, after his old lease was up, he was unable to find housing and had to move in with his sister who lived two hours outside of Paris.

Popular and academic discourses around migration and ethnicity in Paris put an emphasis on the *banlieues*—urban areas surrounding Paris proper (Wacquant 2008). Most *cités*—public housing communities—are located in the *banlieues*. *Banlieue cités* are stigmatized as dangerous, undesirable places and are avoided by middle-class Parisians (Castañeda 2012b; Misra 2017).

While visiting a Parisian housing project (*cité*) in the morning, one can see the peaceful green common areas with a few women and children carrying out their daily activities. In contrast, late in the evening, activity increases as students, the unemployed, and those returning from work come out to socialize. Some gather extra cash any way they can, which often means selling marijuana on the streets. Most of those selling drugs in the *cités* do not choose this trade willingly but do it because they have few employment alternatives (Bucerius 2014). This observation would seem to give credence to the common idea expressed by Parisians and politicians that there is a divide between those who wake up early to go to work and those who wake up late and rely on welfare. Yet things are more complex than simply an individual moral issue.

In a bar next to a housing project in a *banlieue* south of Paris, I interviewed Ahmed, a forty-three-year-old Algerian French man. His father had worked in postwar France and sent remittances to his own parents in Algeria. He also sent remittances to the Algerian National Liberation Front (Front de Libération Nationale, or FLN) when the war for independence began in 1954. Although his father had worked all his life in France, he did not have many assets. Access to public housing was essential for him to make ends meet. His children were born and grew up in these housing projects and had scarce job opportunities. His father spoke imperfect French, and, beyond a few words and phrases, Ahmed did not speak Arabic. Ahmed had visited Algeria only once, when he was forty years old. He was raised Muslim and said, "I am a believer, but I do not practice the faith." When I asked him if he saw himself as Algerian or French, he answered: "[Legally speaking] I am French. I have the same rights as the white Frenchmen. But I am Algerian. My parents come from there. And look at me; I do not look French, now do I?" (Ahmed, February 6, 2008).

Although Ahmed had been born and raised in France, did not speak Arabic, and had visited Algeria only once as an adult, he still identified culturally and racially as Algerian. He largely attributed this to his physical appearance. He felt excluded by those who did not see him as "a true Frenchman" and seemed to have internalized this racism. In fact, Ahmed had made a virtue out of necessity, believing it was completely his choice to identify primarily as an Algerian and secondarily as French. He knew there was a cultural tension in claiming to be both French and Algerian, which are two identities that Parisians consider mutually exclusive. Even so, he still emphasized that he had the same legal rights as any other French person and thus had the right to live in public housing and receive disability support from the state after having an accident at work.

He openly told me that, after his accident in the workplace, he worked in the black market and in the traffic of illegal products, including drugs. He claimed to have customers who came from all over Paris because "my stuff is top quality." He stated that he was "not made for school," that he did not like to "slave away for others" as his father and mother had done, and that he had no access to a decent job close by anyway. Indeed, following the urban planning of Le Corbusier, the *cités* were conceived purposefully as housing areas away from sectors of employment and consumption, the opposite of mixed-use areas in downtown Paris (Castañeda 2012b).

He reported that it was common for police and undercover agents to come to the projects to bust them for selling drugs. He felt the most bitter toward the police, who he said were always close by waiting to bust and imprison him. It was not rare for people from these projects to have spent time in prison. When released, they told others that they had been on a holiday or gone back to the *bled* (Arabic word meaning their hometown, homeland, or North Africa).

Ali, another French citizen of Algerian origin who lived in a private building a few blocks from these projects, refused my invitation to come along to the bar where I interviewed Ahmed because, he said, "The place is full of thieves and criminals." He expressed opinions that were critical of people living in public housing and identifying as minorities, even when in the past he had also lived in public housing. His perspective may have been evidence of what Bourdieu calls "symbolic domination" (the acceptance of stereotypes created by the powerful). Ali had internalized the contempt of French society against North African–origin people living in public housing.

When immigrant-origin individuals were asked whether they felt French or foreign, the majority said French. Rachid, a thirty-six-year-old man born in France to Algerian parents, said he was a "French citizen with foreign roots." Padonne, a twenty-nine-year-old service worker born in France of Tunisian parents, said, "I feel French. I adore France; I would give my life for this country."

Some wanted desperately to become French. Fatine, a thirty-year-old woman, claimed a kind of transient identity, one that might shift over time, saying, "I am Moroccan. but I could become French . . . one can integrate." Similarly, Najib, a twenty-seven-year-old man, said, "I am a foreigner, a Moroccan, but I would be French if I had the chance." Some interviewees mentioned a dual or hybrid identity. Lynda, a thirty-two-year-old woman born in France to Algerian parents, said, "I feel French with a double culture." Sonia, a twenty-four-year-old Moroccan woman, felt "between Moroccan and French." Some of the North African interviewees in Paris reported a cosmopolitan outlook. Othman, a forty-one-year-old Tunisian man working in a kebab restaurant and who has lived in Paris for fourteen years, said, "I am a universal citizen; I belong to humanity."

Many said they felt like strangers despite their legal citizenship. Tarek, a twenty-seven-year-old unemployed man born in Morocco, said, "I feel like I am a foreigner despite my French nationality." Mohamed, a thirty-six-year-old man born in France of Algerian parents, said, "I see myself as an Algerian because I have suffered racism."

Some felt they were strangers and thus refused to naturalize. Farid, a thirty-one-year-old Moroccan man, said, "I am a legally a foreigner, but even if I had French citizenship, I would remain a foreigner." Yahia, a forty-eight-year-old Algerian professional who has lived in Paris for four years, said, "I feel like a foreigner, a second-class citizen, a nonnative." Benamara, a thirty-three-year-old Tunisian, said, "I feel like a foreigner, and I will stay so. I refuse to get French nationality." Saadia, a thirty-eight-year-old Jewish woman born in Tunisia and in constant contact with her family there, said she feels "100 percent a foreigner" in Paris.

Others feel neither North African nor French. Naima, a twenty-one-year-old woman born in France to Tunisian parents, said, "In France I feel like a foreigner; in Tunisia I feel like a foreigner." Abdel, a fifty-nine-year-old Kabyle from northern Algeria who has lived for sixteen years in Paris, said of migrants, "We are cultural schizophrenics," referring to the constant jumping back and forth from French to Algerian cultural references and practices. A twenty-three-year-old said he feels like a "foreigner in Paris. In Morocco, I miss France. I can't live there anymore. I love the French system, but I feel Arab." Thus, despite not feeling fully at home in Paris, moving to North Africa would not be the solution either.

As seen here, integration experiences and the sense of belonging run the gamut. Although most feel French, there is some ambiguity or exclusion experienced by some North Africans and French citizens of North African descent living in Paris. This sentiment echoes the work of Abdelmalek Sayad and Emmanuelle Saada:

> In practice, being Algerian and French [legal citizens] effectively meant being neither Algerian nor French. The juridical splitting thus prolongs the "double absence" of the immigrant population—itself a prolongation of the splitting imposed by colonization, which had made the Algerian peasants into "French muslims," foreigners on their own lands. (Saada 2000: 38–39)

The dissimilation of the emigrant is met by the impossibility of being fully French because of an Arab phenotype, low education and social capital, and often a different religion. Among the sixty-five North Africans interviewed in the Paris metropolitan area as part of this project, the great majority mentioned work as the reason they or their families had moved to France. Family reunification and education were also common responses. One mentioned armed service for France, and another left North Africa for political reasons. Although many did not feel at home in France and often spoke of their desire to return, moving to Algeria was not a realistic option because these second- and third-generation individuals were culturally more French than Algerian (Castañeda, Morales, and Ochoa 2014; Abdelhady 2008).

I attended a protest demanding better public housing in Rue de la banque in 2007, where I met Amira, a Kabyle woman in her late forties. As part of the protest, people set up a camp in the streets. Over the course of my many visits to the street camp, Amira told me about her migration story. She had come to Paris eight years earlier with her older sons, so that they could go to school in France. Her husband stayed in Algeria because he had a relatively good job but not good enough for French consular authorities to grant him a visa. Her young daughters also stayed behind. Amira has not been back since because she has no residence papers.

Amira arrived not speaking French and now she speaks it rather well, after

doing anything I could to learn the language. I have been here for eight years, and I have not been able to find housing. I have applied many times, and I am still in line to get some housing. I live in a "foyer" [emergency housing/long-term homeless shelter]—the problem is that they [the state representatives] do not let my children stay there with me because they say they are too old to live there.

"So what do they do?" I asked.

They are students. They are getting ready for their exams in order to get into a good college and get a diploma and then get a good job. Not like me . . . My oldest son was here yesterday; he slept in the street with us, and he told me he would work hard to get us a house in Paris. I said that all I wanted was a modest house in the Kabylia. He said that he would prefer to stay and succeed in France and that we would go to Algeria only for vacations.

"And what do they do about their living situation?" I asked after she had misunderstood the sense of my original question but had still provided very important information.

> Well, I sneak them in. But if they find out, they would kick me out. They gave us a two-bedroom apartment. But another woman lives in the other room. So my three children and I sleep in one room. My older son said yesterday, "I am glad we are here protesting because I am . . . tired of sleeping in the floor all these years."

This case illustrates the limits of the French welfare state and the housing shortage in Paris. Amira's family, divided in two countries without the ability to travel, forms what we call a transnational household (Castañeda and Buck 2011). The conversation between Amira and her son already points to the different orientations of the first and second generation. The son is already invested in the French rules of the game: he wants to finish college, become a professional, and have a house in North Africa only for vacationing, as many other French people do. Amira, like many other first-generation migrants, wants to go back to Algeria and rejoin the rest of her family after achieving her target savings (Saada 2000; Piore 1979; Abdelhady 2008; Sayad 2006).

Part of the unequal relation between European French citizens and those of color is rooted in the French colonial enterprise. Thus, this chapter provides a brief discussion of how the colonial experience shapes present-day French understandings of race, citizenship, and rights. This chapter then discusses the political and economic integration of immigrants and finishes with some of the effects that cultural exclusion has on youth of color in Paris.

Colonialism and Migration

Migration to France is nothing new. For more than a century, France has been the most significant immigrant-receiving country in Europe (Noiriel 2001; Weil 2002). By the end of World War I, France surpassed the United States as the world's leading immigrant-receiving nation in terms of share of the population (Rosenberg 2006: xiii). Today, approximately 25 percent of the French population has at least one foreign-born parent. At least 30 percent of French residents have an immigrant grandparent (Tribalat 2015). In 2014, over 2 million or 20 percent of the inhabitants of metropolitan Paris were foreign born (INSEE 2017). Yet there is no notion of being "a nation of immigrants," as there is in the United States. Public discourse denies immigrants' contributions to French economic, demographic, and cultural growth (Noiriel 2001). This amnesia of a history of immigration wrongly paints new waves of migration as threatening and unprecedented.

European countries have not only been receivers of immigrants but also senders. Large European emigrations include the colonizing missions that occurred after the discovery of the Americas; 52 million people left Europe between 1824 and 1924 looking for social mobility (Hoerder and Moch 1996: 3). France was the only European country with a positive net growth rate in the period of 1850–1940; all other countries had declining populations due to emigration (Schnapper 1991: 64).

Most immigrants in France come from current and former colonies in the Caribbean, Indochina, Africa, the Indian Ocean, and French Polynesia. In the second part of the twentieth century, the most important sources of migration were the former colonies of North Africa—Algeria in particular.

Located across the Mediterranean Sea from France, Algeria is the largest country in Africa by area. French troops invaded Algiers and its surroundings in 1830 and made Algeria a French territory from 1830 to 1962. Unlike other colonial ventures such as Morocco or Tunisia, which were French protectorates, Algeria was seen as a part of France. As a settlement colony, its population reached over one million inhabitants of European origin by 1954 (Stora 2004: 28, 33). Algeria was populated by people coming mainly from the south of France and from the Alsace and Lorraine territories, which were lost to Prussia in 1871. The newcomers included political exiles and deportees from the Revolution of 1848 and the Paris Commune. Contingents of colonists also came from Corsica, Spain, Italy, and Malta; their naturalization was relatively easy, and their children immediately acquired French citizenship. The white settlers became later known as the *pieds noirs*, which translates to "black feet," but the original meaning of the term is disputed. Today it refers to people of European origin expelled from Algeria.

The Berbers or Imazighen[1] settled in North Africa before the arrival of Arab people in the seventh century. Most converted to Islam after the Arab conquests of the eleventh century CE (Stora 2004). The Kabyles are an Algerian ethnic minority and one of the North African Imazighen tribes (Mahé 2006). In antiquity, the Maghreb had important Phoenician, Greek, and Roman colonies (Mahé 2006; Silverstein 2002). They have their own ancient alphabet and spoken languages. The Kabyles often have light skin and eyes.

Colonial administrations engaged in the classic imperial strategy of "divide and conquer" by creating divisions among the French, European, Jewish, Arab, and Berber inhabitants of Algeria. The so-called Kabyle myth underlines the European origin of Kabyles and the French view that Kabyles were not real Muslims but hidden Christians. There was a real belief in the potential conversion of Kabyles into Catholicism (Mahé 2006). In that framing, the French annexation was the return of the Maghreb and the Berbers to a common Latin, Mediterranean, and European tradition. To mask French colonial rule as liberation, procolonialist French authors and administrators stressed the fact that Arab invaders had reluctantly subjugated the Kabyles and forced them to convert to Islam.

The French colonial government in Algeria gave jurisdiction to Jewish, Berber, and Muslim courts over their local communities. Settlers from Malta and other parts of Europe eventually became French citizens (A. I. Smith 2006). The Crémiuex Decree of 1870 gave French citizenship to all Algerian Jews, whereas Muslim men were given citizenship on a case-by-case basis. There was a tension between equality before the law and what the French saw as insurmountable racial and cultural differences. This difference in rights was against the spirit of the French Revolution and the belief in universal human rights. It was not until 1947 that French citizenship was granted to all the inhabitants born in Algeria, despite their religion and background (Shepard 2006), but it was too late. In 1954, the Algerian National Liberation Front (Front de Liberation Nationale, or FLN) demanded the sovereignty of "the Algerian nation," and the Algerian Revolution began. After eight years of war, Algeria became independent in 1962. In reaction to the contentious political claims of the FLN, the French proactively gave independence to the protectorates of Morocco (1912–1956) and Tunisia (1881–1956) (Filali 2008).

During colonial rule, French settlers, engineers, technocrats, and colonial administrators moved to Algeria. At the same time, a rural indigenous people of Northern Algeria, the Kabyles, moved to France to provide low-skilled labor. Paris became the main destination of Algerian immigrants around a hundred years ago. Algerian political independence did not end emigration. The social networks and chain migration that started at the beginning of the twentieth century, especially among Kabyles, were not cut by independence. On the contrary, the destruction, terror, and turmoil caused by the war resulted in large numbers of people leaving Algeria for the place they had been taught during colonial days was the best place on earth: mainland France. All educated Algerians know the French language, culture, and history, which explains the desire of many to migrate to France. There is much symbolic violence between France and Algeria. As an Algerian merchant told me, "We know things about the rest of the world, yet the rest of the world knows nothing about us." This phrase, whether factually true or not, shows the outward orientation of the Algerian middle class, international inequality among nations, the enduring legacy of colonialism, as well as the devaluation of their culture once they leave Algeria.

Colonial French authorities framed colonialism as part of a civilizing mission where the French troops would bring the enlightenment and a human rights regime to "savage, uncivilized and pagan nations" (see Bowden 2013). Aspects of this framing can still be observed today; for example, in the 2017 G20 meeting, French President Macron spoke about Africa's "civilizational problems" (Anyangwe 2017).

Because of the colonial and historical ties and existing networks, Algeria has been one of France's main sources of guest workers and immigrants for the last hundred years. For example, in 1924 alone, over 70,000 Algerians moved to France to work (Schneider 2008), most of them Kabyles (Sayad 2006, Sayad and Dupuy 1995). Algeria attempted to halt labor migration in 1973, French guest worker programs decreased, and the bulk of the current Algerian migration to France (averaging about 11 percent of annual inflows over the past decade) is dominated by family reunification. Most of the Algerian-origin population in France now consists of the children and grandchildren of migrants.

Even in contemporary Paris, people from Algeria are not all treated the same. Many Kabyles can and sometimes do pass as French given their physical appearance, but their religion, country of origin, and their names often prevent them from fully passing and being treated equally. Yet they are often treated better than darker-skinned Maghrebis, everything else being equal.

Muslim France

Estimates on the Muslim French population vary. Some calculate around 4 million (Simon and Tiberj 2013), others estimate 5 million people, others anywhere between 5 and 11 percent of the population, which would be from 3 to 7 million (Laurence and Vaisse 2006). Despite the idea of a community of Muslims around the globe, referred to as the *Ummah* (Kurzman 2010), in reality, divisions between Muslims persist due to different interpretations of

Islam, as well as over international politics and local particularisms. As I witnessed in Paris, even among Muslims living in close quarters, national and local stereotypes often gained salience and drew real boundaries between, for example, Algerians and Moroccans. Despite external categorization in the same box, national origin and intranational regionalisms draw boundaries internally among immigrants from the Maghreb. Yet, many native Parisians lump them together, as does some of the immigration literature on Maghrebis or North Africans, including this book. This generalization is necessary for academic discussion, but the reader should keep in mind the diversity within these categories.

Maghrebi immigrants are not a unified political group, and even within national groups there are strong divisions along ethnic, education, class, religious, or historical lines. For example, the term *harki*, which comes from the Arabic word *haraka* meaning "movement" and refers to a group of volunteer soldiers, is used to name those Algerians who fought with the French against Algerian independence. Algerians use the term *harki* as a derogatory term against those whom they viewed as traitors, collaborators, and internal enemies of the new Algerian nation (Stora 2004).[2] Not surprisingly, in France the descendants of *harkis* and the descendants of those who fought for Algerian independence have different political outlooks and avoid each other.

Although I use the terms "Algerian-French" or "French-Algerian" to make the concept relatable to readers accustomed to hybrid identities, my interviewees rarely used this conceptualization to refer to themselves. In fact, most French people would strongly oppose this characterization and emphasize instead that all French citizens are simply French. Unlike the United States, in France, hyphenated group identities are seen as denoting racism and denying the egalitarian and republican values of France. In Parisian politics, ethnoracial collective identities are not seen as legitimate avenues for members of these groups to demand inclusion and equal treatment. Despite these noble ideals, this categorical thinking is used in everyday understandings that result in disparate outcomes for these visible minorities. In Paris there is racial discrimination, but there is no political space to talk about how to address this discrimination. Many Parisians talk about brown-skinned North Africans as *Arabes* in a racializing manner. The concept of race is no longer seen as having a scientific basis but is a social construct to create and normalize social distinctions, draw social boundaries, and create categorical inequality (Castañeda 2018). Yet, the belief in the reality of racial/cultural differences (including language, religion, music, food, shared histories, and stories) is a source of imagined and real communities (Anderson 1983; Calhoun 1997).

In France, it is common to categorize people from Algeria, Morocco, and Tunisia with the label *Maghrebi*. In Arabic, *Maghreb* means the place where the sun sets and is mainly a geographical category that refers to countries west of Egypt that include Libya, Tunisia, Algeria, Morocco, and Mauritania. By contrast, the term *Muslim* is a label that underlines religious identity over other possible salient identities. The increasing use of the term *Muslim* essentializes the group and emphasizes the religious aspect of North African immigrants over their specific national origin, their status as postcolonial economic migrants or political refugees, or as Christian, Jewish, or nonbelievers.

People of Algerian descent can be found everywhere in French society: in large cities and small towns; living in public housing and in the wealthiest neighborhoods; unemployed, working in service jobs, as professionals, and as the owners of their own companies (Beaman 2017); hustling in the streets and working at high levels of government and academia. Although a number of individuals and some subgroups may be doing well (such as the many Maghrebi Jews, Kabyles, and *pieds noirs* whom I interviewed and interacted with), a significant number of Arab Algerians and their children in Paris remain stigmatized.

The Legacy of Colonialism

> *It is problematic that the receiving countries do not assume responsibility for the period when they were a colonizing state, that they do not recognize their history.*
>
> **Abdel el Ghadi, fifty-nine-year-old dermatologist from Constantinople, Algeria**

The hierarchies and preferential treatment given to different social groups during colonial times were transplanted into modern France, affecting the integration and the opportunities given to immigrants today. As I discovered, colonial history also shapes present-day contention among immigrants in France in a number of ways. It divides people of different Maghrebi and religious origins into different national and local camps. The violence from the war of independence still incites strong emotions (Pontecorvo 1967; Siri 2007). Parisians who would prefer to leave their colonial history behind are confronted by present-day immigrants, who are seen as either victims of colonialism, as ungrateful children, or as former armed enemies of the Republic.

Before arriving at the airport in Algiers, my taxi driver made a point of driving me by the front of the former French police headquarters where, he told me, "the French army tortured Algerians during the war." As I witnessed, the Algerian war was often brought up in discussions between French people of European origin (especially *pieds noirs*) and French people of Algerian origin. The *pieds noirs* often look back with nostalgia at their years in North Africa and are resentful that they were expelled (A. I. Smith 2006). One of my Algerian respondents reported being asked by neighbors in a Paris *banlieue* while challenging Algerians' presence in Paris, "You wanted independence, so what are you doing in France now?" To which an Algerian informant's mom replied, behind closed doors, "We are here to take revenge and take something back of what the French robbed from Algeria." Although not everyone thinks like this, these exchanges exemplify the continued relevance of colonial history in contemporary immigrant–native interactions.

Institutional Integration: Parisian Citizenship Culture

France has a "republican citizenship regime" (Lainer-Vos 2006). Modern-day notions of citizenship are derived from France's historical project to create a common civic culture. Since the French Revolution of 1789, the normative concepts of secularism (*laïcité*) and popular sovereignty—as opposed to monarchic sovereignty—aimed to create a unified republic in the French territory (Rousseau 1913). The state was given the role to actively create a common culture in order to bring unity to a diverse set of peoples and classes and to forge them into one nation (Weber 1976). This goal is exemplified by Émile Durkheim's call for a political civil religion: a shared love of the French Republic that substitutes local, religious, and family ties (Bellah and Hammond 1980; Durkheim 1893). The distrust of identity being derived from religious affiliation also had historical grounding. French history is full of episodes of violence and divisiveness based on religion, such as the French Revolution, the Vendée revolt, the Jacobin movement, the Vichy regime, and the Algerian War. These bloody precedents help explain the origin and the strongly embedded ideal of a secular Republic (Kuru 2008). The current dogmatic support for a secular Republic can be seen as the synthesis of France's contentious past (Calhoun 2010).

The French republican model of a supposedly culturally homogenous nation-state has been copied abroad and legitimized due to its association with the liberal ideals of democracy, liberty, equality, and universal human rights.

However, the result in France was not an egalitarian society but one in which the values of the Parisian elite became dominant (Bourdieu 1996 [1989]). What Eugene Weber (1976) calls "the official culture" is allegedly secular, but the implicit religion of the French state and society is Catholicism. As Craig Calhoun (2010) writes, rather than secularism as the absence of rituals, France has a set of official rituals and a *Catholaïcité* coming from its Catholic history. The Catholic tradition can still be found in the national holidays celebrated in Paris (six of the eleven official holidays have Christian origins) and in buildings, museums, art objects, and cathedrals that form part of the national patrimony. This may pass unnoticed by the average French person but not by citizens with other religious traditions. The belief in a common origin, cultural homogeneity, and existence of equal rights is strong among a large part of French society. Therefore, individuals who may wear traditional clothing, headscarves, *hijabs*, and other visible religious objects (used either as identity markers or as cultural artifacts) are seen as an affront to the French Republic. To maintain a perceived homogeneity (and power relations), the French government imposes a strong "assimilationist program" on its immigrants that expects a quick and unquestioned acculturation into the mainstream culture of the majority. In this context, religious differences have been used by political entrepreneurs such as the Le Pens to create fault lines (Almaguer 1994) and by natives about supposedly obvious differences between native French and Muslims in France (Lamont 2000: 6).

French popular discourse keeps a colonial gaze and pseudoscientific systems used to classify civilizations in a range from primitive to modern, with the supposed infantilism of people of color posited as a rationale for colonization (Mitchell 2002; Saada 2005; Le Cour Grandmaison 2008). The extreme right has capitalized on these xenophobic perceptions, the colonial past, and the bitter memories of the Algerian War of Independence. The National Front Party's founder, Jean-Marie Le Pen, and his daughter, Marine, identify immigration as the cause of all of France's national problems. The rise of the National Front has been such an embarrassment and a great cause of concern for the French elite, not only because of its openly anti-immigrant discourse but also because of its antirepublicanism. The party has failed to keep the illusion of color blindness with its open call for ethnic whites to unite in their rejection of colored immigrants and has racially defined the "true" French as French-speaking white individuals of Western European ancestry.

For example, far-right National Front presidential candidate Marine Le Pen said in Marseille on April 19, 2017, "Just watch the interlopers from the world come and install themselves in our home. They want to transform France into a giant squat. But it's up to the owner to decide who can come in. So, our first act will be to restore France's frontiers" (*New York Times* 2017). During her campaign, Marine Le Pen promised: to "make France more French," a moratorium on immigration, an end to family reunifications, an increase in deportations, and a reduction of visas. She also said, "I'm opposed to [women] wearing head scarves in public places. That's not France. There's something I just don't understand: The people who come to France, why would they want to change France, to live in France the same way they lived back home?" (*New York Times* 2017). Interestingly, Marine Le Pen frames her policy proposals as defending her home, France, from outsiders coming in to change it.

Macron's success in winning the presidential election in 2017 was largely based on his differentiation from Le Pen while also displaying his nationalism. In an event in the *banlieue* of Sarcelles, Macron said, "There are two projects facing each other. There's Marine Le Pen's project of a fractured, closed France. On the other hand, you have my project, which is a republican, patriotic project aiming at . . . reconciling France." He called out Le Pen's dangerous political opportunism that would increase tension between French Muslims and non-Muslims. "I want to help with Muslim integration. If you follow the line of Marine Le Pen, you create a civil war" (*New York Times* 2017). As Macron said in a presidential debate, "The trap you are falling into, Madame Le Pen, with your provocations, is to divide society. [You are making] enemies out of more than four million French men and women whose religion happens to be Islam." Macron wrote on his campaign website, "Too many Frenchmen confuse secularism and the prohibition of religious manifestations—and some make this confusion their business" (*New York Times* 2017).

Further examples can be found in the 2007 presidential elections. In contrast to Jean-Marie Le Pen, the rest of the candidates from the Socialists to the center and right agreed on statist approaches. The Mouvement Démocrate (MoDem) candidate François Bayrou openly expressed that the solution to the problems in the *banlieues* was a stronger state presence. He admitted that France should go beyond formal equality on paper to a real equality (*égalité réel*). He proposed without irony that French Muslim imams study theology in French universities with a more secular approach and to make Islam more compatible with French values (talk at Sciences Po January 2, 2007). The political discourse of Bayrou shows how ingrained the republican secular ideals are in the habitus of the French political elite. Not surprisingly, the proposals from the candidate Ségolène Royal of the Socialist Party were not that different as she also emphasized a certain "*identité nationale*" during her campaign. Nicolas Sarkozy's presidential campaign had certain openings for discussion about the virtues of diversity and affirmative action inspired by the American model. However, once in office, he established an ethnocentric Ministry of Immigration and National Identity that caused alarm and disgust among some intellectuals and researchers in France. In 2010, he signed a law prohibiting full facial covering in public places, even when only a small minority of women used *niqab* or *burqa*s in France. The French Interior Ministry estimated that there were no more than 2,000 women wearing a *burqa* in all of France (Bouteldja 2011).

This political discourse has real effects on individuals with North African origins. Hela, a thirty-one-year-old French-born Tunisian woman, saw Sarkozy "as a demagogue and an opportunist." Mokhtar, a twenty-six-year-old French Algerian, also saw him as opportunist and as "very offensive." Hourari, a thirty-eight-year-old Algerian, said, "I do not like him because he does not like us." Yahia, a forty-eight-year-old Algerian-born man, said, "I would hope that the politicians either from right or left would not use the immigrant population as the supposed cause and source of all social problems. It is the population of immigrant origin that contributes to the growth of this country." Similarly, Hacen, a thirty-two-year-old Moroccan who moved to Paris as a child, said, "France has never taken her immigrants into account," meaning that France has few policies catering to immigrants as such or making them feel at home. When asked what the worst aspects of living in France were, people I interviewed often mentioned racism. Najib, a twenty-seven-year-old man born in Morocco, said, "Racism; you do not feel at home." Thirteen others also mentioned racism as a negative of living in Paris. Others mentioned humiliation, indifference, and distance among people. Yahia said, "People always make you feel like a foreigner." Seven interviewees mentioned family separation. Six mentioned the lack of economic resources, such as not having enough money, not having a job. Racha, a twenty-nine-year-old woman born in Morocco, said, "We do not have time to live, enjoy life. Everything is about work. There is a lack of communication, and people don't want to listen." Amel, a nineteen-year-old female student born in Morocco, lamented "being far from our roots." Fatine, a thirty-year-old woman from Morocco, said, "I am without family, far from home culture, absence of tolerance." Othman, a forty-one-year-old Tunisian, summarizes it as "being far from home."

Interviews with immigrants and some of their descendants show the psychological toll imposed by this strong demand for acculturation logic. Parisian governmental, cultural, and intellectual elites exert a very powerful influence on what it means to be French, leaving very little room to those who deviate from the norm to present alternative identities and enter these elite circles. For many, this ideology is so culturally embedded that it becomes unconscious—part of their habitus—in a way that makes it almost impossible for them to step outside of this worldview. Evidence of group differences is hard to come by because since 1978 the French government has prohibited the systematic collection of ethnic and racial data on its population. Patrick Simon and others at INED have collected relevant survey data, but the French state and society still have a strong preference for monoculturalism: cultural and religious homogeneity under the guise of secularism. The French political system has very few constructive avenues in which cultural differences may be channeled and negotiated.

Political Integration: Lack of Avenues for Political Voice Along Ethnic Lines

The French are famous for frequent displays of contentious politics, including striking, street marching, rioting, and carrying and displaying banners (Tilly 1986). These events happen routinely and are staged around issues of labor and human rights (Crettiez and Sommier 2002). Contentious politics are everywhere in Paris as subway workers strike and close the metro, bikers ride to demand more bicycle lanes, people protest against the wars in Iraq, Afghanistan, Palestine, or even against the Olympic Games and human rights abuses in China, while taxi, bus, and airport workers strike over labor conditions, and protests are staged against stores opening on Sunday. While I was in France, I attended a number of marches and rallies for immigrants' rights to asylum and housing. The movement of demanding official papers by the *sans-papiers* has been associated in recent years with immigrants from sub-Saharan Africa.

Beur is a slang term that reverses the syllables of the word *Arabe* or Arab in French; it often has a political or identitarian connotation similar to the term *Chicano* in the United States in the 1960s. The last time that the *beurs* made political claims as a group in the public sphere vis-à-vis the state was during "the March for Equality and against Racism" popularly called the *marche des beurs*. The march left Marseille in October 1983 and on December 3, 1983, 100,000 people arrived in Paris, where a delegation was received by the then recently elected President François Mitterrand. Hopes were high, but the resulting changes were few (Barsali, Freland, and Vincent 2003). In the end, the political establishment of the socialist party co-opted these demands without addressing the structural root causes (L'Information Citoyenne 2006).

Young Maghrebis treated this experience as a failed attempt and largely gave up on any illusion for rapid change and acceptance and on organizing marches on such a grand scale in the name of French North Africans. Since then, there have been some individual successes in social mobility but at the cost of the depoliticization of some *beurs*. Although some have become members of the middle class, a great majority face total economic exclusion. However, consumer culture and cultural forms of expression have sapped much of the energies of young Maghrebis (Boubekeur and Roy 2010; Boubekeur 2007).

But less common these days are marches or large public events organized by French Maghrebis, either by first-generation people from the Maghreb or by second-generation French of North African origins, the so-called *beurs*. Neither group rallied large numbers around issues of cultural rights, religious freedom, or identity, at least not to the extent of the large immigrant rights marches across the United States on May Day in 2006. In France, there are small organizations that aim to do just this, but they do not constitute powerful lobbies, political action committees, or organizations with large membership or legitimacy. In 2007 and 2008, I marched in immigrant rights marches with important numbers of French Maghrebis and with contingents from unions, left, and far-left parties and organizations. But they did not receive the same attention from the media as other marches centered on labor and economic issues.

Important exceptions to this general absence of protest were the series of marches organized against the "DNA law" during my time in France (2007–2008). This DNA law initiative sought to conduct genetic tests to ascertain paternity and kinship claims in migration cases. These protests were coordinated by SOS and the Socialist party and were used to proselytize and protest against Sarkozy's government and party. Yet, the language of the public speeches was based on the French republican model and the universalization of the French human rights framework.

Given the failure of the *beur* movement, no political voice for this group has emerged. A major problem of the riots in the French *banlieues* is that rather than solving the social and structural issues in the long term, they instead act as pressure valves for discontent and are only rarely translated into grassroots organizing or policy changes for the better. On the contrary, then interior minister Nicolas Sarkozy reacted to the riots of 2005 by making comments to the media about his intention to clean the *banlieues* of *racaille*,which could be translated as "scum," "thugs," or "villains." As president, he strengthened the security and police apparatus and reduced welfare benefits.

During the campaign for the French presidency, Sarkozy seemed ready to copy some of the American multicultural models such as affirmative action (Sarkozy 2004). However, one could see as soon as he nominated his ministers that he misunderstood the concept of affirmative action. He named some people of immigrant origin (*issues de l'immigration*) to cabinet positions, people who were accomplished individually but lacked any claim of representation or even connection to the larger groups that they were supposed to be part of. So although Rachida Dati, the child of a Moroccan father and an Algerian mother, embraced a strong assimilationist approach to life in France, as Minister of Justice, she promised to strengthen the laws to better control criminalized youth from the *banlieues*.

Rama Yade, born in Senegal, was Secretary of State for Sports after serving as spokesperson for human rights, whereas Fadela Amara was a junior minister for urban policy. These were token appointments of people who embody the French secular republican model. Still, the appearance of "people of color" speaking in the name of the government and the Republic on French television and in the public sphere was a step in the right direction. The trajectories of these "visible minority" individuals are rather elitist, and their background is either Berber or mixed. The main source of minorities in government today is those representing overseas territories and domains. Yet, the French Senate in 2010 had fewer minorities than the Senate of the 1950s, which included members from a large set of colonies (Shepard 2006: 14).

Federalism (Local Autonomy versus Centralization)

In contrast to the American federal system, in France most policies originate in the capital, and political power and national elites are concentrated there. In 1983, the "March for Equal Rights" wound its way from groups in Lyon and

Marseille in a march to Paris to be received by President François Mitterrand at the Élysée Presidential Palace. Yet, this attempt to create a collective civil rights movement was incompatible with the French centralized republican model of supposed blindness to race, ethnicity, or religion.

Although Maghrebi immigrants in Paris or its *banlieues* live physically very close to the centers of power, many social processes reinforce social distance across cultural, symbolic, and social capital. Immigrants are thus kept very far away from the mayor of Paris and the president of the Republic in terms of making their voices heard, despite their geographic proximity (Castañeda 2012b).

Local mayors in the *banlieues* had political clout when many were part of the Communist Party and formed the so-called red belt around the city (Fourcaut, Bellanger, and Flonneau 2007). In previous decades, working-class inhabitants, including the few emigrants from the colonies, enjoyed a patron–client relationship with the local *banlieue* politicians. But in recent years, the Communists lost their offices when many of them embraced anti-immigrant positions in an attempt to protect the shrinking local working class from the labor competition posed by the newcomers and consequently lost the support of both populations. The embrace of right-wing anti-immigrant discourse by the Communist Party ended in the collapse of large areas of the red belt (Beaud and Pialoux 2006, Fassin and Fassin 2006). Some researchers show how these dynamics played out historically in the Parisian *banlieues* (Masclet 2005, 2001). The break-up of the relationship between party politics and the *banlieue* population weakened the power of the mayoral offices in the Parisian *banlieues* at the same time that they faced important budget cuts. Even the left failed to form a coalition that included the visible minorities living in the areas that they used to govern uncontested.

Political Underrepresentation

Minority politicians are not common in France. One could mention names like Christiane Taubira from Guyana and other politicians and elected officials from the *domaines ou territoires d'autre mer* (DOM-TOMs), including the islands of Guadeloupe, Guyane, Martinique, and La Réunion. The percentage of people of non-European origin elected in France is very low, even at the local level. In the municipal elections of 2001, for cities over 50,000, only 3.6 percent of the elected officials had African origins; in the regional elections of 2004, only 2 percent of those elected were of Maghrebi origin; and among the candidates for the 2007 elections only 3 percent of the candidates were of non-European origin (Geisser and Soum 2008).

Of 331 members of the senate in the early 2000s, there were only two Muslims, and of 577 members of the assembly, none was Muslim (Jytte Klausen 2005, cited in Kuru 2008), which makes them especially underrepresented (Hackett 2015). Electoral representation is important because

> where immigrant minorities are not represented in elected office or are only minimally so, they evidently experience very unequal life chances in the attainment of such highly esteemed and powerful positions as mayor, city councilor and parliamentarian . . . While lack of electoral representation is likely to reinforce a sense of outsider status, the ability to elect one's own can nurture and strengthen a sense of identification with, and allegiance to, the society and its institutions, including the rules, procedures, and values of the political system, and indeed can itself be a source of pride. (Alba and Foner 2009)

I interviewed an active and brilliant black Senate staffer, and he continuously showed his discontent with this lack of inclusion across all parties, including the progressive Green Party to which he belonged. Local leaders, grassroots activists, and politicians of color also have a hard time making it onto the electoral lists of any political party (Geisser and Soum 2008).

Historically, social class has been seen as the most legitimate form of political representation in France. INED sociologist Patrick Simon has gathered some important samples that trace immigrants' national originals—yet, overall, national data on social and health disparities along categorical groups are still very limited. Thus, disadvantaged and disenfranchised immigrant and minority groups have a hard time being heard in the public sphere and electing representatives, which emphasizes their collective exclusion and, I argue, leaves them with no other alternative than to sporadically *voice* their claims through contentious politics, for example, marches for the rights of the *sans papiers* (meaning literarily "without papers" or "undocumented") (Siméant 1998), hunger strikes, large-scale squatting by the homeless (Castañeda 2009), and sometimes rioting (Schneider 2014).

In my fieldwork accompanying Magrebins who lived in Paris and the *banlieues*, I observed how adult Maghrebis in France are disenfranchised not only from the state but also socially from one another. Although many families are divided transnationally, family ties, trust, and solidarity are strong. Yet, their internalization of anticommunitarianism makes them keep to themselves and distrust other Maghrebis. Because of all of this, they cannot engage in collective action, except in reaction to provocative violent attacks by the police against youth. Typically, these attacks are on youth who, because of their school networks, are socially well connected with other working-class youth from the same neighborhoods in the *banlieues*. As Loïc Wacquant (2008) rightly notes, most contemporary French *banlieues* are rather diverse in terms of income, ethnicity, and religion. Although this differentiates them from the historical concept of the ghetto, it also renders them less cohesive and less prone to engage in collective action (Castañeda 2012b).

French Algerians have not formed an interest group in the way that farmers, worker unions, or business interests have. Their lack of organization is to be expected because many are poor, discriminated against, and discouraged from associating with coethnics in other parts of the Parisian metropolitan area.

The French Muslim population is what Bourdieu would call "a class on paper" (Bourdieu 1998): in theory they should be a class and act together, but they are not a cohesive social group, and thus they are not a source of political power. Economically many are members of a "class in itself" but "not a class for itself." Yet, it is relevant to talk about them as a collective because they share many similar experiences. They are often disenfranchised from main society as well as from each other. Many are disillusioned, and because most of them are not strict Muslims they face high levels of anomie[3] despite having internalized a strong French republican ethos. This ethos is designed to avoid anomie and intended to create a collective pseudoreligious allegiance to the state (Durkheim 1893). Instead, their lack of meaning and social belonging leave some of them vulnerable to radicalization in prison and online. A few are indeed recruited to extremist pseudoIslamic groups, as we witnessed in several terrorist attacks carried out in France or in those who traveled to radical Islamist training camps abroad. Without legitimate opportunities for collective action and collective political voice, those excluded often resort to violence.

Collective Voice: Riots and the Lack of Institutional Channels for Collective Claim Making

The lack of political representation results in, among other things, frequent confrontation between youth and police. Riots in recent French history have been fueled the extreme abuse of power by some police officers, resulting in the deaths of young members of the local community (Schneider 2008, 2014). These events drive the victims' friends into the streets.

During a 2005 police chase, two minors got electrocuted in a power station in the Parisian suburb of Clichy-sous-Bois (Schneider 2008). Local protests and riots ensued, and the police responded aggressively (Lagrange and Oberti 2006). The riots extended to 274 towns across France and lasted twenty days and thousands of vehicles were burned. This was a major event that brought negative attention to immigrants, North Africans, and *banlieue* residents (*New York Times* 2005).

I will now describe some of the typical features of these events. In 2007, I witnessed the aftermath of a riot when I visited the northern Parisian *banlieue* of Villiers-le-Bel a few days after riots had taken place there. The smell of smoke still hung in the air. Villiers-le-Bel is eleven miles from the center of Paris. It has 27,000 inhabitants. Riots erupted after a police car hit and killed two adolescents riding a small motor scooter on November 26, 2007. Friends of the victims, Moushin, age fifteen, and Larami, age sixteen, blamed the police but felt that the officers would go unpunished as had previously been the case for similar events (Moran 2012).

Feeling they had no recourse for justice, people took to the streets, threw rocks at the local schools, and set fire to a school library, the police headquarters, and over thirty cars (see Figure 3.1). Federal antiriot police squads moved through the streets like an invading army conquering enemy territory. Most adults stayed indoors; some watched timidly from their windows, while others slept, indifferent both to the claims of the youth and to the police abuses. Those who did not know the victims or their families just wanted order restored and to return to their regular lives. Many people from the neighborhood testified against their young neighbors. In February 2008, thirty-eight suspects were apprehended in a massive raid by almost a thousand police officers who descended on Villiers-le-Bel in a large show of force, accompanied by TV cameras. The message broadcast nationally was that future riots would not be tolerated and that participants would be punished. In July 2008 participants in the riots were sentenced to jail for one to three years. In December of 2009, *Le Monde* reported that the two policemen were acquitted of any responsibility; Moushin and Larami were declared fully responsible for their own deaths (*Le Monde* 2009).

Another example of the criminalization of minority youth is that most of those implicated in the Villiers-le-Bel events were between eighteen and

Figure 3.1. Burned police barracks at the Avenue de la Concorde, Villiers le Bel, in the Parisian periphery.

SOURCE: © Castañeda 2007.

twenty-five years old. These events are often framed by the French media as related exclusively to immigrants, but this is not the case, as reports on the 2007 rioters mention the participation of "whites," "blacks," and Maghrebis, all French citizens. Similarly, only 120 of the 4,000 people arrested in the "French riots of 2005 had been born outside France, yet the rioters were universally referred to as immigrants" (Katz 2008: 203).

Social Boundaries and Collective Violence

Although emotions and anger play significant roles in symbolic attacks against state and private property, this does not mean that fires like the ones set in Villiers le Bel were the result of crazy mobs acting out of passion and irrationality, as Frédéric le Play would have us believe the dangerous masses do. Nor do we see at play "Algerian pride" or other stereotypes of cultural characteristics typically attributed to children of immigrants. Instead, we see examples of the real structural forces that oppress immigrants and minorities in France. Symbolic violence works in slow and lacerating ways. The community combats institutionalized differences when police transgressions become all too obvious in their direct attacks on specific members of a community. These naked attacks on individuals, based on a categorical grouping (youth of color is an intersectionality that is commonly criminalized), activate symbolic boundaries. This creates solidarity and rage along categorical lines that drive people with certain characteristics and networks to act in violent ways (Tilly 1998).

The gap between realities and expectations within a post-colonial context partly explains the riots across France. As Loch writes,

> In the French case, the experience of the discrepancy between, on the one hand, internalized French values and, on the other, social exclusion and racist post-colonial discrimination, leads to frustration and moral indignation . . . a gulf between identification with republican values expressing equality and solidarity, and actual social and political exclusion, further reinforces the discrepancy between rights and the reality of the integration model, and hence the resulting rage is vented in riots. (Loch 2009: 795–796)

Thus, male French citizens of Algerian descent are seen as problematic by other French people and in turn are an example of what Portes and Rumbaut (2006) call "reaction formation," or a rejection of a group that rejects them— and I observed how many working-class and unemployed French Algerians tend to be contentious in everyday interactions with other Frenchmen.

When French youth riot and attack public buildings and private property, it should not be seen as innovative or outside of French cultural frames and repertoires of contention. They are borrowing from the repertoires of contentious politics historically performed by people in France (Tilly 2008; Traugott 1993). French history is full of small riots and rebellions against physical symbols of the state, like public buildings, as well as private property. In France, the aspects that are most celebrated from the 1960s are the riots, the occupation of the streets and universities, and the construction of street barricades made with paving stones during the student movement of 1968 (Seidman 2004).

Banlieue Residents' Opinions About Rioting

Rather than rely on media reports and op-eds to understand the effects of the riots on public opinion (Clare and Abdelhady 2016; García and Retis 2011; Benson 2013), I asked sixty-five Maghrebis throughout the Parisian metropolitan area what their opinions were of the riots. Although some public housing youth participated in the riots as a form of contentious politics, most *banlieue* residents disapproved. Most Maghrebis, whether born in France or abroad, did not participate in any rioting, and most of them disapproved of the riots. Many openly disapproved of the riots or blamed second-generation youth, marking a moral differentiation from themselves. Regarding the possible motivations behind rioting, close to 10 percent pointed directly to aggressive policing and racial profiling. Many also pointed to unemployment, systemic discrimination, and state neglect as causes for the riots. Racism and the inflammatory comments by Sarkozy were also mentioned as causes for the extent and spread of the 2005 riots.

Showing a tension between first and later generations, Tarek, a first-generation Moroccan, said, "The rioters were born here." A twenty-six-year-old second-generation Algerian said, "It is understandable. It is good that this was not worse." Mohamed, a twenty-three-year-old Moroccan, said, "I am in favor and against. On the one hand, it is not right that they burn the cars of their neighbors. On the other hand, they are right because they are not otherwise heard by the government." Revarig, a sixty-one-year-old French citizen of Tunisian origin, said, "I am against them. The riots hurt regular people. There is always someone who pays. It is us in the *banlieues* who are affected and lose financially." Many said that rioting does not work, does not change a thing for the better. Mohammad, a forty-six-year-old Tunisian, said, "It was violent, and they are right. It is a way to express themselves." Nabil, a twenty-five-year-old second-generation Tunisian, said, "It is too bad they happened, but they prove that there are problems." Sonia, a twenty-eight-year-old third-generation immigrant with Algerian grandparents, said, "I was not there, but I think that this translated the unease between the youth, especially those of foreign origins, and the government, and French society more generally." Huma, a thirty-four-year-old professional Kabyle, said, "It is mainly a problem of policing. The kids are too young to be already worried about unemployment directly, but they worry about a bleak future, and police violence is real. The riots result especially from the criminalization of youth and from confrontation between youth and police, as in 1968 or as in other countries."

When asked further about possible causes, Mohamed, seventy-five, blamed "Sarkozy; he said bad things, like getting rid of the scum with a pressure washer." For Habib, a twenty-four-year-old son of Algerian and French parents, it is due to "incomprehension." Nabil, a twenty-five-year-old second-generation Franco-Tunisian, said, "People do not feel French. I feel French, but not the others." For Sonia, a twenty-eight-year-old third-generation immigrant of Algerian origin, riots are due to "the unease at integration of French youth of foreign origin in French society." Racha, a twenty-nine-year-old Moroccan woman, says riots are due to "the lack of listening to others, the lack of economic means, and the lack of work." Huma said that "people are afraid of youth, and the youth take advantage of that image to riot. It is a reaction to the fact that when women pass them, the women grab on hard to their purses." Sofiane, an eighteen-year-old man born in France of Algerian parents, said, "It is simple. The riots were caused by the deaths of the two young men," bringing it back to police brutality. So, only a few *banlieue* residents participated. Most *banlieue* residents, including those of immigrant origin, disapproved. Yet many were quick to point at real issues of racial profiling, violent policing, discrimination, and lack of political voice as reasons why some would want to participate.

The state often reacts to riots and looting by increasing police presence and sending antiriot police and soldiers. The state established a curfew during the 2005 riots, something that had not been done since the days of the Algerian war (Loch 2009: 800). Since the riots across France in 2005, military-type curfews have come to be seen as legitimate and expected. This has only increased with a growing number of terrorist attacks in recent years and the state responses to them. Yet these strategies often escalate the violence rather than decrease it. They also harden social boundaries and categorical inequality (Tilly 1998, 2005; Castañeda 2018) making future confrontations more likely. Some suspect police violence as the cause for the mysterious death of twenty-four-year-old Yacine Ben Kahla on September 14, 2017 (Misra 2017). On February 2, 2017, policemen stopped and assaulted a young black man known as Théo in the *banlieue* of Aulnay-sous-Bois. In response, there were riots and car burnings.

Yet, despite riots along with activists, minority organizations, and a few studies showing large disparities along race and religious lines, the French state, politicians, and society at large have kept their emphasis on assimilation and the reluctance to systematically gather data on ethnicity and social and health outcomes or to protect religious freedom.

The attacks against *Charlie Hebdo* and a Jewish store, and then the Bataclan music hall massacre, in Paris in 2015, as well as the attack in Nice on the anniversary of the French Revolution on July 14, 2016, mark a new type of contentious performance in contemporary France. Exploding bombs and mass shootings had not been seen in Paris to this degree since the Algerian Revolution. Today, like then, terrorist acts may be occurring due to the confluence of three elements: (1) international politics over the control of land (Algerian, Syrian, and Northern Iraqi, respectively); (2) a small minority within a local population living in mainland France with links to contentious groups in North Africa and the Middle East with sympathies to their political causes; and (3) the marginal position and constant exclusion of these minority populations within France, making it easier for minority youth to be radicalized.

Conflict between Muslims in France and secular French is avoidable. The current polarization, punctuated by increased acts of violence, is the result of the creation of social boundaries between Muslims and non-Muslims initiated by the latter. Pundits and politicians fearing the Islamization of France have been calling for a war on Islam in France and radical Islam abroad (Deltombe 2005; Caldwell 2009; Bawer 2006). Sadly, they are creating a self-fulfilling prophecy and creating a trope from a few disenfranchised individuals whose heinous acts gain a large visibility and further reinforce us–them boundaries. The best bet to reduce tensions and violence would be to integrate the descendants of North African immigrants into the French mainstream by providing them with the same humanity and opportunities (Castañeda 2012c; Alba and Foner 2015; Silberman, Alba, and Fournier 2007) afforded to French citizens of European origin.

Economic Integration: Labor Markets and Categorical Inequality

In 1995, 46 percent of immigrants in France were unskilled laborers, whereas only 26 percent of French workers were unskilled. In the same year, 20 percent of immigrants were unemployed whereas only 12 percent of citizens were. In 1998, the immigrant unemployment rate skyrocketed to 31.4 percent, and immigrant youth faced a 43 percent unemployment rate. These high levels of unemployment continue to disproportionately affect citizens of African origin who average a 30 percent unemployment rate for adults and a 50 percent rate for black and Maghrebi youth (Schneider 2008). Furthermore, "Those of African or North African origin earn half the national average and are four times more likely to live in poverty. High school and university graduates of immigrant descent are twice as likely to be unemployed (11 percent) as those with French parents (5 percent)" (Schneider 2008). Immigrants in France, particularly those from North Africa and their children, are more likely to be unemployed (Alba and Foner 2015). Access to jobs is lower for individuals who have a Muslim last name or an "Arab phenotype." Muslims with similar CVs to non-Muslims were less likely to be interviewed (Adida, Laitin, and Valfort 2016). Along similar lines, "The Integration of the European Second Generation" (TIES) study shows a worse employment situation for second-generation Turkish immigrants in France than in other European countries (Fibbi and Wanner 2008).

In Paris, Maghrebis are more discriminated against in the labor market than blacks are. Many of my Muslim North African informants reported feelings of uselessness, ennui, and low self-efficacy, which I contend are the direct result of the lack of jobs, job discrimination, and forced dependence on welfare. In my Parisian sample, there are a number of underemployed immigrants who have unstable temporary contracts or jobs well below their capacity, despite having extensive experience and educational credentials. The differentials in the labor market that I found through my research are similar to those reported in a quantitative study based on a survey of 55,000 people who had completed their education by 1998 (Silberman, Alba, and Fournier 2007). As Table 3.1 shows, the probability of being unemployed, underemployed, and undereducated is much higher for those of Muslim Maghrebi origin than for others in France. *Pieds noirs*—white former colonizers of Algeria and their children who were expelled after Algeria gained independence—have achieved higher levels of education than other French, yet are still more likely to be unemployed and underemployed. Table 3.1 shows unequal social

Table 3.1. Education and employment for French subgroups.

		Maghrebin	*Pieds noirs*	*French*
Higher education (greater than baccalaureate +2)	Male	6.3	22.6	17.6
	Female	9.2	26.3	22
Employed	Male	72.1	81.4	87.4
	Female	65.8	77.6	79
Unemployed	Male	18.7	10.6	7.2
	Female	20.8	11.4	10.2
Inactive	Male	4.4	2.4	1.6
	Female	7.5	4.2	5.3
Employed below perceived level of competence	Male	38.2	32.7	26.7
	Female	34.7	32.1	25.8

Table elaborated by the author from data reported in Silberman, Alba, and Fournier 2007.

outcomes by social groups, as a man of Maghrebin origin is 2.6 times more likely to be unemployed than a Franco-French man (T. B. Smith 2006: 266).

The authors of the study shown in Table 3.1 do not have the data to disaggregate by national origin, but in my year of fieldwork in Paris I found that, among the Maghrebi, the situation is surely worse for Algerian men because they are most likely to be unemployed or with limited prospects of upward social mobility. Moroccans, Tunisians, and Berbers in general face relatively less exclusion. Among my interviewees, lighter skin and eye color, higher education, and higher willingness to integrate coincided with higher employment and earnings.

The French Welfare State

In contrast to the United States, France tends to be proud of its strong welfare state. After the Second World War, the French welfare state did provide broad and generous benefits to the average citizen. Generous policies were designed to help mothers and children, aiming to increase birth rates and promote population growth. In the aftermath of the Second World War, (the "*trente glorieuses*," or the "glorious thirty years" from 1945 to 1975), France was rebuilt and thus experienced rapid economic growth. The middle class expanded, and by 1975, the French economy had grown enormously, becoming one of the largest in the world.

According to social historian Timothy B. Smith, France is a great place to live if you are married, over age forty, well-educated, employed, or retired—which combined describe around 60 percent of French citizens (T. B. Smith 2006: 23–24). Indeed, you could hardly do better anywhere else in the world. Paris boasts a great public transportation network, an enviable public health care system, and a high quality of life for this group. Most French citizens see their welfare state as *solidaire*, redistributive, and concerned with social justice and equality (T. B, Smith 2006: 10). But since the 1970s the French welfare state has not been particularly redistributive toward its poorest citizens; it is relatively ungenerous to women, youth, immigrants, and children of immigrants. The official unemployment rate for the young hovered around 30 percent in 2000 and was unofficially estimated to be as high as 75 percent (T. B. Smith 2006: 22). Youth unemployment was at least 25 percent in 2015.

In 2005, 7 percent of French workers were "working poor" (L'Observatoire National de la Pauvreté et de l'Exclusion Sociale 2008: 14). Opinion surveys show that a majority of the French population is concerned about falling into poverty or know someone already living in poverty. In the Eurobarometer Survey of 2007, one-fifth of French citizens said they had great difficulty "making ends meet." In a 2007 survey organized by the NGO Emmaüs, 47 percent of those surveyed feared becoming homeless in their old age (L'Observatoire National de la Pauvreté et de l'Exclusion Sociale 2008: 21).

Those living alone, such as single people, widows and widowers, and unaccompanied immigrants, are especially susceptible to living in poverty. Single people between thirty and fifty-nine years of age are twice as likely to live in poverty as the rest of the population. Of single people aged sixty and older, 40 percent live in poverty (L'Observatoire National de la Pauvreté et de l'Exclusion Sociale 2008: 71). The precarious economic state of the young and the elderly can be understood, at least partially, as simply a part of the life cycle in which the young and the elderly come to the points in their lives when their income is the lowest (Carter and McGoldrick 1999). However, this is also a structural problem given that over 21 percent of those under twenty-five seeking work cannot find it. Young single people used to not be able to receive benefits such as the Revenu Minimum d'Insertion (RMI), which is an unemployment income for those unable to find work (L'Observatoire National de la Pauvreté et de l'Exclusion Sociale 2008: 71), although the more recent *Revenu de solidarité active* (RSA) provides a basic income to those 18–25 who had worked for two years.

The French welfare state is a generous one, but it is most generous for those who are employed. Although universalism is the model for citizenship, particularism is the driving principle of social policy in France (T. B. Smith 2006: 265). French citizens themselves perceive France as "more unjust than just" as 68 percent of the population said in 2000, 72 percent in 2004, and 69 percent in 2007 (Bréchon and Tchernia 2009). This questions the French ideal of solidarity because "the French welfare state is anything but solidaristic . . . The disadvantaged—women, immigrants, and new young participants in the labor force—do not benefit from the current system" (Adams 2006: 458).

The experience of poverty and duress is relative, so while objectively the unemployed citizen immigrants in France are, due to the strong welfare state, in far better economic condition than their counterparts in the United States or Spain, they still feel marginalized. Though the poverty rate—at 60 percent of the national median income for France in 2013—was 15.5 percent, it was 38.1 percent for immigrants born outside of the European Union (Inequality Watch 2015). The proportion of unemployed immigrants and their children in

France is much higher, and cultural and structural obstacles to employment in France often cause feelings of social isolation and even resentment against the state in the Parisian *banlieues*.

Objectively speaking, most immigrants and minorities in France are doing well as a result of state-sponsored welfare programs, yet everyday solidarity and private charity are low. French citizens feel that they are doing their part by paying taxes and that it is up to state officials to deal with immigrants, refugees, minorities and those in need (Bréchon and Tchernia 2009). It is the American laissez-faire attitude that leaves many services to nonprofits, outside the government's purview. In France, these tasks are seen as too important to leave them to individuals' good intentions. Immigration officials and social service workers meet frequently with authorized immigrants and individuals of North African origin and have funds to provide aid. An unintended consequence is atomization because the contemporary centralized bureaucratic French government recognizes only individuals and not social groups. It deals directly and constantly with immigrants as individuals covering basic necessities through social programs. This requires much time and effort in terms of paperwork to be completed and red tape to cut through to stay eligible for support. In France, many immigrants receive benefits such as health care, housing, and/or unemployment financial support, but they often told me assertively that they would prefer to be given the chance to work.

Social Integration

Paris has been a great land for refugees and self-exiled political and cultural elites for a long time. Although the French authorities have tolerated governments in exile escaping coups or planning a revolution at home, large groups of economic migrants are expected to intègrate and leave behind their allegiance to their country of origin. There is little space for identity politics in Paris; the contemporary French media uses the word *communitarist*, or communitarian, as an insult and see it as a threat to the nation (Montague 2013). Paris provides anonymity and safety for newcomers escaping their countries because of their sexual orientation and/or political or religious persecution. Yet, it is often hard for newcomers to connect with other Parisians. French citizens believe in helping others through the welfare state more than citizen to citizen, through charitable acts or civic organizations (Bréchon and Tchernia 2009). This contributes to the social isolation of North Africans, particularly those who do not have work acquaintances. As a result, immigrants become marginalized, depressed, or discontent; a few are vulnerable to radicalization against the state, and sporadically a few individuals commit acts of terror. The terrorist attacks from very few members of this categorical group further stigmatize North Africans in Paris and create a negative feedback loop of further social distancing.

Some have achieved success and full integration. I interviewed individuals with North African parents who are as successful as any other Parisian could be, with top posts in the governmental administration and corporations. Yet, Arab Algerians and their children in Paris are disproportionately poor, excluded, and stigmatized.

Interethnic Friendships

Native Parisian informants often told me how they preferred to befriend people like themselves and how much harder it would be to be friends with someone from a different background—especially someone who does not speak French fluently. Strong expectations of homophily and cultural homogeneity shape hiring processes,

> high levels of religiosity in a self-proclaimed *laïc* [secular] society, male-favored gender norms in a society in which women have struggled for equal rights for a half century, French linguistic weakness in a society that glorifies its language all feed into beliefs that Muslims will present problems as co-workers in French firms. (Adida, Laitin, and Valfort 2016: 92)

The strong preference that Parisians have for their own culture puts a heavy burden on immigrants and their children who look different or have different religious practices, and this can lead to social exclusion.

Parisian neighborhoods have strong identities, local flavors, and widespread reputations. People can quickly assume social class by knowing where someone lives in the Parisian metropolitan area. The *banlieues* are especially stigmatized and are often falsely assumed to be the places where immigrants and minorities almost exclusively live (Castañeda 2012b). Employment discrimination often begins with an applicant's name and address, limiting the employment prospects and thus social mobility of *banlieue* residents of color.

Liberté, Égalité, et Fraternité?

When I asked what Maghrebis thought of the French national motto of *Liberté, Égalité, Fraternité* (Liberty, Equality, Fraternity), only 11 of 65 interviewees had something neutral or positive to say about it. For Othman, forty-one, it was this that made him move to Paris from Tunisia. Yet Mohammed, a thirty-six-year-old second-generation Algerian, saw it as a lie. For Lynda, a thirty-two-year-old woman born in Paris to Algerian parents, these values "were not always applied." For Yahia, a forty-eight-year-old immigrant from Algeria, the phrase "is not applied to everybody." Nabil, a twenty-five-year-old Franco-Tunisian, said, "It would be great if everybody enjoyed it, but not everyone does." For Mohanmed, seventy-five, "It has never existed." Ahmed agreed about its nonexistence in practice. For Sonia, a twenty-four-year-old Moroccan, "They are lies." For Enzo, an eighteen-year-old Franco-Tunisian student, "It is like saying 'Water, Gas, Electricity'; it does not mean anything." For Sadok, a sixteen-year-old student, there is liberty but not equality or fraternity. Sonia, a third-generation professional, "It is an ideal but not the case today."

Although many immigrants in the United States and Spain have a hard time paying the bills, their employment and ability to send remittances to help their families grants them a certain sense of agency, empowerment, and source of pride (Castañeda, Morales, and Ochoa 2014). Moreover, work occupies their time and energy. Even in poorly paid dead-end jobs, employment allows new immigrants in Spain and the United States to interact with other immigrants as well as with natives, and this often results in larger social networks, greater access to resources and information, and an increased rate of voluntary acculturation and integration into the receiving society. This also happens in Paris for those employed, but the high number of unemployed Algerians reduces these opportunities for many individuals.

As Loch points out, "France [is] characterized by a strong state and weak mediating organizations linking citizen and state" (Loch 2009: 801). In Paris, immigrants have a direct personal relationship with the state bureaucracy, but this ends up eroding group solidarity because the French welfare state bureaucracy deals with applications one by one and "cannot hear" the collective voices of immigrants and ethnic communities. This weakens the social capital of immigrant groups as well as their ability to act collectively.

The discontent of French descendants of immigrants from Africa stems not from value dissimilarity with the French mainstream but just the opposite; they are discontent precisely because they have internalized mainstream French civic values, but they do not reap the same benefits as majority groups (Loch 2009). In the view of young Maghrebis, the mythic France does not measure up to reality when they come face-to-face with the labor market, state institutions, and many of their fellow citizens.

Many French rap songs, and increasingly books and memoirs, complain about injustices faced as people of North African origin in Paris (Amrani and Beaud 2004: 80). I have heard the same feelings expressed in interviews. The second-generation distances itself from the values of their first-generation immigrant parents of sacrifice, humility, and hard work regardless of pay. As citizens, they hope for more and are angry when they are not given the opportunities that they and their parents thought they would enjoy. This may be the case even when engaging in a counterculture as a rationalizing response and appearing to reject mainstream values (Willis 1981). French citizens of Maghrebi parents are not willing to work under the same conditions as their parents, and even those who would cannot do so given the decrease in industrial, mining, and construction work in the last generation. Second and subsequent generations of Maghrebi immigrants in France, now all French citizens, face a cognitive dissonance between their understanding of French culture and the way many French treat them as being different. Some may become angry in particular interactions, and a few may even participate in riots not because of a rejection of the French system and its ideals but because they believe strongly in them. Even riots are a form of contentious politics and come from the immigrants' internalization of French values, their desire to be fully French, and their rage at the injustices and relative deprivation that many of their parents did not have to experience because their frame of reference was still the Maghreb.

Maghrebis wish for more incorporation and belonging (Tribalat 1995; Terrio 2009; Ribert 2006; Venel 2004). Most French Maghrebis are not particularly religious, are extremely distanced from each other, and, in many cases, are disenchanted with their political disempowerment and lack of economic prospects.

In conclusion, many Parisian residents of North African origin feel discriminated and marginalized and view their culture as belittled by mainstream French culture. They often feel pressured to be more French than other French. Even when they conform, they do not always receive the same opportunities as whites. Despite citizenship and a social safety net, many children of Arab North Africans are not socially integrated. They lack political voice and urban belonging.

4 Barcelona
Deliberate Integration

SPAIN DID NOT BECOME AN IMMIGRANT DESTINATION until the 1970s (Rius Sant 2007; Flesler 2010). A period of rapid economic growth up until 2007 created a demand for workers. The internationalization of the Catalan economy happily coincided with increased immigration. Barcelona is the economic and political capital of Catalonia, an autonomous community in the Iberian Peninsula vying for independence. Barcelona's tourist and economic activity are among the highest in the area. Many locals speak Catalan and have a historical memory that often puts them at odds with Madrid. Barcelona became one of the main destinations of internal and international migrants at the turn of the twenty-first century. Since its democratization after Franco's dictatorship, Spain has had to openly deal with issues of cultural diversity and local prerogatives. In the case of Catalonia, its arguments for minority cultural rights within Spain have been extended to immigrants within Catalonia. At the same time, Catalan nationalism creates social boundaries for those not born in Catalonia.

A referendum for Catalan independence was held on October 1, 2017. The Spanish government called it anticonstitutional and refused to recognize the results in favor of independence. On October 27, 2017, the Catalan Parliament voted to declare independence. Spanish Prime Minister Rajoy swiftly dissolved the Catalonian government and imprisoned Catalan politicians, claiming that it was necessary to defend the nation. Rajoy called for new elections in Catalonia on December 21. Although an anti-independence party was the largest winner, proindependence parties won a majority of congressional seats. This is another episode in a long history of attempts to declare Catalan independence without success (Keating 1996; Sobrequés i Callicó 2010).

Language and Integration: The Catalan Question

On a visit to Hospitalet, a neighborhood on the outskirts of Barcelona, a local teacher told me, "*El barrio se ha puesto muy mal*" ("The neighborhood has gotten very bad"), referring to the growing number of immigrants. I mentioned that, in the past, Catalans had made the same complaints about immigrants from other parts of the Hispanic peninsula, to which this man answered, "My grandmother was from Murcia [meaning she came from outside of Catalonia], but the internal immigrants adapt fast to the Catalan culture," something that previous generations of locals denied. This quote shows us how the children of internal migrants are often among those more openly opposed to new international immigrants (Astor 2016). Then a friend in common intervened, saying, "When I hear immigrant kids speaking in Castilian, I tell them to speak in Catalan. They understand me and can speak to me in Catalan, but after I leave, I can hear them again speaking in Castilian among themselves" (fieldnotes, February 2007). Castilian language is what is known elsewhere as Spanish. The Portuguese, Basques, Catalans, and other groups in the Iberian Peninsula call Spanish *Castellano* and see it as the language of the Crowns of Castile and Leon. Catalan is the language of Catalonia, where Barcelona is located. Much of the Catalan vocabulary derives from Spanish or French; nonetheless, Catalan is its own language with an official dictionary, grammar, local dialects, and accents (Sobrequés i Callicó, 2010).

A Mexican immigrant talks about his reaction to Catalonian culture:

> I used to live in Solsona, a small town where the Catalan culture is felt much more strongly than in Barcelona. In Barcelona, there are people from all over the world . . . One hears less Catalan than one would in a small Catalan town, where you hear it all day. There are no menus in Spanish in the restaurants . . . Many people support Catalan independence, which comes from their history . . . it has an economic rational too . . . and also that during the years of the Franco dictatorship, he prohibited the use of Catalan, and the older generations are very traumatized by that. Because it was forbidden, people have fought hard for the language . . . so, for example, once, a Catalan architect invited my wife and me to a family party. We arrived first, and we talked all in Castilian, but later on, as the extended family kept arriving, it all switched to Catalan, but neither my wife nor I speak Catalan. . . . I used to think that this was disrespectful and inconsiderate . . . but now I understand that for them it is normal to speak Catalan with each other and that it would be weird to speak in another language to each other. The grandfather was asking why, if I

had already been living in Catalonia for three months, I didn't speak Catalan. (Pepe, a twenty-three-year-old Mexican man with Catalan roots[1] studying architecture in Barcelona and planning to stay)

So, contrary to what people assume, migration to Catalonia from Latin America does not mean that there are no cultural differences. Another Mexican gives us her experience of difference in Spain:

In Spain, I never stop being "the foreigner" in social groups. My Mexican accent seems curious to people, and sometimes I become the center of attention; after all this time [living here] it bores me that this keeps happening. It does not happen because I am Mexican but because I am a foreigner. I think most Spanish see Mexicans as good happy people from a beautiful country . . . Spanish culture is different yet very similar to Mexican culture, but it is difficult to feel fully at home when people start talking about there being "too many immigrants in Spain" and see how they are not welcome. We Mexicans look like the South Americans, and in Spain, there are many Peruvians, Colombians, Ecuadorians. Some Spanish people think that South Americans are taking jobs away from them. I have not been impacted by discrimination directly. However, when my aunt and uncle, who have dark-brown skin, came from Mexico to visit, I noticed a couple of instances when people stared at them, gave them dirty looks, and even made some negative comments. That did not make me feel at ease. (Claudia, a thirty-year-old professional woman from Queretaro married to a Spaniard)

As the preceding vignettes show, language is an important part of identity for both immigrants and natives. One would assume that acculturation is harder for North Africans in Spain. Yet, the dozens of Moroccans I interviewed proved adept at learning not only Spanish but also Catalan. Language is indeed another example of ways in which Muslim Moroccans are willing to integrate culturally. Schoolchildren of North African descent tend to become fully trilingual in Arabic, Spanish and Catalan. Children of Maghrebi parents raised in Barcelona may speak Arabic with their parents. They speak to each other in Spanish and can communicate with local authorities and merchants in Catalan when required. Immigrants and their children learn Catalan.

For example, Hassim, a tall and fit young man who has been living and working in Tarragona for fifteen years told me, "I have bought my own house. I feel at home here. My daughters learn Catalan at school and speak Spanish with me." Still, Catalans worry that the influx of immigrants will dilute

Catalan culture as well as their claims for fiscal, political, and cultural autonomy (Rius Sant 2007: 246).

Latino interviewees assumed before migrating that they would experience a closer cultural affinity with Barcelona and Spain than they actually did (Cook-Martín and Viladrich 2009; Lacomba 2016). Moroccans on the other hand, assumed a farther cultural distance than that which actually existed and as a result were more tolerant than Latinos were of locals correcting their *Castellano*. Latin American immigrants pose a special concern to some Catalans because they are more reluctant to learn Catalan. Indeed, most of the professional Mexicans living and working in Barcelona for many years refused to learn, or be spoken to, in Catalan and resented that distinctions were made between Catalans and non-Catalans, which made them feel unwelcome in Barcelona.

Social Integration: Immigrants Finding a Home in Barcelona

The Spanish national identity was formed in reaction to the eventual distrust and exclusion of the Moorish, Jewish, and colonized indigenous peoples (de Zayas 2006; Flesler 2010; González Alcantud 2002). Today, many Spaniards still distrust Moroccans and prefer Latin Americans because of their cultural similarities (Calavita 2005: 127). As was evident from most of my interviews with local Spanish and Catalan people and from attending antiracist marches, immigration is welcome or at least tolerated. Although older generations may still be influenced by General Franco's strong republican and ethnonational discourse against outside influences, the younger generations are far more tolerant and have a high level of participation in civil society's efforts to embrace immigrants, except for a small number of neo-Nazi youth groups (Salas 2003).

Arab North Africans are aware of the tense history between Spain and the Maghreb, mass expulsions, and anti-Muslim sentiments. This results in an exaggerated anticipation of discrimination that would be met after immigration. When they arrive, they are proven wrong and report that they actually faced less personal and institutional discrimination in Barcelona than they had expected, especially when they compared their experience to that of friends and family living in other countries such as France or Italy. Moroccans are among the most stigmatized groups in contemporary Spain. Surprisingly, despite frequent openly racist comments, the Moroccans interviewed report feeling quite at ease in Barcelona. They work hard, and they hope their children will profit from growing up and studying in Barcelona. Barcelona was also the city, among the three discussed in this book, where the young male immigrants interviewed had the highest number of social contact with locals and where I recorded many cases of recently arrived Moroccan men dating local women.

Moroccans are objectively fairly well accommodated in Barcelona because they are able to join the labor force, begin a new life, participate in the formal or underground economy, and retain many cultural practices from their hometowns. When I asked Moroccans about their identity, they reported cosmopolitan traits, emphasizing their humanity and the equality of all people. Furthermore, they showed they were eager to perfect their Spanish, and it is indeed quite common for their children to be fully fluent in both Spanish and Catalan. Interestingly enough, many Spanish citizens will tell you that there is a perception of a problem with the integration of Moroccan immigrants; nonetheless, the great majority of Moroccans in Spain are well integrated.

Contrary to what one might wrongly assume a priori, Latin Americans moving to work in Spain felt that there would be an almost perfect cultural affinity with the Spanish and that, because of this, they would receive a very positive welcome. This was not always the case. Accents, skin tone, and the use of different words to refer to food and objects initially cause much apparent tension and discomfort between Spaniards and Latinos. It is necessary for Latinos to relearn aspects of formal Castellano Spanish to fit in better. Many Mexican elite expats particularly resented this. Mexican professionals I interviewed often felt discriminated against at work or were attacked verbally in public. Furthermore, some Catalans viewed Latinos as another factor that would dilute the Catalan population and the use of the Catalan language in Barcelona, lowering the legitimacy of their claims for increasing political and cultural independence from the rest of Spain. Nonetheless, the Latinos who stay in Barcelona have jobs, contribute to the local economy, and have diverse networks. Immigration to contemporary Spain today is a result of Spanish imperialism, and assimilation occurs in the context of a long history of nation building. Aside from the question of complete independence, the prospects for the Catalan culture look good because newcomers appreciate the local culture and acculturate through time.

Colonial History and Immigration

During the Middle Ages, many kingdoms and fiefdoms existed in present-day Spain. In 795 Charlemagne established the *Marca Hispana* or Spanish March, also known as the Barcelona March, as a buffer zone between Franks and Moors (Griffith 2017, Sahlins 1989). The County of Barcelona was part of the Crown of Aragon since the eleventh century CE. The reigns of Alfonso X of Castile and Jaime I of Aragón, as well as the Caliphate of Córdoba in the south of the peninsula, were multicultural places. Cohabitation among Jews, Muslims, and Christians of different European ethnicities (Visigoths, Hispano-Romans, and so on) was an everyday fact.

The contested marriage between the young Fernando of Aragon and Isabel of Castile in 1469 resulted in the union of the Kingdoms of Castile and Aragón around the banner of Catholicism (García de Cortázar 2007). Despite having been excommunicated for being cousins and marrying without the initial approval of the Pope, Fernando and Isabel called themselves the Catholic Monarchs. The merging of Castile and Aragon occurred after a failed war with Portugal and France and after Isabel had secured her contested claim to the throne. In the need to legitimate their mandate over Castile and Aragon, the Monarchs set into a nation-building and imperial agenda that resulted in the subjugation of the neighboring Christian Kingdom of Navarra in 1512 and the annexation of the Canary Islands as part of an agreement with Portugal.

The drive for the creation of what would be later called a nation-state, led the Catholic Monarchs and their *converso* (Jews who had converted to Catholicism) religious and policy advisors to implement the eventual expulsion of Jews, decreed in 1492. In the same year, they conquered the Moorish Kingdom of Granada. The *reconquista* took control away from the different Moroccan Berber and Arab kingdoms that fought among each other and reigned on the south of the Iberian Peninsula intermittently since the Moorish invasion of 711. Also in 1492, Christopher Columbus, sponsored by the Catholic Monarchs, left Spain in search of a route to India and instead reached the Caribbean and later the Americas. The Moorish colony in the Iberian Peninsula was called Al-Andalus. Few Arab females came along with the armies, and many children were the product of Moorish–Spanish relationships (BBC 2009). After the reconquest of 1492, around 300,000 former Muslims and 60,000 Jews converted to Christianity, though the Inquisition doubted their true conversion and persecuted them. Over 200,000 Sephardic Jews left Spain, scattering around the Mediterranean and Latin America. Not until June 30, 1982, was a law passed in Spain inviting these exiles' descendants to return.

In brief, the Iberian Peninsula has been inhabited by many different cultures. The people who populate this region are the result of a mix between Nordic tribes, Mediterranean peoples (Greeks, Phoenicians, Romans), Berbers,

Arabs, and Jews who once lived in these lands as discrete ethnic groups that cohabited and intermarried. The process of nation formation made many of these religious and ethnic groups mix and identify themselves as Spanish. Regional differences still exist, though; for example, the Basques and Catalans have kept distinct languages and traditions, despite Franco's banning of their languages. The centralization, brought by the dictatorship of General Francisco Franco (1939–1975), has been increasingly weakened by democratization, the growing federalism, and some provincial and local autonomy. Still, some Catalans still refer to Madrid or Castile as the "conquering empire" and demand complete independence.

Due to the colonial legacy of the Spanish protectorate over Morocco (1912–1956) (Mateo Dieste 2003), there are a large number of people who speak Spanish in the northern Moroccan provinces, and in addition there is a similarity of food, architecture, and climate. Political borders and the Strait of Gibraltar cannot erase centuries of back-and-forth between these two sides. Moroccan immigrants know this and thus see themselves as the latest wave of population movement and cultural exchange.

Although some are quick to dismiss historical events, the way newcomers frame this history matters in the subjective expectations of integration. While doing fieldwork through Morocco, I was surprised by the commonplace argument that Moroccans, Spaniards, and Latinos were brothers because of their intertwined histories. Moroccans often say that Moroccans and Spaniards are *kif kif*, meaning similar and equivalent, sharing a close history and similar cultural traits. Ali, a forty-five-year-old Moroccan who has lived in Barcelona for seventeen years, said, "I feel as close to the Spanish as I do to Moroccans." One could say that the unspoken difference is religion, but some Moroccans were fast to say that the Spanish and Latinos understood religiosity and the right to have a religion and thus were similar. As a forty-four-year-old woman told me in 2017, "People in Barcelona are fraternal and tolerant, not like in France or Belgium. Here I can cover my head, and nobody forbids it." Moroccans also pointed to similarities to Latin Americans. A Moroccan man told me that, due to a colonial past, Moroccans and Latin Americans tend to have a longer historical memory than Europeans and Americans.

I asked Abdlah, a Moroccan man who lived in Barcelona for ten years and now has a small fruit business in Montpelier, France, where the best oranges were from. I expected he would proudly say Morocco. Instead, he responded in an egalitarian and cosmopolitan manner, "All of them are good. They all come from the ground. Same Mediterranean climate. People take orange trees from Valencia and plant them in Morocco. It is all the same."

The Backlash against Franco's Dictatorship and Cultural Homogeneity

During the thirty-six-year (1939–1975) dictatorship of General Francisco Franco, Spain was a very centralized state with Madrid in clear hegemony. But, since democratization, there have been loud calls from the provinces, especially from Catalonia and the Basque country, for more autonomy or total independence (Díez Medrano 1994; Griffith 2017). This has created a federal system where the independent provinces have much more say about local policies, economic development, tax systems, and immigrant integration policies. Catalonia has always been one of Spain's most prosperous provinces (Díez Medrano 1994). It developed rapidly after Spain's entrance into the European Union. Barcelona is one of the metro areas that has attracted the largest number of immigrants, second only to Madrid (INE 2007). Catalonia instituted many local policies to accommodate new immigrants and cultures (Aragón Medina et al. 2009) in a way that is compatible with their own long-term claims for multiculturalism vis-à-vis Madrid, in calls for space, respect, and rights for the Catalan language and culture.

Franco's regime imposed Spanish as the sole official legal language and prohibited the legal use of Catalan, Occitan, Basque, and other local languages. Since the death of Franco in 1975, Catalonia has sought increasing political independence and cultural pride. This was done partly by framing themselves within Spain as parallel to Québec within Canada—and thus indirectly inspired by the work of influential intellectual proponents of multiculturalism such as Charles Taylor, Will Kimlycka, and others on the Québec issue. This was similar to global discourses on multiculturalism that mobilize a different language and culture to claim provincial autonomy and minority rights. In 1978, along with Galicia and the Basque country, Catalonia was recognized by the Spanish government as a historical nationality and was given the Statute of Autonomy (Keating 2007). In 1985, alongside other regions, Catalonia was designated as an Autonomous Community by the Spanish government, and, as such, Catalonia's regional governments became responsible for their own schools, universities, health, social services, policing, cultural policies, and urban and rural development. The relative autonomy of Catalonia means that the local government has been able to create and implement its own immigrant-integrating policies. Influenced by its own discourse on

Catalan minority rights, Catalonia had a certain degree of empathy for immigrants and felt the need to offer a similar program for local minority groups to be coherent.

In Barcelona, the government has institutionalized policies and provided funding to organize events that showcase with pride the cultures of the newcomers. Thus, there are North African community centers throughout Catalan cities that provide spaces for cultural activities based on the practices of the Maghreb, as well as educational programs that teach the Spanish and Catalan languages, how to use computers, and how to apply for office jobs. Although not a panacea, this direct involvement of Spanish national and local authorities results in the incorporation of certain elements of the immigrant population. For example, I visited offices for Maghrebi immigrants in both Madrid and Barcelona. Often the offices were brand new and well kept. One of them displayed art for sale created by Maghrebi immigrants in an upscale art gallery–type setting. The centers had native Spanish social workers, secretaries, and directors. There were computers that some immigrants used for personal and work purposes. These centers are a combination of a social service agency and a community organization. The presence of the local government was visible, at the same time, outreach was done in a respectful way that was open to the Latino and Muslim immigrants' cultural and practical needs; visitors were welcome regardless of nationality, religion, or accent. There was no need to check in at the front or talk to a staff person first, so newcomers felt welcome to use the space.

With the growth of immigration to Spain in the last two decades, progressive multicultural policies by the Generalitat de Catalunya actively highlight the immigrants' own cultures, stressing that immigrants enrich Barcelona and Catalonia in general. Nonetheless, there has been tension surrounding these policies. Some natives feel that this is unfaithful to their own culture because of the increasing number of Spanish speakers who refuse to recognize the local symbolic and political importance of using the Catalan language. The refusal of some new Barcelona residents to speak Catalan, along with the history of Castilian oppression and the increased dependence on tourism, make Catalans further distrust Latin American immigrants. Indeed, most Latin American immigrants see themselves as immigrating to Spain and not to Catalonia and are initially reluctant to acculturate to Catalan culture, as these immigrants feel closer to Spanish culture. Catalan traditionalists consider them to be a proxy for Castilian cultural homogenization pressures inside of Catalonia. Thus, Catalan politicians like Jordi Pujol believe that new immigrants "could again slow down or postpone the process of normalization of the Catalan language" (Rius Sant 2007: 218).

History is relevant because new immigrants are used as proxies in this economic, political, and cultural competition between the Spanish state and Catalonia. The degree to which Catalonia can mold immigrants into Catalans, the way it successfully did in previous decades with the children of many economic migrants from within Spain (Astor 2009), affects the duration of its claims for autonomy. If immigrants from other parts of Spain, Morocco, and Latin America refused to learn Catalan and instead exclusively spoke Castilian, they would lessen the demographic and cultural claims of Catalan independence. Many migrant parents I talked to view the knowledge of the Spanish language as a valuable skill to have that opens more labor markets for them and their children. They often complained about the number of courses taught in Catalan in public schools, a complaint that Catalan social workers and state intermediaries did not receive well and chose to ignore. Yet, due to different expectations of similarity before migration, Moroccans appear to be more promptly willing than Latinos to incorporate into Catalonia. Catalan culture and language are not at risk because formal education is carried out in Catalan, and most people growing up in the area, including the children of internal and international immigrants, become bilingual in Catalan and Castilian and have a strong local identity. For Abdul, a twenty-year-old man born in Morocco who works in a bar in Badalona, one of the main benefits of growing up in Barcelona is his ability to speak Catalan and Spanish. Many immigrants often wear the Barcelona soccer-team T-shirt partly because they feel urban belonging and pride for their city.

Fostering Urban Belonging and Institutional Integration

Spain has inclusive policies at the government level (Aragón Medina et al. 2009), and immigrants are willing to assimilate, but, like others, many Spanish citizens show certain parochial, nationalistic, and anti-immigrant views. The difference in immigrant incorporation in Spain, then, is not due to a lack of xenophobia or opportunistic politicians, but, rather, policy precedents, social interaction, and immigrants feeling more driven to assimilate than in Paris. Furthermore, Spanish national politics has moved to the left, whereas in France, politics has moved to the right. Spain does not have a xenophobic right-wing rising political force, unlike the United States, France, and other

European countries. Spain's policy makers have had time to consciously learn from the experiences of other countries and to choose their own model to follow. Thus far, the Spanish have used enlightened and tolerant policies that have allowed space for a de facto incorporation of immigrant groups. Yet the economic crisis took away abundant jobs, a crucial element of immigrant integration.

Spanish experience with immigration is a new one. The fast growth of manufacturing, construction, and tourism sectors at the end of the twentieth century made foreign labor a necessity. Spain does not have a republican model like France, and, although it does not have a points system when selecting immigrants, it has a top-down multicultural model of immigrant integration like Canada's (Bloemraad 2006a). National governments, especially under the socialist Presidents Felipe Gonzales (1982–1996) and José Luis Rodríguez Zapatero (2004–2011), were good at carrying out many middle-sized administrative regularizations and amnesties. The 2003 Historical Memory Law allowed the grandchildren of Spanish emigrants and political exiles to apply to obtain Spanish citizenship; 90 percent of the over half a million individuals applying through this legal route are from Latin America (González Enríquez 2014). Sephardic Jews and immigrants from Latin America, Portugal, Andorra, the Philippines, and Equatorial Guinea have access to citizenship after two years of residency in Spain. This provision benefits mainly Latin Americans. In contrast, Moroccans have to live in Spain for ten years to be able to apply for citizenship (González Enríquez 2014).

The timing, tempo, and composition of Moroccan migration to Spain, which is largely a labor migration, has taken a very different form than what brought Moroccans to France. Morocco is very close to Spain, and the abundance of jobs brought many Moroccans to the country looking for work. Because Moroccan migration to Spain is a relatively new phenomenon, the members of the immigrant second generation are young (Portes, Vickstrom, and Aparicio 2011: 392).

State And Society Openness to Multiculturalism

Barcelona's city government has an office in charge of immigrant affairs, and this policy area is taken very seriously. The Barcelona municipal governments have long been aware of the economic benefits of immigration. They also see immigrants, along with tourists and foreign investment, as a way to make Barcelona a global city. Government officials have learned best practices around immigrant integration from other cities and countries and have become a model in the process. Yet society is still adapting to this new reality, which is why I place Barcelona in between New York and Paris in terms of its openness to multiculturalism and diversity.

Political Integration

In Spain, new small political parties such as Unión Progreso y Democracia, Coalición por Melilla, and Renacimiento y Unión have appeared, representing Spanish residents of Maghrebi origin. This last party, Union and Renaissance, writes in its newsletter: "We are Spanish, Spanish citizens, our country is Spain, and our constitution is the Spanish one, therefore we are de jure and de facto citizens, neither first class citizens nor second class citizens" (Bakkach El Aamrani 2009). Despite some reservations from many native Spaniards, the Spanish of Muslim origin choose to underline their belonging to contemporary Spain and seek to join future governments and institutions on an equal footing. Besides politicians from Ceuta and Melilla (Spanish enclaves in North Africa), Mohamed Chaib, born in Tangiers and a Catalan congressman for the Socialist Party of Catalonia (Partit Socialista de Catalunya), was the first deputy of Muslim and immigrant origin (Rius Sant 2007). Chaib has also played an important role in civil society by founding and supporting the nonprofit Asociación Socio-Cultural Ibn Batuta (ASCIB), which has joined many other associations to help and integrate immigrants and to create bridges between Catalans and Moroccans.

Still, in Spain, one could say that most initiatives are preventive and top down as bottom-up organization has been actively discouraged. Immigration laws forbid foreigners, especially undocumented ones, from organizing meetings in public and private places and organizing marches. Although in the past these limitations have been found unconstitutional, politicians—especially those from the Christian Democratic Popular Party and during the government of conservative José María Aznar (1996–2004)—have continued proposing anti-immigrant and "immigrant contract" bills. Leaders of Maghrebi humanitarian organizations have also been tried "for aiding illegal immigration" (Rius Sant 2007).

After the newfound prosperity of Spain in the 2000s, the government spent considerable energy and resources to cater to the needs of immigrants. In recent years, new initiatives at the national level have included the

Comisión Interministerial de Extranjería (Interministerial Commission for Alien Affairs), the Foro para la Integración Social de los Inmigrantes (Forum for the Social Integration of Immigrants), the Observatorio Permanente de la Inmigración (Permanent Immigration Observatory), the Consejo Superior de Política de Inmigración (High Council for Immigration Policy), the Fundación Pluralismo y Convivencia (Pluralism and Coexistence Foundation), and the "Strategic Plan for Citizenship and Integration" that the Spanish government approved in 2007 (Bezunartea, López, and Tedesco 2009). Furthermore, the Barcelona municipal government has hired various successful immigrants as influential advisors on minority policies. It seems that a positive legal framework with resources devoted to aid in immigrant integration, along with positive subjective feelings by immigrants themselves, result in a very positive combination that can facilitate structural assimilation, as is the case for Maghrebis in Spain. The necessary next step for full integration is for natives to dispel their distrust of foreigners. Continued interaction in the city can achieve this.

Economic Integration: Labor Markets and Categorical Inequality

Carlos, a working-age Peruvian, told me that in the early 2000s recruiters would go to Peru, Ecuador, Bolivia, Colombia, and Morocco to look for prospective employees to go work in Spain. Carlos told me that "mainly foreigners work here; the only Spanish people are the kitchen chef and the general manager." This hierarchy reflects the wages paid across categories that reproduce inequality; lower-paying jobs are assigned to an out-group, thus reinforcing their supposed inferiority, until it is made to appear natural (Tilly 1998). Another example of this pairing of categorical groups with exploitation can be seen in the truck-driving sector in Spain. As Carlos told me, "I am getting my Spanish commercial truck driver's license soon. As a truck driver, you can make good money. They pay well here, around €3,000 a month plus benefits." Thinking about the protectionist American Teamster Union that opposes the entry of Mexican truck drivers into US territory, I asked, "Do they employ foreigners to drive Spanish trucks?" He immediately answered, "Yes, they often go to Peru to look for drivers. They also get you papers. I have friends who are doing it. But I prefer to get employed here because they pay people they hire in Spain €3,000, while they pay only €1,500 to the people they hire in Latin America!" This clearly exemplifies the inequalities within labor value based on where somebody is hired. Despite having a stable job, Carlos lives day to day, supporting himself in Spain while sending money back to his family in Peru.

At one point, he asked me what I did; "I am a sociologist," I answered. Carlos replied:

> I thought you were coming from the workers' union. They come often, and they help us a lot. For example, we are supposed to get two consecutive days off every week. Once a colleague got one day off later on the week than he was supposed to—and not continuously to his other day off—something that violated Spanish labor law, so he complained to the union. They came and asked the manager for the schedules. The manager was shaking. He showed the schedules to the union representative, who saw other cases where the employees were given the nonconsecutive days off, and he reprimanded the manager: "Why do you take advantage of these foreign workers who do not know their rights?" For example, when you get married you are supposed to get fifteen days off with pay for "matrimonial rest," but they did not want to give them to me until the union representative came and reminded them that because I had gotten married while working here, I had the right to these extra vacation days. Some days later, the manager told me I could take two weeks off.

This passage demonstrates how Spanish labor unions defend their members' rights through advocacy and by insuring that immigrants' labor rights are upheld without negative repercussion for those filing complaints. This increases the voice of immigrant workers in their workplaces and reduces divisions between native and foreign-born workers who share labor rights and union representation even though salaries are unequal.

The Spanish Welfare State

In 1981, French President François Mitterrand attempted to simultaneously reduce working hours and increase wages, social benefits, and taxes, but in an already integrating Europe he suffered the "backlash of currency markets" (Castells 2000: 139) and was forced to devalue the franc and backtrack on many of his policies. The Spanish socialist government, elected in 1982, learned from this experience, and the government of Felipe Gonzalez took a middle ground social market economy between neoliberal economic policy and social democracy (Castells 2000: 139). Spain is a weaker welfare state than France is. At the same time, the nature of Spain's society and the size of its economy have changed drastically since Spain became part of the European Union. The funds for economic and social growth provided by the European Union have resulted in an overall increase in the standard of living for most Spaniards. Spain changed from a country of emigration to a country of immigration.

In Barcelona, immigrants are traditionally required to register with the local police station, regardless of their legal immigration status. This registration results in their administrative incorporation to the city and is often accompanied by rights and benefits. Yet, after the economic crisis, state funding for immigrants and citizens has been drastically cut (Castañeda 2012a).

Changes After Economic Crisis

As jobs have decreased after the global financial crisis that started in 2007, integration has become more difficult. Unemployment benefits have also been drastically cut. Interviewed migrants reported telling their family and friends in their home countries to stay there because it was hard to find new jobs in Barcelona. However, in 2008, relatively few migrants chose to return to their countries of origin. Most of them said that they would try to weather the storm. Some thought that, in the long term, their employment prospects still were better in Barcelona than in their hometowns. Yet in follow-up fieldwork conducted in the summer of 2011, I found that many of the immigrants whom I had interviewed in 2007 and 2008 had left Barcelona due to the economic crisis. I heard many stories about people moving back to Morocco and Latin America where the economy was stronger than in Spain. Even when the economy was not necessarily stronger, people went back; for example, some Cubans who were living in Spain returned to Cuba because they could not get any jobs in Spain. Some Venezuelans were in the same situation. Doing fieldwork in Switzerland in 2008, I interviewed many immigrants and European-born children of Latin American immigrants who had moved from Spain to Switzerland in search of jobs. In 2017, many immigrants remain in Barcelona, but I heard statements like this from a man working in a Halal meat shop, "I am going back to Morocco. Before I would send my family money. Every week, I would be, 'here you go,' but not anymore."

The economic crisis gave rise to massive marches on May 15, 2011, and the establishments of encampments in public plazas in Spanish cities, including Barcelona (Castañeda 2012a). The activists and issues brought included stopping austerity measures and the accompanying cuts to public services and programs including education, housing, and health, as well as demands for immigrant rights and regularizations (Castañeda 2014a). Immigrants themselves had an active role among the so-called *Indignados* movement, establishing immigrant shadow cabinets and bringing protest tactics from movements in their countries as well as spreading the occupy method to future protests (Castañeda 2015).

Who Are You?

Often when I asked Moroccans, "Who are you?" They answered, "a human," "a person like everyone else," "normal," or, less often, "a Muslim," "a resident of Barcelona," and sometimes even "Spanish" or "Catalan." Although these may be socially desirable answers, choosing to give them is in itself a political act that displays a nonconfrontational identity, a strategy very different from that of Algerians and Moroccans in France. When I asked one Moroccan what he did during his free time, he answered, "the same things as a Spanish person." When asked about how they thought Moroccans in general are treated in Spain, most Moroccan respondents said "badly," at least by some Spanish people and especially when compared to European or Latin American immigrants. But when asked about their own personal experiences, the most common answers from these respondents were "good" in general or, when particularizing, that "some treat them well, and others do not." Herein lies the paradox; Moroccans *do* suffer discrimination, and they know the negative stereotypes that Spaniards and Catalans have about "the Moors," but after living in Spain for some years, they have an even more positive opinion of Spain than before migrating (Aparicio et al. 2005). Another counterintuitive finding is that Moroccans reported the highest levels of satisfaction and thankfulness for living abroad, even when they were undocumented, employed in the informal economy, or had faced many hurdles. When asked which Spanish values they had learned, most said "tolerance" and "to cohabit with different people." It seems that many Moroccans in Barcelona (and Madrid) had found the political freedoms and economic mobility that they lacked in Morocco and had also experienced multiculturalism beyond the superficial and instrumental contacts that take place between locals and tourists in Morocco. In summary, in the case of immigrants in Barcelona, the interventions of the municipality, economic integration, and social contact with other Barcelona residents are more influential to their perceptions of Barcelona than any residual racism they may have experienced.

The initial reception experienced by these immigrants also helps shape their perceptions. State–Church partnerships in Spain are historically prevalent and problematic. Indeed, Catholic organizations have organized many migrant relief efforts sometimes with underlying hopes of conversion. In Barcelona, I attended a Sunday Catholic religious service conducted in Tagalog for immigrants from the Philippines, another Spanish former colony, and I also visited the offices of nuns in Barcelona who helped newly arrived Moroccans to obtain food and clothing. Given the multicultural policies and resources promoted by the state and the active participation of the Church and nonprofits, Barcelona gives Moroccan immigrants the impression that both civil society and the state are "on their side" despite the residual racism encountered at times. A powerful image in a local newspaper showed a Catholic nun in full habit voting with the help of a smiling election volunteer wearing a headscarf (Morán and Chirino 2009).

Many Barcelona locals complain about the tensions and problems posed by the "Moors" and "Arabs" and may openly make racist comments and spout generalizations about Muslims, while at the same time exchanging jokes, drinks, and greetings with their foreign-born friends. In this case, making racist comments does not preclude socialization and friendships with individuals from a racialized group.

In 2008, I interviewed dozens of immigrants. Most had parents and family members back in Morocco. When I asked them if the fact that they had been born in Morocco mattered, Ahmed, a tanned forty-eight-year-old Moroccan businessman, said, "No, not for me." Mustafa, a documented thirty-year-old man working on construction, said, "Not much; except for a few cases, people are respectful."

Ahmed, a forty-four-year-old undocumented Pakistani married to a Moroccan woman, said he did feel discriminated against and mistreated when selling beer in the streets at night. Beni, a twenty-nine-year-old Moroccan documented worker, said, "Moroccans look different from Europeans." Mosanet, a thirty-five-year-old Moroccan, said, "They stare at you because of your skin color." Ahlam, who is twenty-eight, unemployed, and undocumented said, "Yes, people think I sell drugs."

Among the positive aspects of living in Barcelona, they highlighted that in Barcelona many groups live side by side respectfully, and they reported that the city was an example of cohabitation among people of different origin. Ahlamn, a twenty-eight-year-old Moroccan-born man living in the Raval neighborhood, said, "The Spanish think differently than we do, but there is peace."

In 2017, there were many more Moroccan women in the streets, more families, and many looked very middle class with luxury clothes and cars. Although many chose to cover their heads, many Moroccan women and girls have their hair uncovered and are almost indistinguishable from Spaniards.

Unfortunately, sometimes social boundaries remain real, and interaction can end in physical acts of violence. A well-known case occurred on October 7, 2007, when a young Spanish man boarded a subway train while talking on his cell phone, boasting about having hit a "moro" (Arabic) man. Then, suddenly, and without any provocation, he attacked a sixteen-year-old female from Ecuador. The aggressor called her names, hit, and kicked her. The security camera on the subway train recorded the entire event, which was broadcast widely on the media. Ecuadorian President Rafael Correa and the minister of Foreign Affairs had already scheduled a visit soon after the incident. While visiting Spain, they asked the Spanish government to punish this act. The Ecuadorian President was careful to state that this was an isolated incident and that the Spanish generally welcome and respect Ecuadorians. On October 28 over half a million people demonstrated in Madrid against racism and condemning the attack. Later, on March 18, 2009, the attacker was sentenced to eight months in prison plus a fine of €360 and was additionally forced to pay €6,000 as compensation to the victim (*El País* 2009). This event exemplifies the state and civil society condemning violent racist acts.

Upper-Class Latino Immigrants

At lunch one day in Barcelona, I found myself sitting next to a man about my age who appeared to be Latin American. I tried to converse with him, but he seemed uninterested. After lunch, when he opened his wallet to pay, I noticed he had a Mexican ID. After I told him I was born in Mexico City, he still acted coldly, and the only information I was able to get out of him was that he lived and worked in Spain and that he had not visited any local Mexican restaurants. He seemed to be an example of an integrated Latino who had strongly assimilated and who had experienced a process of *dissimilation* from other Mexicans (Jiménez and Fitzgerald 2007); he appeared to have distanced himself and had started to forget some of his first cultural practices and interests. Such Mexican migrants to Spain are largely invisible. They are often young and single; they obtain visas, work as professionals, and focus on individual advancement. Although they are integrated into the Spanish labor market, they remain at an arm's length from local society. Some Mexican professionals complained to me about the social closure of the Catalan elite. Some of these Mexican professionals said they would prefer to live in Paris, New York, or London but said that they were "stuck in Spain" where it was easier for them to obtain legal residence or even citizenship because of having a Spanish grandparent. Experiences of immigrants in Barcelona vary by class and personal circumstance, ranging from total integration and assimilation, to complete exclusion, to biculturalism, and partial integration.

Conclusion: Subjective Belonging Versus Objective Preferences and Lower Discrimination

The limited life chances of many Parisian residents of North African descent contrast with the expectations that they have of the French state and society. This mismatch leaves some of them with a great sense of perceived injustice and relative deprivation (Loch 2009). They also lack sanctioned avenues for collective public, cultural, and religious displays. The difference between expectations and actual opportunities is the opposite for North Africans in Barcelona, who in my interviews, surveys, and elsewhere (Metroscopia 2010), report feeling relatively welcomed. In contrast, Latinos in Spain report feeling less welcome than they had expected before migration. Yet, before the 2008 economic crisis, they could have had jobs and natural interactions with natives, which in time would have eased their acculturation.

Given the cultural, religious, and linguistic commonalities between Spain and Latin America, one would expect Latin Americans to experience a more welcoming context. Yet an interesting set of counterintuitive results emerged from interviews; Latin American immigrants have a very positive image about their prospects for economic and cultural integration in Barcelona, Spain. The reality faced by most immigrants is not as rosy as they had anticipated, but, after a few years of voluntary readaptation, they find themselves in an objectively good position and subjectively start feeling at home. North Africans in Spain also experience both rapid economic and voluntary linguistic assimilation. Unlike their Latin American counterparts, before migrating, they expected racism and substantial struggles to keep cultural practices. Given this difference between expectations and reality, both documented and undocumented migrants reported an urban belonging. Furthermore, before the current economic crisis, Spain had several administrative amnesties and regularizations of the status of particular undocumented individuals, as well as wide access to work visas and residency permits alongside an intense and frequent social contact between natives and ethnic groups. The context of reception in Barcelona is such that immigrants can change gradually in a way that positively allows their structural integration into Catalonia. As I discussed, integration to Barcelona is further mediated by the fact that many in Barcelona speak Catalan in addition to Spanish, and that many support political independence from Spain.

This analysis of immigrant integration in Barcelona shows how feelings of belonging can occur even in a social context punctuated with sporadic racism, as long as there are job opportunities, supporting public programs, and a real immersion in urban life. This is another example of the importance of including the voice of the population in question and not just gathering objective measures about their well-being or analyzing media discourses and incidents. Urban belonging in Barcelona was high among all the foreign born, yet it surprisingly took slightly longer for Latin Americans. Economic opportunities decreased after the economic crisis, and some immigrants returned to their countries of birth or migrated to other countries, yet the peaceful cohabitation and respect of diversity largely remains in the streets of metropolitan Barcelona.

5 Religion and Immigrant Integration

HUNDREDS OF PEOPLE GATHERED IN SAINT PATRICK'S CATHEDRAL on New York City's Fifth Avenue on a winter morning in 2006. The mass attendants came in a procession carrying religious images and banners. Cardinal Edward Egan, Bishop Josu Iriondo, Monsignor Robert T. Ritchie (the rector head of Saint Patrick's Cathedral), and the rest of the cathedral's staff received the procession with attendants from the five boroughs of New York City and neighboring states. Faith and tradition brought all these people together. Everyone went inside for the service, during which the church leaders spoke solemnly about the importance of the group in attendance, praising its worth, union, numbers, commitment, dignity, rights, religious values, political potential, and growing demographic importance. After mass was over, the Church officials wished a farewell to the attendants on the front steps of the cathedral, in front of the news media, tourists, and local onlookers.

What kind of gathering was this? At first glance, this would seem like a purely religious event, but the date was not an official holiday like Christmas or Easter. The group walked in with a collective identity around similar religious beliefs. This identity was reinforced before, during, and after the service through the different practices that the members engaged in. As it had done for Irish, Italian, Polish, Puerto Ricans, or Cubans before (Hagan 2009; Orsi 2002; Pedraza 2007), the Catholic Church held an event catering to traditions from a particular group of people—Mexicans, in this case. The day was December 12, the day celebrating the Virgin of Guadalupe, the spiritual mother of Mexicans and the object of continuous adoration by millions of Mexicans

Figure 5.1. Poster for the torch relay from Puebla to New York, 2017.
SOURCE: Asociación Tepeyac de New York, Facebook page.

worldwide who annually make processions to her temple on the Tepeyac Hill in Mexico City.

The overwhelming majority of church attendees that day were Mexican. There were around 500 people dressed in white clothes showing their membership in Guadeloupian Committees (Gálvez 2009; R. C. Smith 2006); most of them were second-generation US-born youth of Mexican origin. Joel Magallan—the director of Associación Tepeyac, a New York–based Mexican community group—coordinated the event. This mass was the culmination of a torch relay, beginning in the Mixteca region of central Mexico, to Mexico City, and all the way to New York City. From the beginning to the end of this relay, a torch is carried by foot, involving the participation of thousands of devotees following in cars and buses. The torch relay is based on an Aztec tradition of renewal (Gálvez 2009). This tradition has merged with that of the adoration of the Virgin of Guadalupe. Because the torch travels all the way from Central Mexico to New York, traversing long distances, facing the elements, and continuously crossing state boundaries, the torch run is a symbolic reenactment of the emigration process, this time reframed in the light of religious sacrifice and spiritual transcendence.

The torch has been going to Saint Patrick's Cathedral almost every year since 2000. Mexican consular authorities and different Mexican celebrities participate each year as guests of honor. Some Mexican national periodicals cover the event. For those participating in New York City, this is not only a religious event but also a political one. As Gaspar Orozco, Consul for Communities, told a reporter from a Mexican national newspaper, "[This celebration

Figure 5.2. Procession arriving at Saint Patrick's Cathedral on Fifth Avenue, December 12, 2006.

SOURCE: © Castañeda 2006.

of] the Virgin of Guadalupe is a symbol of the space that Mexicans have won in this great city" (Torre 2006). The Mexican Consulate and the Catholic Church joined in this grassroots event, which was not originally

> developed by the Church or by a charismatic activist or group of activists attempting to "politicize" Guadalupan devotion, but rather emerges from the everyday experiences of Mexican immigrants as they go about their business of going to work, keeping their families together, participating in church activities, and sweeping shrines to the object of their devotion. (Gálvez 2009: 7)

Given their numbers and the extent of their devotion, Church leaders were happy to join and welcome these worshippers and to expand their congregation by accommodating a tradition compatible with the goals of the Church.

During the mass, Monsignor Ritchie, the Rector of Saint Patrick's Cathedral, delivered a sermon with political undertones: "The Virgin is interested in just laws, in more immigrants in New York, a city of immigrants. It is an honor that you have brought her image to New York." After this, he asked for better laws to protect immigrants and offered a prayer for "the immigrants who have lost hope of returning to their country, and for those who have died on their way" (Torre 2006). Monsignor Ritchie was wearing a robe with a large image of the Virgin of Guadalupe printed on it, covering him from his chest to his toes.

At the end of the service, the attendants then marched to the close by Dag Hammarskjold Plaza in front of the UN headquarters and held a rally to celebrate their organizational achievements in honor of the Virgin. As they ate tamales, Joel Magallan and the leaders of the respective neighborhoods, parishes, and boroughs spoke to the crowd of young men and women. They told them that their duty "was to put the image of the Virgin and Mexico high—*en alto*—to make them proud by their actions in New York so that people knew that Mexicans are hard workers, good students, and devout Christians." In New York, they had the possibility to construct a new collective identity other than the one they had in the Mixteca region. In their participation in community events like this, they could enjoy an identity with more worth and self-respect than what they often encountered in their New York workplaces and schools (Gálvez 2009: 3, 4). Yet, like the image itself, their faith and devotion to the Virgin was portable and traveled with them.

The organization of weekly religious practice, common belief, and a yearly ritual creates the social capital necessary to talk about a real community of faith, which can be displayed publicly in an important American cathedral. By participating in this event, Mexican immigrants can show their worth, unity, numbers, and commitment (Tilly 2005), a potential social movement, a collective political actor that the state and civil society have to take seriously (Tilly, Wood, and Castañeda 2018).

In contrast to the daily social invisibility that many Mexican undocumented workers experience, by walking the streets together with their families and conationals as "good" Mexicans they become active residents of New York City—*citizens de facto* (Gálvez 2009: 7). This transformation has implications for urban belonging. The ability to retain their culture and religion allows Mexican immigrants to integrate into their new society and to gain a certain political voice and public visibility, one that is proud but not confrontational. This allows them to reinvent their traditions while adding values, cultural tropes, practices, and repertoires for political contentious performances learned in the United States. The collective religious celebrations that they may have taken for granted in their hometowns now bring them together in a way that no politician, community leader, or neighborhood in New York could. Public religious events allow working-class and undocumented Mexicans to build a positive identity despite their marginal position in New York City (R. C. Smith 2006). This religious channel also opens a way for political voice, the construction of a positive identity, and integration into the host society that prevents members from taking on more contentious identities, such as gang or criminal identities. Local churches in neighborhoods with a concentration of Mexicans have reacted in analogous ways to the example discussed here. Mexicans are permitted to practice their religion and their traditional cultural practices in New York—and this creates a positive collective identity.

Mexicans in Paris

I attended the same celebration in Paris in 2007. I headed to the famous Cathedral of Notre Dame in the historical heart of Paris. Despite the imposing building and a large Christmas tree in the front, there were no outward signs that a religious event was taking place inside right then. In New York, the celebration of the Virgin of Guadalupe takes place throughout the day. Participants often skip classes or work to attend. Those who must go to work attend local services in their neighborhood parishes as early as the night before, early that morning, during the evening, or late at night. In Paris, the service took place in the evening to accommodate professional work schedules. The celebration was private, as Notre Dame was not officially open to tourists at that time. I found out about the Parisian celebration through an e-mail listserv for graduates of the Monterrey Tech—a Mexican private university network. Dozens of Tech graduates work in transnational companies in Paris.

In striking contrast to New York, the participants in the mass at Notre Dame arrived alone or with a few friends or family members. They avoided talking to others. There was a mariachi band participating during the service, and the participating members of the Church hierarchy spoke positively about the Virgin and the Mexican people. There was neither mention of migration nor any political undertones directed to any state or public outside of the church walls. After the service was over, the Mexican crowd dispersed. I was looking forward to meeting more members of the Mexican diaspora living in Paris, but, unlike in New York, nobody lingered outside the cathedral after the service to socialize. Are these differences due to class? Or was it that

Figure 5.3. Notre Dame Cathedral. Despite the claims of secularism and disapproval of religious signs in public, Christmas trees and other decorations are indeed visible in Paris.

SOURCE: © Castañeda 2007.

the Mexicans in Paris had internalized the norm that—contrary to the public aspect of mass attendance in Mexico—in France, worship was something private and individualistic, not to be taken into the streets nor seen as a legitimate cause to identify collectively and socialize with others? Were they wary about appearing communitarian? This lack of group cohesion and low community organization could also be partly explained by the fact that the great majority of participants had visas, jobs, and European friends and spouses and were seemingly living up to the French model of immigrant integration.

Mexicans in France are a relatively small community. They are neither a marginal group nor a visible community in the French public imagination. Some educated Parisians saw educated Mexicans as more similar to them than working-class North Africans. Mexican students, artists, writers, politicians, and members of the elite had strong connections with members of the French business, diplomatic, and cultural elite, which I observed directly through participation in a number of organizations. These are groups of Mexican Francophiles and French Mexicophiles, fluent in the other's culture and language, having often studied or worked abroad. The French and Mexicans in these groups do not underline a religious commonality or a common "Latin culture";[1] they focus instead on the cultural differences they were familiar with and appreciated. There were also connections between the Mexican and US expatriate communities through these organizations, especially among people who had studied and lived in the United States, American expats, and French graduates of American universities who shared a certain academic and professional culture with English as the lingua franca.

In secular Paris, religious affiliation is not the best manner for Mexicans to express worth or to generate respect. They could live in France due to individual abilities, personal connections, or professional or artistic skills valued in Paris. The most valuable asset one had was the economic, cultural, social, and symbolic capital embodied in the individual. Networking happened along professional or business lines or through alumni associations. This is another example of how immigrants' religion, class, habits, institutional practices, cultural contexts, and political opportunity structures work in different configurations to shape political voice and immigrant integration.

The Catholic Church and Immigrants in the United States

One could assume that Latino immigrants would be welcomed to the United States solely on the fact of being Christian and therefore seen as "compatible" with the dominant culture. But many of the thirteen colonies were founded by religious groups escaping persecution by established European churches. Previous waves of immigrants to the United States faced exclusion partly for being Catholic: Germans, Irish, French, Polish, and Italians. Historically, Catholic people in America were seen as backward, unsophisticated, alcoholic, and lacking proper religious discipline (Massa 2003).

Although Latinos are becoming an important part of the US Catholic Church (Ospino 2014), one should not overemphasize the Catholic affiliation of Latinos. There are Latinos of all faiths, and most Catholics in twenty-first-century America are non-Hispanic whites (Pew Research Center 2014; D'Antonio 2007). However, it is the case that Latinos are a source of Catholic growth. Thus, the Catholic Church in the United States has decided to have a Hispanic ministry to cater to Latino immigrants.

Partly reacting to the needs of their members and partly looking to expand their membership, the Catholic and other Christian churches have acted openly and behind closed doors to get legal and informal rights for immigrants (Hondagneu-Sotelo 2008; Yukich 2013). Churches started the sanctuary movements of the 1970s and 2000s protecting political and economic refugees from Central America and Mexico, respectively, helping immigrants find hospice and protection from the problems in their countries and from immigration authorities in the United States (Smith 1996; Rabben 2011). Many immigrants remain or become engaged with the Church after migrating, and many find a collective voice and civic participation through religious institutions (Mooney 2009). Religious belief and practice can be part of life for Latino religious immigrants in the United States.

Another example of the historic involvement of the Church with immigrants' lives: in 2006, Cardinal Roger Mahoney, Archbishop of Los Angeles, addressed Latino protestors in both English and Spanish who were marching against a proposed tough anti-immigrant law (H.R. 4437, the "Sensenbrenner Bill"). He told them, "So I'd like to request that unless you have an American flag, that you roll up flags from other countries and do not use them because they do not help us get the legislation we need" (Norris 2006). This did not mean that Mahoney was not sensitive to the pride of his followers toward their country of origin but rather that he was conscious about the way that the displays of Mexican and other flags are misread and misconstrued by commentators and ultimately counterproductive to their cause. Secular immigrant activists also took notice of this; in the 2006 May Day proimmigrant

Figure 5.4. The Mexican flag, with an image of the Virgin of Guadalupe in the center instead of the traditional seal with an eagle standing on a cactus devouring a serpent. New York, Day without an Immigrant March, May 1, 2006.

SOURCE: © Castañeda 2006.

rights march and rally in New York City, I witnessed organizers distributing American flags. Thus, sometimes the same person would be holding the American flag in one hand and the Mexican one in the other. Some created their own flags, not only putting an American flag on one side and the Mexican one on the back but also replacing the eagle in the center of the Mexican flag with the image of the Virgin of Guadalupe. This shows the central role that religious symbols can have in marking identity in the Mexican American community, as we also saw when Cesar Chavez marched under the banner of the Virgin protesting on behalf of the farmworkers.

Besides the sanctuary movements and the Migrant Rights Marches of 2006, there are many other examples inside the United States of the Catholic and other churches helping, organizing, and speaking in name of undocumented immigrants suffering hardships (Hondagneu-Sotelo 2008). Promigrant stances by the Vatican are not new. The Vatican encyclical *Gaudium et Spes* in the 1960s called for the respect of minority cultural rights (Paul VI

1965: 84). These stances have had a real effect on institutional practices of the Catholic Church worldwide in relation to immigrant and refugee rights and transnational parish dialogues (Fitzgerald 2009a; Levitt 2007; Costes 1988: 33). Many practices and stances of the Catholic Church in regards to migration and cultural and minority rights are similar worldwide; what changes are the social contexts and the space that is given for political voice along religious affiliation in different cities and citizenship regimes (Mooney 2009).

The Relation of the Catholic Church and Immigrants in Spain

For decades, Spain was a country of emigrants. The Spanish Catholic Church created branches abroad to cater to the spiritual and material needs of the Spanish diaspora. The Spanish Church was interested in keeping these migrants among their flock; the best way to do so was to allow them to keep their religion and their ties to their Spanish parishes, to which they sent remittances. The Spanish Catholic Church's strong relation with Spanish emigrants abroad and the call of the encyclical, *Gaudium et Spes*, predisposed it to notice and cater to immigrants' needs within the Spanish territory. The Spanish Catholic Church also took the initiative to serve not only fervent long-time Catholics from Latin America or the Philippines but also people from North Africa, regardless of their religion. Interestingly, but consistent with this argument, it was the groups affiliated with the Catholic Church that first started raising the issues of protection of Moroccan immigrants and providing services for this collectivity. As early as 1974, the Spanish Bishop's Commission on Migration complained that Moroccans in Spain were treated much worse than Spanish working in other European countries (Rius Sant 2007: 26, 32).

There have been a historic number of Christians and Jews in North Africa who have also emigrated and a small number of recent Maghrebi immigrants who converted to Catholicism. Some of the locals I talked to say immigrants may convert instrumentally so that the Church can help them with immigration papers to France or Spain on the premise of religious persecution in the Maghreb. The bulk of contemporary immigrants from the Maghreb (either Arabs or Berbers) are Muslim. Yet, some of their needs are catered to by priests, nuns, and lay people in the rooms of Christian religious buildings that are not dedicated to prayer. Catholics help them for humanitarian and religious reasons. For example, in Annaba, Algeria, I met a French priest and a Mexican seminarian who managed the church where the Berber Saint Augustine of Hippo (354–430)—author of *Confessions* and *The City of God*—worked during much of his life. The Basilica of St. Augustine has a large house for the elderly and the sick with mainly Muslim residents.

In Barcelona, I visited and volunteered in a number of soup kitchens and shelters staffed by nuns and volunteers that catered largely to Moroccan immigrants. There was a short Catholic prayer before the meals, and some Muslim immigrants refused to return because of this. There were religious services and proselytizing events for Christians or people interested in converting. There were also secular talks on personal growth, integration, and how to solve practical problems for Moroccan Muslims and to other immigrants who needed help.

I visited a Catholic religious center that catered specifically to children living in a poor neighborhood in downtown Barcelona, including many children of Moroccans and Filipinos. The staff, belonging to a Catholic order, helped them with their school tasks and provided tutors, technical training, computer labs, and optional confessional services. Conversations I had with the head priests showed their true intentions. They thought that they would win the war for minds, hearts, and souls in the long run because, even if the parents of these youth were devout Muslims, their children, growing up in Spain, in close contact with Catholic religious and academic institutions, would end up understanding Catholicism. Some of these second- or third-generation immigrants could grow to be devout Catholics in a way that most young native Spanish are no longer interested in being. Similarly, some priests and churches saw new immigrants from Latin America and Africa as their best hope to keep the Church alive into the future, something similar to the view that many Catholic priests have about the importance of Latinos in the United States.

While visiting the office of the religious nonprofit organization that helped children of immigrants succeed in school and integrate in Barcelona, the person showing me around said half-jokingly, "These are the offices. You can put your things here, but do not leave anything valuable—these *chavales* (kids) are in the process of domestication. They are a work in progress, so it is better to be cautious." The guide mentioned that he had invited some Moroccan children to go to the chapel to pray, and that they answered, "No, that one is only for Christians." And he said, "No, that is for everyone." Then he told me, "After I convinced them, my boss told me that no Muslim should go inside because if their parents find out, they would be furious, and they would never bring them back to the center. He told me that we should be patient. That in twenty years when they are independent from their parents, they can tell them that they do not share their religious views anymore." This exemplifies that the long-term goal of this particular group was conversion. The comments denote a mix of racism, classism, ethnocentrism, and paternalism, along with the belief that all men and women could be equal. (This is not that different from the approach of many Catholic priests during the colonial days. Integration in Latin American colonies occurred through cultural assimilation, religious conversion, violence, and intermarriage while keeping Spanish people and culture at the top.) Still, the practice of not bringing Muslim students to places of prayer respects their current religious beliefs and the parental authority, even when parents are not present. This center provides concrete help and resources. It allows parents to work while their kids do their homework, play sports, or learn new skills. This missionary work shows that priests and staff take these children seriously as people and spiritual actors.

I heard stories from other North Africans about Moroccans claiming conversion to Catholicism to get asylum in Spain. Some interviewees in Spain told me that they were happy to convert to Catholicism because they could pray to God, their same former God, but in a public and accepted way. A minority of Muslims justify converting to Catholicism to get material and social benefits, and they may be happy to do so because they then can practice their religion openly. Yet most Moroccans in Barcelona stay Muslim. Furthermore, it is possible to convert back to Islam; native wives of Muslim men in Barcelona and Paris sometimes would convert to Islam. Religious identity and practice are fluid and change through the life course for some. As a forty-four-year-old Moroccan woman in Barcelona told me in 2017 after I told her I was born in Mexico, "There are many Mexicans in Barcelona. I know a girl who converted to Islam seven years ago; she just married an Arab. I also know another one, the same. They like it after they learn that Islam is a serious religion, a religion of peace. There are stories about terrorists. There are terrorists of all colors and religions. People think that men with long beards are terrorists, but even goats have beards." In this discourse, this pious woman noted the importance of religion to her but also how her religious community creates bridges rather than boundaries between people.

At first sight, one could think that Latino immigrants would be especially welcomed to Spain because they are largely Catholic. This is somewhat the case, but for many native Spanish people, ethnicity, culture, and Spanish dialects trump common religion. Religion could bring Catalans and immigrants together, but, as exemplified by religious services in Tagalog for Filipino Catholics in Barcelona, even the Catholics are divided into different services and churches depending on their ethnicity and national origin. In practice, a Catholic commonality has its limits in forming bonds with the newcomers. At the same time, in local public opinion, they do place Latinos closer to Spaniards than Muslim people (Cea D'Ancona and Valles 2010). Still, progressive elements within the Spanish institutional Church have been some of the most active and effective advocates for immigrants in general, including Muslims. The event described next exemplifies this trend.

On Saturday, January 30, 2001, just before a proposed anti-immigrant law would go into effect, a group of 328 immigrants, mainly from Morocco, Pakistan, India, and Senegal, approached the Catalan Catholic priest Francesc Vidal, the head of the Pi Church in Barcelona. The families convinced him to provide sanctuary for them inside the church to protect them from imminent deportation. Other parishes in Barcelona followed suit. Many people went on a hunger strike, lasting until February 3, 2001. The next day, around 50,000 people participated in a march and rally in support of the immigrant workers and their families. The immigrants counted on the support of the organization Papers for Everyone, whose members had the initiative to take to the streets after negotiations failed to pass a progressive law that would have legalized more workers beyond the Ecuadorian and specific cases that could be regularized. Labor unions (CGT), Caritas, SOS Racisme Barcelona, Ibn Batuta, Asociación de Trabajadores Marroquíes (ATIME), CITE de Comissiones Obreras, and others supported these workers, who locked themselves down (*encierros*) in Catholic churches to protest against the difficulty of getting residence and work permits. As a result of these contentious performances, most people involved were regularized along with 20,352 Ecuadorians in a parallel set of negotiations (Rius Sant 2007; xxiii; Varela Huerta 2007).

The Catholic Church in France

In the 1950s, there was a large arrival of Italians, Portuguese, Spanish, and other European (mostly Catholic) groups into France who came in large numbers, but only a few priests came along to tend to their needs, so the French Catholic Church had to make changes to accommodate them (Costes 1988: 39). In the 1960s, the numbers of Algerians settling in metropolitan France started growing at a faster pace than before. Catholic clerics in Paris started helping Maghrebin immigrants without looking to convert them. As result of this aid, personal ties were established with these newcomers. As the conflict in Algeria escalated, many Catholic priests supported the claims for independence of the Algerian FLN (Costes 1988). After the war ended in 1962, many families from Algeria, of all religious denominations, moved to mainland France, and many priests continued taking care of the Muslim newcomers, often acting as spokespersons for them. Indeed, they were one of the few groups who stayed close to their everyday lives and saw to their needs directly. It was the Catholic hierarchy who were the first ones to call for the opening up of religious centers for Muslim worship in France (Kepel 1987: 117). In 1972, a chapel in Lille was given to the Muslim community to turn it into a mosque.

Many French Catholic liberals were close to the Muslim community, advocating for it and acting against racism and discriminatory treatment by the government and society, to the point that just before the "March for Equal Rights" of 1983, the Catholic Church, along with some Jewish and Muslim religious authorities, signed a communiqué supporting the march and its claims. This was repeated in 1985 in a public, and widely publicized, act that included Catholic, Jewish, and Muslim leaders as well as the Human Rights League and a number of civil associations, among them le Mouvement contre le Racisme et pour l'Amitié entre les Peuples (MRAP), La ligue Internationale Contre le Racisme et l'Antisémitisme (LICRA), and even the historically anti-Catholic Masonic League (Costes 1988: 84).

According to Gilles Kepel (1987), humanitarian concerns for Muslim immigrants started to decline in the 1980s after the enrichment of the oil states in the Middle East and the Islamic Revolution in Iran (Deltombe 2005), which made many French, including Catholics, fear an expansionist Islam—a view that had always been held by many *pieds noirs* and soldiers who fought in Algeria. Regardless, many French Catholic bishops spoke publicly against the rise of the extreme right xenophobic party Front National in the early 1980s and its racist discourse. Yet current geopolitics render Muslim–Catholic–Jewish partnerships more difficult because many of my interviewees commented that international politics influence their boundary-making processes.

The 1970s and 1980s in France saw also an increase in the coming of age of the second generation, the children of Muslims from the Maghreb, Portugal, Italy, and Spain. At the same time, the world entered into an economic crisis that lead to less employment for young people. This in turn resulted in increased policing of the neighborhoods of the mobilized youth and often sent

them to police commissariats, tribunals, and prisons; many of these youth
were even deported to the countries of their parents, places where they had
never been (Costes 1988: 39; Rosenberg 2006). In the 1990s, a Catholic Priest,
Abbé Pierre, played a key role in the *sans papiers* movement, giving sanctuary and shelters in his church to both homeless and undocumented workers
(Siméant 1998).

Islam in France

In contrast with the interests of the American and Spanish churches in gaining new converts, in France the goal was not to win converts into Catholicism
but to combat any public symbols of Islamic practice. Most immigrants in
France understand and adapt to this expectation. The secular French repub-
licanism does result in the decrease of public religious expression, and most
Muslim immigrants comply with this expectation. But a woman's choice to
cover her hair using the veil became a highly publicized issue that underlined
differences between Muslims and others in France. A growing Islamopho-
bia resulted (Deltombe 2005), including the law in 2004 banning headscarves
in schools and the law of 2010 banning face coverings in public; today some
women wear the veil as a protest. This reaction formation reinforces social
boundaries, in this case along religious identification.

Some Muslims in Paris feel that their religion and cultural traditions
are disrespected, under attack, and even denigrated. Their religion has been
systematically problematized and stigmatized not only discursively but also
with real policies like Sarkozy's banning of burqas in public spaces throughout France. In Paris, there is a public and political discourse that puts Muslim religion and culture as inferior and even opposite to French culture. The
French Muslims I interviewed tended to have a lower sense of belonging and
relatively felt more discontent than Muslims in Spain. French society imposes
the Parisian elite culture through the educational system as well as the physical force of the state as embodied in the police force (Bourdieu 1984 [1979],
1996 [1989]).

Many French people would object to the use of the descriptive term
French-Muslim because French citizens should identify simply as such and
not have hyphenated identities (Silverstein 2004; Kastoryano 2002).

Public policies and prejudices clearly affect Muslims in France. In France,
there is no funding provided for religious events or institutions as such, yet
the state provides funds to maintain church buildings and cathedrals in the

name of safekeeping the French national historical and architectural patrimony; because of the *laïcité* law of 1905, it owns all the churches built before
1905 (Bowen 2007). Meanwhile, "Muslims have faced several municipal and
bureaucratic restrictions on building mosques" (Kuru 2008). Therefore, it is
not surprising that there are only 1,685 mosques in all of France; if one says
there are at least 4.5 million Muslims in France, then there is only one mosque
for every 2,670 Muslims. This is a lower ratio than in the United Kingdom,
Germany, or the Netherlands (Kuru 2008). Thus, Muslims have a harder time
finding a place to congregate and follow basic religious practices than do
Catholics, Protestants, and Jews, who have a longer historical and physical
presence in France, resulting in more places of worship and supportive institutional infrastructure.

History plays an important role in understanding *laïcité de combat* (com-
bative secularism). The French monarchy and the Catholic Church had a
strong alliance, and thus people identify a strong presence of the Church in
the public sphere as a reminder of the monarchy of the old regime. After the
Revolution of 1789, over 3,000 priests were guillotined. The Revolution did
not eliminate the Catholic Church, which again became influential during
the monarchy of Napoleon III. It was not until the foundation of the Third
Republic in 1870 that the term *laïcité* (secularism) became a widespread code
word for anticlericalism; for example, Léon Gambetta's slogan "Clericalism,
that is the enemy!" Schools became a battlefield between Catholic and secular
education. With the retreat of public funding, many Catholic schools closed
or submitted to being taken over by the state in exchange for a more secular
bent (Kuru 2008). Since then, the hegemonic view has been a secular one, and
in most sectors of both the right and the left, secularism is something worth
fighting for. Muslims are seen as the new threat and thus the state must put
in place policies to stop any religion from gaining political power (Caldwell
2009). France may need a *"laïcisation de la laïcité"* because many hold secularism in a dogmatic quasi-religious manner (Jean-Paul Willaime, cited in
Kuru 2008). Islam in France must be understood not only as a new religion in
the land but also within the framework of the French traditions of skepticism
of religious identifications.

Islam is not the cause of contention of most immigrants and their children in France. The *banlieue* riots discussed in the Paris chapter had nothing
to do with Islam. Indeed, different imams tried to act as mediators, calling
the youth to stop the rioting after the first night of events in 2005, but they

failed to have an impact. Sometimes, some immigrants may be attracted to militant Islam, but this is an effect of anomie, exclusion, and social isolation (Boubekeur 2008). Some extremists aside, some interviewees claimed that a proper understanding of Islam has an attenuating effect on generalized forms of violent performances in the Parisian area. The exaggerated government reaction to terrorist attacks—with states of emergency and break-ins into apartments in public housing apartments in the *banlieues*—creates a downward spiral that increases distrust and animosity along a religious boundary (Castañeda 2018; Bail 2008).

Gender and Religion: Strange Bedfellows, Feminism and Islamophobia

For believers who come from a culture where religious practices and symbols are an important part of meaning making and everyday life (as is often the case for Mexicans, Moroccans, and Algerians), religion plays an important part of a person's identity. Thus, when the receiving state and society attack their religion, they take it as a personal insult. Maghrebi men in Paris are not particularly religious; most of them choose to drink and smoke to fill their idle time or to socialize with their French friends. But some of the laws against religious symbols worn by women have pushed many 1.5- and second-generation women with Muslim parents to further embrace Islam as part of a reaction formation to the state's pressures to assimilate and dissolve all outward signs of nonconformity to France's republican, secular ethos.

The attempts of the French state to ban headscarves and *burqas* is understandably seen as an attack not only against women who wear them but also against the cultural identities of all Muslim women and men. As a result, some women redouble their efforts to pass as non-Muslim, thus strengthening the social boundary (Tilly 1998) and signaling that being non-Muslim is preferred. Others seem to internalize the attacks, falling prey to symbolic violence (Bourdieu 1991). Yet others may be further polarized and pushed to embrace a more dogmatic practice of Islam. Despite these insults and provocations by the political, intellectual, and media elite, riots or large protests have not been seen around the issue of Islam and religious freedom itself. This could be because many of them embrace secularism and because the French Muslims are divided—they are not a community in the strict sense of being connected. Maghrebis are also divided along gender in part because of the patronizing discourses and a "white savior complex." In this view, Western "civilized" men are viewed as needing to intervene to "save" Muslim women from the oppression of Muslim men, a collective fantasy since the colonial days that has been mobilized lately by the controversies around the "burkini" (Kaufmann 2017).

France's former Secretary of State for Urban Policies, Fadela Amara, is the child of immigrants from Kabylia, Algeria. She got her political start in the March for Equality of 1983 and then in the civil society organization SOS Racisme. She later founded Ni Putes, Ni Soumises—an association originating in the Parisian *banlieue* whose role was to support women from the Maghreb who did not want to closely adhere to gender roles that require a certain retreat from the public sphere; rather, these women saw themselves as modern, independent, and feminist (Amara and Zappi 2006). This movement sees a need to empower women in neighborhoods where the pressure to conform to strong Islamic principles can sometimes be oppressive. Nonetheless, it would be a mistake to generalize these claims as speaking for all women of Maghrebi origin. It is false that wearing a headscarf is always a sign of oppression and submission to men, or that this is the main problem faced by women coming from the Maghreb. Many of my interviewees had no conflict with being female, Muslim, and French; and they were mostly concerned about jobs and equal treatment by non-Muslim French. A woman said, "Instead of providing jobs and opportunities for us and our husbands, we are portrayed in the media as dupes." Some of my interviewees voiced their frustration that the government took the demagogic, divisive, and colonialist view of intervening to save women of color from men of color.

Fittingly, the discourse framed by Amara and her civil association Ni Putes, Ni Soumises was one that was compatible with French political discourse, one that could be further translated as a movement against communitarianism and "the backward culture" of Muslim men. These arguments are also expressed in many best-selling novels about Maghrebi female victims and in many novels and autobiographies written by French and Maghrebi women against the abuses caused by some Muslim men. The faults of these few men are then generalized by much of the French public and applied to all Muslim men. This discourse is used as a cultural and moral weapon that justifies their criminalization and has reinforced symbolic boundaries along ethnic and gender lines, hardening social boundaries against interfaith marriages between Muslim-French men and Catholic-French women. This further fuels the frustrations, depression, and anger of Arab men (Ben Jelloun 1977; Hajjat and Mohammed 2016; Dendoune 2007). This example suggests that, despite their original intentions, these sorts of organizations further splinter positive ethnic group formation and collective claim making. The pose to defend Muslim women in France from submission turns often into another form of symbolic violence that further stigmatizes and marginalizes North African working-class men.

Through the 1990s discussions on the veil, with the ban of "conspicuous religious symbols" in public schools in 2004, and the laws banning head-covering clothing in public that went into effect in 2011, France shows its intolerance for religious and cultural difference. Although this decision is anchored in the secular republican tradition in the eyes of many French people, it also results in the government signaling and showing its authority over a particular group: Muslim women. The result will be further discrimination, feelings of marginalization, and exclusion felt by Muslim females and males, as well as the radicalization of some believers, who may feel attacked and may now have a higher stake in keeping their religious practices despite, or due to, a hostile environment. Secularist and antiterrorism laws will be counterproductive in their supposed intent of increasing integration by religious minorities and will only serve to amplify contention and violence.

French Islam: A Decentralized Network

Because of the secular culture and the general French disdain for religious expression in public, French children of Muslim parents tend to be more isolated and estranged from other coethnics and coreligionists and do not turn collectively to religion as a balm for the symbolic wounds inflicted by the dominant culture. French mosques are relatively minor institutional settings for emotional and material support, especially in comparison to other immigrant groups in France or in other countries as discussed earlier.

A major difference between Muslim Maghrebis and Christian Latinos is the role religious institutions play as centers for socialization and political organization. The French see the organization of Maghrebis and other immigrant groups around Islam as suspicious. Furthermore, Islam does not have the same level of institutional organization as the Catholic Church because there is a decentralized structure of mosques and an individualized practice of Islam. Religious observance for Muslims happens in a more individual and less hierarchical fashion than for Christians or Jews. The imam is a moral figure, but routinely obtaining his advice and guidance is not paramount to being a good Muslim. Indeed, most Muslims whom I interviewed in France did not go to a mosque frequently nor speak with imams regularly, even when they considered themselves to be religious. They often said that, in Islam, imams do not play such an active role in the social and family life as priests or rabbis do in their respective religions. Maghrebi immigrants do not necessarily pray five times a day or visit mosques very often, but still many resent what they see almost as religious persecution by *secular fundamentalists*; in a sense they just want to be left alone to practice their faith themselves, their way. As Benamara, a thirty-three-year-old Tunisian-Moroccan, said, "I hope that in the future Muslims will live in peace and that the atheists will leave us alone."

In contrast to Paris, religion brings immigrants together much more openly in Barcelona, where Maghrebis are quick to point out their commonalities with other Muslims, even if they do not know them, and act accordingly, helping other Muslims in a way that was rare to find among my interviewees in the Parisian metropolitan area. Given the strong ideology against communitarianism in France, many Maghrebi young adults live relatively individualized lives and belong to few friendship networks beyond their family. Furthermore, there is a large social isolation for those unemployed people with no school friends living close by. Muslim people receiving unemployment benefits in France prefer to stay at home and keep their social contacts limited. They often reported feeling that the limited economic resources they had would limit their ability to entertain guests and return favors in the way that is expected of Muslim Maghrebis who are known for their legendary hospitality.

The French State and Islam

The French state prefers to have official interlocutors. It deals with one official rabbi who is to represent all Jews in France (one of the largest Jewish communities in the world). In the same vein, it has named a head imam based in the Paris Mosque, which has been from the start a state project to centralize and organize Muslims in France to govern them through intermediaries, as in colonial Algeria. There have also been proposals to educate imams in state-sponsored madrasas, where imams would learn to combine Muslim faith in a way that would be compatible with the republican values of France. But all these top-down approaches have been unsuccessful, and none of my interviewees feels represented by the institution of the Paris Mosque and other artificial initiatives to create a cohesive French Muslim community ex nihilo. Mosques or imams rarely act as intermediaries among newcomers, established foreign-born Muslims, French-born Muslims, and secular France. France lacks enough local neighborhood religious institutions and public spaces to create social capital around common religious faith. This ends up further impoverishing immigrants not only in terms of economic but also in terms of social, cultural, and symbolic capital.

The Paris Mosque plays an important symbolic role because of its classical architecture, its central location, and its antiquity. Rather than representing an embrace of Maghrebi immigrants, the Mosque was inaugurated in 1926 in thanks to the North African soldiers who fought for France during World War I, at a time when the Muslim population in metropolitan France was small. Another symbolic institution could be the Museum of the Arab World, but many Maghrebis complain that it represents Arabic high culture from Egypt, the Arabian Peninsula, and other Middle Eastern countries and that it does not represent the everyday culture of the Maghreb or the contributions of French Maghrebis.

The Muslim associations in France are the Union of Islamic Organizations of France (the Union des Organisations Islamiques de France, or UOIF), the National Federation of Muslims of France (FNMF), the European branch of Turkey's Directorate of Religious Affairs, and the oxymoronically named French Council of Secular Muslims (CFML), which supported the ban on the headscarf. In 2002, as interior minister, Nicolas Sarkozy founded the French Council of the Muslim Faith (Conseil Français du Culte Musulman, or CFCM) as an umbrella organization to control these associations. The CFCM was given jurisdiction over the construction of mosques, training of imams, appointment of Muslim chaplains, regulation of lamb slaughter for Aid al-Adha, the organization of hajjs to Mecca, and so on. This was part of an attempt by the French government to create what it overtly calls an "Islam of France" rather than an "Islam in France." Yet this was a failed attempt by the state, as these institutions have not addressed the concerns of the people who rioted in 2005 or the concerns of the immigrants from the Maghreb or their children. These associations are top-down structures with little popular support and are not an avenue for political voice. This may be due in fact to the low religious collective socialization around Islam among the average first- and higher-generation French, arising from their acculturation to French norms.

Islam in Spain

I asked a middle-aged woman from Morocco if celebrating Ramadan in Barcelona was hard, and she said, "If there is faith and will, one celebrates wherever one is. My religious faith does not stop in my country; it comes with me wherever I go." Doing fieldwork in Barcelona, I found tight small networks of Muslim Moroccans[2] who also had frequent contact with people from Pakistan and other Muslim countries. This does not mean that they did not have non-Muslim friends or that they aggressively looked to impose their religion on others. The respect of religious fervor and practices has resulted in considerably more spaces (compared to those in Paris) for a constructive space for Islam and *Moroccaness* that made many of my Moroccan informants happy to be in Barcelona and able to cling to cultural practices that make their transition easier. This also made them increasingly eager to absorb, learn, and imitate Catalan practices and outlooks. Moroccan youth were happy to join the late-night tapas-eating and wine-drinking practices of Barcelona natives the same way that many tourists and expats did. Some believe that Moroccan cultural incorporation into Spanish regions will, down the line, also dilute the practice of Islam by the second and third generation of Moroccan immigrants partly through the loss of the Arabic language. Indeed, I witnessed how many children of Moroccan couples were sometimes spoken to in Arabic but always responded in Spanish; sometimes parents even needed to talk to them in Spanish—a similar process to what we see in the United States and elsewhere.

Mosques in Catalonia

In 2010, there were over 718,055 Moroccan immigrants and 1,446,939 Muslims living in Spain. Catalonia has the largest number of residents coming from Muslim countries in all of Spain—over 326,697 Muslim immigrants and 30,518 naturalized Spanish citizens (Observatorio Andalusí 2010). There are 145 dedicated places to pray in Catalonia (Observatorio Andalusí 2010). In Barcelona and throughout Catalonia, organized vocal opposition and contentious performances against the construction of mosques have taken place in thirty different municipalities (Astor 2009). Locals see mosques as immigrant magnets. Using the name *mosque* is a misnomer here because in Barcelona and Catalonia one most often talks about *oratorios*, or prayer rooms, located in storefronts, private apartments, empty garages, or industrial areas and warehouses. Although Catalonia has the largest number of Muslims in Spain, it does not have a proper mosque with minarets. As in Switzerland and the Netherlands, these buildings have recently been framed as signifiers of a "Muslim threat" at home (Haenni and Lathion 2009).

Growth in immigrant businesses and Muslim residents has been accompanied by a growth in oratories, which cluster around Muslim-owned businesses in downtown Barcelona (Serra del Pozo 2006). Ethnic entrepreneurs rented previously vacant storefronts and bodegas in declining business areas throughout Barcelona and contributed to economic revitalization (Serra del Pozo 2006). Yet, some working- and middle-class Spanish, especially older internal migrants to Barcelona, look with envy at the special resources that the government provides for immigrants and have complained about preferred treatment given to immigrants (Astor 2009). There have been some controversies and popular opposition to the construction of large mosques with visible minarets. A main source of contention is over space and public resources and over the neighborhood cultural image. Many do not want to change the implicit hegemony that Catholicism has had in Spain for the last 500 years since the expulsion of the Moors and Jews in 1492 (Astor and Griera 2016). As a reaction to the connection between the local Catholic Church and the Franco regime, Spain has seen a lower interest in religious practice in young Spanish Catholics. Many churches in Barcelona are being turned into cafes, museums, and offices. This could open some room for other religions to take place in Barcelona. A decrease in church attendance may create the groundwork for an active multicultural and religiously plural society to exist again in the Iberian Peninsula.

Conclusion: Freedom of Religion, Politics, and Social Incorporation

Mexican pioneers, self-appointed community leaders, and political entrepreneurs have created small New York–based organizations, that is, Asociación Tepeyac, Casa Mexico, Casa Puebla, and Mixteca, with the help of private, foundation, city, and state funding. These organizations are relatively small and perpetually struggle to get funds to stay afloat; they are often the sites of turf wars, personality feuds, and political maneuvering. There is an organizational field of Mexican and Latino community organizations, and some immigrants do go to one of these organizations when in need. Mexican communal institutions may engage in the near future in direct political brokerage, as Puerto Rican and Dominican organizations have done. They act as places for organization, socialization, politicization, and integration into American society, eventually moving from issues affecting the country of origin to pressing matters at the place of destination. These groups, along with the Mexican Consulate, Mexican State Chambers of Commerce, Mexican transnational companies, clubs, and groups of Mexican students and professionals, as well as the Catholic Church, compete to represent and speak in the name of the Mexican community in New York and thus to get the attention of New York, American, and Mexican politicians. Hometown associations and other Mexican organizations in New York fill a great need by the population and local politicians to dialogue with the "Mexican community." But, as Patricia Hill Collins rightly points out, many studies, politicians, and spokespeople overemphasize the cohesiveness of "communities," often for personal and political reasons (Collins 2010).

Among these organizations, Associacion Tepeyac, which organizes the Guadalupan celebrations, is the one that has the largest number of affiliates and the one that can mobilize the largest numbers, interestingly around religious festivities. This type of association can gain political traction in New York but not in Paris, where organizing around religion has less legitimacy. To better understand the French context and the immigrant reaction, think what could happen if a US president or politician proposed to ban any display of the Virgin of Guadalupe in public spaces. The mobilization and reaction would be huge given the large role that the Virgin plays in the identities of Mexicans. The thought of banning the Guadalupe image in the United States is not only inconceivable but would also cause the disapproval, politicization, and solidarity of members of other ethnicities and religions (Hondagneu-Sotelo 2008).

On paper, the three countries have freedom of religion and separation of church and state. However, this freedom and separation is differently actualized. Formal principles alone do not explain the differences, but history does: struggles against the Catholic Church in revolutionary France, which led to state-sanctioned secularism as the civic religion; the multiplication of Protestant faiths in the early United States has led to a civic religion that embraces all of them. Catholicism had a hegemonic role in Spain for five centuries, but the transition to democracy put into question the close alliances between state and church. The separation of church and state was inscribed in the 1978 Spanish constitution and made real with the end of state subsidies to the church. Some of the pushback against Muslim immigrants in Paris is due to French inherent secularity, especially when compared to New York and

Barcelona. So, the avenues of religious expression differ in each city, thereby influencing different forms of inclusion or exclusion and the agent, manner, and object (who, how, and to whom) of claims making. Socially sanctioned collective religious practices can create institutional infrastructures, social capital, mutual aid, and places to draw transcendental meaning, respect, and dignity, all of which can help in easing the sense of belonging and integration of poor immigrants into their new cities.

6 Urban Belonging
Objective Milestones and Subjective Interpretations

You will always miss something from your hometown. The ideal place does not exist. You have to create it yourself with time.

S. M. J., a Mexican woman born in 1981 in Mexico City to parents from Puebla, who has studied abroad and has lived in various cities in Germany and the United States

Every time I go back to Mexico, I feel a little nostalgia about not living there anymore, but each time I am more convinced that I made the right decision to move to New York. I love Mexico, but there are major problems with unemployment, insecurity, governance. Socially there is a lot of classism in Mexico. That is what I like the most of New York, the mixing of classes and cultures . . . I don't suffer negative discrimination in New York, but there is a stereotype about what Mexicans look like; when I tell people in New York that I am Mexican, people often say that I do not look Mexican because I do not have indigenous features or because I am not short, etc.

Pamela, a twenty-eight-year-old Jewish Mexican lawyer who lives in New York

In New York you are respected. In Paris life is tough. No jobs. I would not live there.

Kadur, a forty-three-year-old Algerian man living in New York with family in Paris and London, May 6, 2017

THE INTERACTION BETWEEN IMMIGRANTS and the context of reception determines social, political, and economic integration and urban belonging. This context includes employment opportunities, formal and informal markets, laws regarding immigration, and natives' attitudes about immigration as well as about race, local and centralized state institutions, residential segregation patterns, and avenues for political voice through political organizations, including both those that previously existed and those that immigrants created. Important factors affecting immigrant integration also include the role of the state in regulating immigration and labor markets, the historical relationship between the sending and receiving countries, the possibility for immigrants to speak as a group, and the degree of tolerance for other cultures. An example of this is tolerance for those with foreign accents and different religious practices—coupled with real opportunities for social, political, and economic integration. These different phenomena often act simultaneously, reinforcing or countering one another.

I have now outlined the process of integration by presenting examples from major immigrant and ethnic groups in three global cities. Although all three cities are in liberal democracies within developed economies, they offer very different contexts of reception to immigrants. This renders this particular three-city comparison revealing. A broad comparison of the variables across my cases is summarized in Table 6.1. Each state–society relationship, citizenship ideological model, and institutional arrangement has varying effects for the larger minority groups in these different cities. Each city has things to improve on, lessons it can learn from the others, as well as things to celebrate. The findings along the dimensions in the table, discussed throughout the book, point to the importance of civil society and local socialization patterns in fostering processes of both belonging and exclusion, which are then translated into diverse forms of contentious politics and urban belonging. There are stimulating paradoxes between objective measures of material well-being and subjective feelings of malaise given differing social expectations. Findings show how different social boundary configurations create parallel pathways of simultaneous exclusion and inclusion along these domains. Note that the discussions of political systems and citizenship regimes are often done at an abstract and national level, whereas interview data and description of immigrant socialization are grounded and city based. The results listed in Table 6.1 represent each city, not the whole

Table 6.1. The social context that shapes immigrant incorporation and belonging.

Context	New York	Paris	Barcelona
Historical memory and oppositional identity	Medium	High	Medium
State and society openness to multiculturalism	High	Low	High
Avenues for political voice and collective action	Medium	Low	Medium
Support for migrant and ethnic organizations	High	Medium	High
Economic incorporation (pre-2007 financial crisis)	High	Low	High
Feasibility of undocumented life	Medium	Low	Medium
Social integration and urban belonging	**High**	**Low**	**High**

Note: The social contexts compared here are prior to the 2007 economic crisis. Levels do not imply value judgments but comparative degrees.

country. Each case is compared in relation to the others and within its own logic. As Harriet Martineau (1856) discussed, we should be careful to avoid being ethnocentric when analyzing other "societies." The ideotypical categorizations of immigrant integration processes across fields presented in the tables in this chapter are immanent critiques—that is, they are based on the local ideals of equality and the real challenges of incorporating foreigners; they are not universalist normative judgments.

The domains in Table 6.1 are key components in shaping belonging. This list was developed inductively from fieldwork, interviews, and surveys, as well as deductively through secondary sources, official data, and a theoretical analysis of the social forces at work. These factors summarize my findings and reflect relative values or rankings. Altogether, these factors explain immigrant social integration in a contextual, relational, and complex way. "Historical memory and oppositional identity" refers to the past relationships between the country of origin and the host country, including colonial relations and warfare. Whether there is an "openness to multiculturalism" both in the state and the society greatly determines how tolerant of cultural differences an average individual in society is. Whether there are "Avenues for political voice and collective action" explains why immigrant groups may apparently behave more contentiously in one social context than in another. Whether political organization takes place along ethnic lines and if state and society provide "Support for migrant and ethnic organizations" show if there is a tradition that allows ethnic groups to act politically as a collective and to organize events to maintain cultural practices and produce a positive sense of identity as a minority. "Economic incorporation" is related to the probability of employment in 2007, whether in the formal or semiformal economy. These dimensions shape immigrant incorporation and belonging.

Historical Memory and Oppositional Identity

The brief recount of historical events presented at the beginning of each city chapter serves as background for locating useful comparisons between immigrant-receiving countries and important emigrant-sending communities such as Mexico, Algeria, and Morocco. This is relevant because historical accounts produce different attitudes toward integration to the host country. Colonial history plays a big role in explaining historical and contemporary migration flows, categorical inequality, and everyday conflict (Shepard 2006: 4). The official histories of receiving and sending countries often present colonial history in diametrically different manners. The way these histories are understood, addressed, or ignored in national public spheres can play a big role in the political, moral, and symbolic contentions among newcomers, minorities, and the majority group. This matters because, at times, historical collective memory can make it difficult to identify with the new place of residence; for example, for Algerians in Paris the traumatic memory of the Algerian–French war creates barriers between immigrants and the native French. The war of independence still marks Algerians, and, even when their families have been French citizens for many generations, they often underline their Algerian identity over their French one. Moroccans, in contrast, used the historical links between Spain and Morocco as a rationale for their desire to integrate into Spain. Both Mexican immigrants and American natives often mention playfully the idea of the *reconquista* of the Southwest, yet they often deny any present or historical colonial ties between these two countries, failing to acknowledge the intertwined, often neocolonial, relationship between Mexico and the United States (Dear 2013).

State and Society's Openness to Multiculturalism

The more committed cities are to a multicultural model, the more material resources they can allocate to welcoming migrants and making sure that they integrate on their own terms. Thus, it is important to view in parallel the various degrees of openness to newcomers.

Interethnic relations in New York can vary for Latinos, who, depending on their class origins, interests, and local demographic realities, may spend anywhere between almost none and 80 percent of their time in Latino networks, according to my survey data. But even the Latinos who live in ethnic spheres share the general culture and aspirations of the American mainstream. Even if there are many more barriers to becoming a citizen in the United States, when allowed to become citizens, Latino immigrants gladly participate in the American political system. Although there are always reasons for discontent and contentious politics, there are also avenues to address such concerns through both formal and informal channels that do not normally include rioting or antistate violence.

Barcelona is an interesting case of elite and state enlightenment in relation to multicultural policies, practices, and programs that are effective in the integration of immigrants. Yet, intriguing tensions exist between ideals of democratization, autonomy, minority rights, and the rights of newcomers, particularly among the Catalan inhabitants of Barcelona, who wish for a Catalan majority and their own cultural hegemony.

Avenues for Political Voice and Collective Action Along Ethnic Lines

In the United States, avenues of political voice and organization that benefit from the legacy of the civil rights movement and the country's multicultural ideology aid the overall status of Latinos. Without having the largest voice of all groups, Latinos still have a political voice that is heard in the streets, in politicians' offices, and in the public sphere. The existence of a language around racial and ethnic discrimination as well as racial politics provides sanctioned avenues for political voice and participation. This is particularly true for Puerto Ricans and Dominicans. Mexicans are also establishing places for cultural and political inclusion in New York.

There have been some promising changes in French society and the creation of government agencies against discrimination (HALDE); as a reaction to the 2005 riots new associations openly advocate for people of color (CRAN organization of black French or the Indigènes de la République), and other groups advocate for a more diverse elite (Club Century 21). Yet, labeling these groups as *communitarists* works as a coded attack:

> This linkage between awareness of how race operates as a social construct to marginalise visible minorities and accusations of particularist intent has been used to reinforce the image of French universal exceptionalism against the demands of minority activists by framing minority demands as communitarianist intent. Communitarianism has become an effective discourse to delegitimise public inquiry into race-based institutional inequality and effectively minimises minority political agency. (Montague 2013: 220)

The French political system and civic culture discourages communitarianism (ethnic or racially based collective civil rights claim making) and thus robs disenfranchised migrants not only of political voice but also of collective action and social capital. Many unemployed Muslim immigrants and citizens are disenfranchised and distanced from one another and from the French mainstream. The lack of a legally sanctioned way to talk about group discrimination and cultural and religious differences in Paris limits the avenues for a political voice for North Africans. This is true particularly for disenfranchised youth, who often live in the *banlieues*. Groups and institutions that foster North African and Muslim association have been accused lately of aiding radical Islam; for example, the May 22, 2015, cover of the popular French magazine *Marianne* called ethnic and immigrant organizations "accomplices of Islamism." Articles inside the issue criticized immigrant organizations, left-wing groups, and Beur FM of threatening the French Republic by being open to Islam.

In Spain, by contrast, Moroccans in Barcelona have social clubs, friendship networks within and across national groups, and a moderate political voice as city residents. Moroccans in Barcelona rely on certain spokespeople to prevent stigmatization of Muslims in the printed media, and the Catalan government has instituted several policies and programs to include newcomers from Morocco while respecting and protecting their cultural differences.

Federalism

Different degrees of federalism and avenues for political participation along ethnic lines result in the use of different contentious repertoires by new immigrants and their offspring. The decentralization of policy making makes the objects of their claims more accessible for local groups, including minorities who undergo extreme difficulties to make their voices heard more easily than they could be in a highly centralized state where a distant and cold national bureaucracy must run everything, as is the case in France. The opportunity to organize along ethnic lines allows for avenues of cultural and political expression that create integration and political participation. Although not perfect, community advocacy is better than avenues for political voice that are closed to immigrants. Possessing individual rights and entitlements is not enough to have one's complaints heard through sanctioned avenues. This individualistic/statist approach to rights results in widespread and recurrent riots in France.

Contentiousness

As a reaction to the riots of 2005 in France, many observers noted that the French integrationist secular model was not working and that a more multicultural and tolerant model was necessary (*New York Times* 2005). If these suggestions were put into effect, the French citizenship regime would be moved closer to the liberal American model. For example, the Paris Institute of Political Studies (Sciences-Po) has started a modest "affirmative action" program (Descoings 2007). But it was a very controversial decision that was seen as going against the expectation to be blind to ethnic differences in France (Sabbagh 2002). For some this controversy highlighted the need for statistics to show group differences in outcomes (Simon 2004). For others, this represented the fall of this university. Racist and elitist criticisms included: "Mr. Director, you have made Arabs enter Sciences-Po"; "One should not mix"; "You have made the bed of communitarianism"; "This will be the boat people of Sciences-Po"; "You are making Sciences-Po into a [*banlieue*] university, with Arabs, drugs, and rapes"; "You will ruin the value of this diploma"; "This is a step backwards to the principles of French meritocracy" (Descoings 2007). Nonetheless, graduates from this program include success stories (Delhay 2006) and real exceptions in a system where graduation from a few elite schools is key to the elite reproduction (Bourdieu 1990). Since the affirmative action program, the perceived value of a Sciences-Po diploma has not decreased; for example, President Macron studied at Sciences-Po, as did François Hollande and Nicolas Sarkozy.

None of these groups is more or less contentious than the others, but they are all contentious in different ways. In France, centralism, the lack of avenues for ethnic/racial organization, the dearth of opportunities for informal and infrastate economic existence, plus the ideology of secularism all conspire to make the French Muslim pattern of contention sporadic, violent, unorganized, and antistatist performances that fit in with French historic contentious repertoires (Traugott 1993; Tilly 1986; Shorter and Tilly 1974; Crettiez and Sommier 2002). By contrast, in the United States, federalism, the established nature of organization on a racial/ethnic basis, the thriving undocumented economy, religious tolerance, and a more gender-balanced pattern of immigration make the Latino style of contention one of sustained, organized, nonviolent claims making directed at the state as an ally, which is in conformity with established American "civil rights" repertoire. The state may react to popular protests for migrant rights in a way that alters the nature of the citizenship regime. For example, after the use of Mexican flags in the immigrants' rights marches of May 1, 2006, in New York and other American cities, many media commentators, and later immigrant organizers, pointed out the divisive nature of using foreign flags. In quick response, the organizers distributed American flags in the following immigrant rights marches I attended in New York. This further Americanized these events and gave them a legitimacy that was then translated into the electoral arena, as communicated by marchers who chanted, "Today we march, tomorrow we vote."

Spain lacks both of these two styles of contention. Immigrants from Morocco come with little experience in political organizing and collective action. Despite xenophobic and anti-immigrant sentiments in Spanish society, proactive and protective governments both in Madrid and in Barcelona have learned from experiences abroad and created a model for successful incorporation.

Support for Migrant and Ethnic Organizations and Events

A symbolic, limited, and yet revealing way to measure openness to multiculturalism and immigration is to assess the amount of resources provided by a government to immigrants for cultural and social events. New York's historic Ellis Island is a contemporary symbol of immigration, and the city also hosts numerous events and parades such as the Puerto Rican Day Parade, the Dominican Day Parade, the Mexican Day Parade, and the New York City Immigrant Week. Although not all New Yorkers participate in these events, they are not surprised to see Fifth Avenue or another street closed for an immigrant, ethnic, cultural celebration. Events like this are simply considered just another aspect of the character of New York City and its cultural landscape, and, correspondingly, immigrants from all corners of the globe feel welcomed in New York City. As an observer noted, "They close off streets to traffic, and people just put up with it!" In addition, government resources are dedicated to welcoming immigrants via ethnic and mutual aid societies that are often at least partially funded through government grants.

In France, it is taboo to fund ethnic and race-based organizations as such. Certain organizations are funded for cultural activities not through ethnic or communitarian appeals but through funds provided for distressed regions (Doytcheva 2007). In this manner, the support of non-French cultural events is provided without favoring specific ethnic or religious events. However, this results in a lack of connection between spatially segregated ethnic groups and people from other parts of Paris. For example, I attended a street fair in the *banlieue* of St. Denis, just across from Paris on the other side of the *périphérique* beltway. It had stalls selling products from many of the countries of origin of the area's inhabitants. Although designed to celebrate cultural diversity, the bulk of the costumers were other immigrants and a few whites who lived in the area, not downtown Paris residents.

Barcelona's city government spends considerable resources on events designed to create appreciation for the cultures of immigrants within specific

Table 6.2. Organizational environment.

Dimension	New York	Paris	Barcelona
Model of integration	Laissez-faire; multicultural	Civic republicanism	Multicultural
Population composition	Multiethnic	Majority French European	Multiethnic
Legitimacy of minority religious and cultural practices in public	High	Low	Medium
Legitimacy for making claims on an ethnic basis	High	Low	High
Legitimacy of immigrant organizations	High	Medium	High
Legitimacy of ethnic organizations	High	Low	High

neighborhoods, as well as on large celebrations. For example, a Citizen Party is held on December 13; December 18 is celebrated as the International Day of the Migrant. On October 12, there is a commemoration of the first encounter between Europeans and Native Americans brought about by Columbus's discoveries, now celebrated throughout Spain as the Día de la Hispanidad, during which immigrant cultural groups from Latin America march and showcase their folk dances and costumes.

As Table 6.2 shows, each city has its own context of immigrant integration, ethnic politics, and expectations of immigrant integration. Support and funding for organizations closely parallels integration models; for example, by law, Paris could not provide funding for ethnic organizations before 1981. Particularistic associations receive less funding than others but there are place-based exceptions for high-need *banlieues* in the Parisian metropolitan region, as well as frequent exceptions for nation-specific cultural events in the name of universal values. The framing of associations around a unique immigrant community or an ethnic identity is viewed as suspicious (Bordes-Benayoun and Schnapper 2006: 202). Parisian officials and citizens prefer NGOs framed around class, neighborhood, foreign relations, diplomatic, or set as universal, that is, benefiting the general urban population (Doytcheva 2007).

Economic Incorporation

For the majority of people I interviewed, the main reason for migration was to seek employment. Before the economic crisis started in 2007, getting a job in the United States or Spain was not difficult. Before the economic crisis, the employment level for Latinos in New York City was very high, although Puerto Ricans sometimes suffered from negative racialization and were discriminated against in the labor market. In fact, employers in the service sector and restaurant industries actively seek Latino workers. A similar situation existed in Barcelona, where jobs for immigrants were readily available and companies in their countries of origin often actively recruited them. Not surprisingly, these jobs are not well paid by Spanish standards, but they typically provide enough to sustain the immigrant and still remit home between $200 to $500 dollars monthly. The unemployment observed in the data collected in Barcelona in 2007 and 2008 for this book reflects the already cooling economy, a major cause of which was the bursting of a construction bubble. However, access to jobs was more difficult in France, where there is chronic underemployment and relatively high instability in the form of short-term labor contracts in a society where long-term contracts and job security used to be the norm.

Since the crisis, getting a job has been harder across the board, and people have remigrated or settled for lower wages, but the relative employment levels stayed the same as before the crisis: Latinos favored in the lower end of labor market in New York and Barcelona, and North Africans overrepresented among the unemployed in Paris. Interethnic tensions may also be a bit higher after the crisis because native New Yorkers and Catalans may have a harder time getting a job than before the crisis. Yet left-leaning movements like the Indignados in Spain are clear that both natives and immigrants are affected by economic policies implemented by national governments (Castañeda 2015, 2012a).

Employment is an important avenue by which immigrants become incorporated into a polity. Economic incorporation into well-paying skilled jobs is the fastest avenue for cultural integration. Yet, the informal economy also plays an important role in the lives of immigrants and minorities. Economic informality may seem problematic and undesirable to the local government and host society, but it takes away much of the political responsibility from local governments for poverty, exclusion, and discrimination by providing much-needed money. Individual "hustling" to survive turns poverty and exclusion into supposed issues of individual moral responsibility. In contemporary public debates, it is easier to blame the "undeserving poor" than it is to look at processes of social exclusion.

New York's informal economy gives employment to the disenfranchised. In Barcelona, provincial governments have looked the other way as the size of the informal economy of "under the table" commerce and contracts have grown, largely as a way to reduce company costs after the oil crisis of the 1970s (Rius Sant 2007). In France, the state has more control over the economy, and there are relatively few opportunities for the French of Arab descent to engage in an informal economy, with the exceptions of Arab immigrant neighborhoods like Barbès or the small-scale drug trade in the *banlieues*. Hustling to survive, although stressful and risky, creates niches for immigrant integration and adaptation that the formal labor market and a strong welfare state cannot meet when discrimination and limited economic growth occur simultaneously.

These mechanisms of incorporation of immigrants into formal and informal economies affect their overall structural assimilation and sense of urban belonging. I argue that when political but not economic incorporation occurs (as in the case of some French-Maghrebis), it is likely to lead to disaffection and contention. On the other hand, when economic incorporation occurs without political citizenship (as is the case in New York), people may enjoy an urban belonging without the accompanying guarantees of legal citizenship, and their upward mobility is arrested. The role of unions, political parties, and other institutions in bringing these two forms of citizenship together is crucial. Before the economic crisis, immigrants in Barcelona enjoyed economic incorporation and some local political voice as registered citizens of the city. The fashion in which the local and national state and private institutions deal with minorities and new immigrants shapes the way they are integrated into their new society. Successful immigrant integration is therefore a context-dependent process in which the immigrants' agency remains important but is shaped by avenues for inclusion and participation that surround them.

Although work and income are crucial they are not the only things immigrants consider in deciding to stay in a new country. As a middle-aged Pakistani man, who had ten years living in Barcelona and who had lived five years in Paris before that, told me, "In Paris, you make 3,000 euros a month, you spend 3,000 euros a month. In Barcelona, you make 1,500, and you spend 1,500. It is the same, working to survive. But Barcelona is better because people are friendlier. In Paris, people are closed. They do not want to talk to anybody."

Undocumented Life

The "problem of illegal immigration" is often discussed in the US media because it is so widespread—around 11.9 million people in the United States were considered "illegal immigrants" in 2008, about 4 percent of the total US population (Passel and Cohn 2009). Despite the constant risk of deportation, life as an undocumented immigrant in New York is indeed possible. Through personal networks, niche markets, and other mainstream means, undocumented immigrants can have access to housing, credit, cell phones, and, most important, employment. The same was the case in Barcelona in the 1990s and early 2000s (before the economic crisis). Not so in Paris, where official documents are required for bureaucratic processes with the state, as well as when dealing with private companies and with landlords. These requirements increase rates of naturalization in France, where since 1981 there have been a number of regular small- and large-scale legalizations (Silberman, Alba, and Fournier 2007; Weil 2002). It is, therefore, not surprising that there are fewer undocumented interviewees in Paris than in other cities. There are some undocumented immigrants in France, exemplified by a contingent from sub-Saharan Africa who have gained media attention through the political movement of the *sans papiers*, those who are, literally, without papers (Siméant 1998; Castañeda 2009; Kennedy and Tilly 2008; Ticktin 2011). Despite the many regularization campaigns that the Spanish government has carried out, several Moroccans remain undocumented. Yet, the data show that this status does not have a large impact on their access to employment, education for their children, general government services, and overall gradual social integration (Rius Sant 2007).

The state's attitude toward citizens who organize on the basis of ethnicity (*groupness* based on national origin, culture, or religion) is a major factor in explaining integration and the avenues of political participation, contention, and activism (Hondagneu-Sotelo 2008). The immigrants' ability to exist relatively easily in an informal economy or without papers is an additional factor to integrate. Restrictive state policies against living unofficially in an undocumented status, as part of an ethnic enclave, or as part of the informal economy create constant fear of deportation, extreme stigmatization, and exclusion.

A state with a permissive attitude toward economic informality coupled with a tolerance for undocumented existence leads to a more stable pattern of ethnic organization and more institutionalized channels of political participation for immigrants. This is the case in New York and, increasingly, Barcelona. Although the lives of undocumented Latinos in New York City are not easy, they can still find their place and a certain political voice in what could be called a bottom-up organic way that is determined more through their social networks and economic conditions than through direct state intervention. Indeed, government requirements and the associated fees and regulations are higher for those who have or seek legal status than for the undocumented who ignore these bureaucratic requirements. Undocumented status, although increasingly costly in the United States from a policing and symbolic point of view, is sometimes more viable in terms of employment and small entrepreneurial ventures (*economic integration*). In contrast, being undocumented in Paris is economically costly because it places such immigrants outside the reach of most jobs, as well as outside the important welfare state and bureaucratic world, thus resulting in further relative deprivation. In Barcelona, irregular status, while problematic, is relatively without stigma. Of the three cities studied, precrisis Barcelona had the best access to labor markets and government programs for undocumented immigrants. Furthermore, since 1968 there have been more than thirteen cyclical regularizations of undocumented immigrants in Spain (Rius Sant 2007). By contrast, in the United States there has been only one large amnesty in 1986.

Social Integration and Belonging

Civil society and local socialization patterns foster processes of belonging and exclusion that get translated into different forms of cohabitation and contentious politics. Different social boundary configurations create parallel pathways of simultaneous exclusion and inclusion along different arenas and social circles.

Latinos in New York face exclusion due to their own or their family members' undocumented status. North Africans in Paris must fully integrate culturally into the Parisian elites' societal norms or risk being marginalized or chronically unemployed and excluded, despite their access to legal citizenship and social rights. Barcelona's city governments provide resources and spaces for immigrant collectives. Thus, employed Moroccans feel at ease in their new home and are optimistic for their children. In contrast, Latino immigrants in Spain complain about an unexpected cultural distance from the Spanish and, while having to adapt for a number of years, they also see cultural and economic opportunities develop.

In Paris, the major obstacles facing the offspring of immigrants to enjoying a right to the city are unemployment and stigmatization (Castañeda 2012c). In New York, obstacles include a lack of legal papers and low-wage salaries. In Barcelona, they consist of local intolerance and cultural stereotypes. Practical everyday citizenship, including employment, cultural rights, freedom of religion, avenues for political expression, and legal citizenship are necessary to fully enjoy a right to the city and the country where new residents live. These findings remind us how important everyday interactions, expectations, and a sense of belonging are.

Integration Processes Compared: Context Conduciveness to Social Integration and Belonging

Table 6.3 is a product of this relational study of migrants and their social environments, including habits and dispositions formed in both the sending and receiving societies. The difficulty of habitus adaptation to new cultures shows how probable it is for new migrants to successfully navigate their new societies given their premigration habitus. Contextual factors help explain immigrant integration and their mode of collective action and claim making vis-à-vis the receiving state. Table 6.3 sketches the local implications derived from national immigration policies and citizenship regimes on the social life of specific immigrant groups in Paris, Barcelona, and New York. The different forms of incorporation between and among immigrant groups provide important information about how and when political organization and collective action take place, and when they are not seen as necessary or feasible. Different historical, institutional, and cultural contexts lead to various types of political voice and participation. There is an interaction between agenda setting in public policy debates around migration issues and the claim making and political organization of immigrant groups and organizations.

Although some contentious events by immigrants may be widely reported by the media in a sensationalized fashion, the root cause of these actions is not always visible and may escape some observers of immigrant–native relations. For example, in Paris, de facto religious discrimination oppresses and isolates immigrants from North Africa, causing the French and some of its Muslim population to be caught in a downward spiral of friction and isolation from one another. If French Muslims cannot practice their religion and are not allowed to integrate economically and culturally under their own terms, then more contention will be the result. Barcelona has learned from other

Table 6.3. Findings from city comparisons.

	Findings		
Dimension	New York	Paris	Barcelona
Institutional integration and ideological preferences of the receiving state	Legality, ethnic-racialization, liberal multiculturalism	Republican, strong preference for cultural and religious homogeneity, secularism	Racial and religious homogeneity, Recently tolerant
Terms along which civil society can legitimately organize	Ethnicity	Class	Culture
Access to residence papers	Low	Low	Medium
Access to government services, including health care, education, housing, and welfare	Yes, when legal; partial access for the undocumented depending on city and state	Yes, when legal; minimum services for the undocumented and uninsured	Yes, when legal; Catholic charities and civil society organizations
Policing	Medium	High	Low
Economic integration: Access to job markets and social mobility of the first/second generations	Easy access to low-status jobs; little access to high-status jobs	Easy access to low status jobs; little access to secure jobs; little access to high-status jobs; easy access for the highly skilled	Easy access to low-status jobs/little access to high-status jobs
Path to citizenship before/now	Short (IRCA 1986)/long	Long/short	Short/long
Political integration and participation	Sporadic, reactive, local grassroots, transnational	High but fragmented, done at the individual level vis-à-vis the national government; lack of ethnic political clubs	Low; deemed as secondary and unnecessary
Migrant habitus adaptation	High	Low	Medium
Social integration and urban belonging	Medium high	Medium low	Medium high

experiences and explicitly has adopted some of their best policies to create an inclusive and multicultural city.

Economic incorporation is often granted to undocumented migrants in both Barcelona and New York, but not in Paris to unemployed French citizens of Algerian Arab descent. The current lack of avenues for political voice can result only in a more visible contentiousness among North Africans than

Latinos. In turn, this creates opportunities for many politicians to draw on common misunderstandings and rampant xenophobia, as well as blaming immigrants for many social ills to attract votes, instead of working toward greater civic unity, as more intellectual, conciliatory politicians do. For the latter, hard policy work is needed to escape the false conceptualization of migration as a zero-sum game, to work out accommodations that aspire to the moral high ground, and to find the most pragmatic solutions that benefit the largest number of people. Immigrant rights are always in peril, and, as in all democratic politics, policy reforms and outcomes of the struggle depend on the actions and positions of the actors in the field, lobbying, and contentious politics.

The political voice of these groups varies. The political voice of Latinos in the United States partly benefits from the legacy of the civil rights movement. Despite being a discriminated minority, Latinos do have a political voice that is heard in the streets, in politicians' offices, in the public sphere, and most recently as a voting bloc, which became widely recognized after the 2012 U.S. presidential elections. Nonetheless, white nationalists are using this language and these strategies to support the status quo of white supremacy. Moroccans in Barcelona have social clubs, friendship networks with compatriots and natives, and a political voice as city residents. In contrast, Parisians' distrust of ethnic or religious organizations takes away from disenfranchised, unintegrated migrants' political voice, collective action, and social capital. This also disincentivizes the formation of social clubs and large friendship networks. French citizens of Maghrebi origin speak fluent French; are familiar with French culture, history, and traditions; and receive benefits from the French state; I call this "objective integration." Yet, I found many unemployed French Maghrebi who lived at the margins of the French mainstream and alienated from one another.

Findings from the field stress the importance of material conditions as well as expectations and feelings of "subjective integration." The results show how immigrants' subjective understandings are at odds with the aim of national policies, integration programs, and theoretical assumptions. For example, Moroccan immigrants feel at home in Barcelona more quickly than Latin Americans do, despite their command of Spanish and the policies that openly give preferential treatment to Latin Americans over North Africans (Rius Sant 2007). Although Latinos are discriminated against less often than Moroccans in Barcelona, before migrating, Moroccans were expecting a

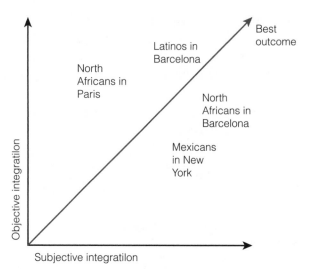

Figure 6.1. Heuristic graph of integration

much stronger exclusion and policing than they experienced in the tolerant and multicultural streets of Barcelona. In contrast, Latin Americans were not expecting to be made fun of due to their accent and manner of speaking and having to learn a new Spanish dialect—much less Catalan.

Another counterintuitive finding is that, despite lacking papers and social provisions, undocumented Mexican workers in New York often have better employment prospects than sanctioned migrants from North Africa in Paris. Although immigrants in Paris have better social provisions, citizenship, and rights on paper (objective integration), they report feeling disconnected from mainstream society (subjective integration).

Moroccans and Latin Americans walk the streets of Barcelona and engage in leisure activities among natives, European citizens, ethnographers, and tourists, thus making Barcelona their own. Moroccans in Barcelona and Latinos in New York tend to fare better than their North African counterparts in Paris do. Yet, the receiving contexts and the immigrant generation matter. This is in agreement with other literature comparing immigration to Europe and the United States (Alba and Foner 2015. 2016a,b); see Figure 6.1.

The best possible scenario for natives and immigrants' well-being and peaceful cohabitation is when structural integration and respect for cultural and religious differences accompany legal citizenship and its safety net and political rights. None of the three cities studied provides by itself all of these ideal conditions. However, doing so would prove most beneficial, not only for immigrants and their offspring, but also for the receiving cities and states, because it would allow immigrants to contribute to their new societies to their fullest capacities.

Given the comparisons discussed in this book, I argue that citizenship is complete only when economic, cultural, and political inclusion occur simultaneously. It is not enough for the immigrant to want to integrate; the receiving state and society must provide a welcoming context for a gradual integration and negotiation of cultural differences.

The systematic comparison between immigrant communities in different cities provides a wider perspective to see local immigrant integration in a larger framework. For example, while the bureaucratic and urban practice vis-à-vis immigrants in New York and Barcelona is one of cultural difference, the civic discourse in France is one of equality. Yet one of the main grievances of the children of North Africans living in Paris is how the official and educational discourse of equality and fraternity differs from their everyday experiences of discrimination and exclusion in the streets and the labor market. This shows how policy intentions and official discourses may differ widely from integration outcomes and immigrant perceptions.

By taking the point of view of immigrants as indicators of social mobility, I found that on the ground, tolerance of cultural differences is much more conducive to economic, political, and social integration. Comparing immigrants' urban belonging in these three cities shows that a multicultural arrangement is much more successful in integrating people into their new cities than one emphasizing equality but failing to deliver it.

Objective Conditions and Subjective Evaluations of Integration: A Path Forward

Immigrant is a categorical name given by elites to a portion of the working class. Giving immigrants access to universal programs is the best way to avoid criticisms of preferential treatment or exclusion and not to pit native-born, working-class individuals with foreign-born workers. Immigrants are one type of city residents, so what is good for all residents (high quality public education, public parks, affordable public transportation, access to affordable housing) is beneficial for immigrant integration; conversely, what is good for migrants is good for city residents (compliance with minimum-wage laws, participation in social security programs).

The objective economic situation for the average Latino immigrant in the United States is one of hard work for an income that typically fails to suffice for all the needs, plans, and aspirations of new immigrants and their families. Thus, transnational families are formed, with some family members remaining left behind in the country of origin and workers sending remittances. The transnational family often lives in limbo both economically and legally (Gonzales 2015; Castañeda 2013a), with a heavy emotional burden and gendered expectations and sacrifices (Hondagneu-Sotelo 1994; Hondagneu-Sotelo and Avila 1997; Castañeda and Buck 2011; Dreby 2010).

The objective economic situation of average Arab immigrants in France is often better, even when they are unemployed, than that of newly arrived labor migrants in the United States or Spain. However, the impersonal way through which these positive outcomes are propagated in France leaves many immigrants deeply alienated and with feelings of relative deprivation. Immigrants ask for a *French Dream*—an American Dream of unfettered opportunity served up *à la française*. Natives often forget the strong psychological challenges that immigration presents to the immigrants. An unwelcoming context of reception for immigrants prevents the quick assimilation that especially the French state and society expect in their Republican and integrationist ideal.

Given the current arrangement, many legal immigrants and their descendants are taken care of in terms of a minimum income and social housing by the French welfare state. However, rather than having a sense of urban belonging, feeling *chez eux* or "part of the family," some immigrants instead feel isolated and stigmatized. Interestingly, and maybe even counterintuitively, the direct connection with and identification of the state as the main provider of entitlements and social rights raises the demands and contentiousness of immigrants and the poor, as exemplified in the case of demonstrations for public housing in Paris. In this way, comparing citizenship requirements, public policies, and the objective welfare conditions of immigrant populations, as well as the expressed subjective understandings of specific individuals, assists us in discovering different attitudes, expectations, and contentious actions that immigrants and minorities often have vis-à-vis their society and state.

A multicultural model makes it easier to accommodate linguistic, cultural, political, and religious differences and paradoxically serves to further assimilate immigrants. Another interesting hypothesis resulting from this study is that the more space for active immigrant cultural life there is, the lower the level of actual transnational experiences is and the more incorporated further generations become. The data from Spain seem to prove this point: despite Morocco's closeness, interviewees were less likely to visit Morocco than French descendants of Moroccan and Algerian parents (Castañeda, Morales, and Ochoa 2014). Moroccans in Barcelona before the 2007 economic crisis felt an urban belonging, which overcomes the allure of self-identification based on the country of origin and thus results in a weaker transnational field.

In conclusion, immigrants in New York and Barcelona feel that they have more potential opportunities than Paris immigrants do, despite the actual economic benefits and welfare programs available in Paris. Objective economic well-being, especially through welfare programs, alone does not predict immigrants' happiness. Immigrants in the Parisian metropolitan area show more contentiousness, although they benefit from a strong welfare state. On the other hand, immigrants in New York and Barcelona are more positive because there are more opportunities for mobility, cultural expression, and interaction with locals. But they work long hours and receive low wages; many face deportation because of the federal unwillingness to give them residency papers despite being part of the urban social fabric.

Cities can learn from these experiences and promote policies of cultural tolerance, economic opportunities in the job and credit markets, and programs to help newcomers set up a home. Cities play an important role in providing urban citizenship and belonging (Gebhardt 2016; Smith and McQuarrie 2012; Però 2007). Based on my findings, policies that would encourage feelings of urban belonging among immigrants are:

- Fair seasonal guest worker programs, not tied to one employer, for economic migrants who wish to stay in their hometowns but temporarily have access to labor markets abroad.
- Provision of residency papers to immigrants with several years of residence in a city.
- Support for immigrant and ethnic organizations and events.
- Support for the education of young immigrants, despite their legal status, through initiatives such as the Dream Act, DACA, and DAPA (Castañeda 2013b).
- Normalized residential documentation and immigration status through regularizations and amnesties.

- Provision of safety nets for all.
- Increased affordable housing in central urban areas.
- Providing asylum based not on individual evidence of persecution but on sending-country conditions of insecurity.

Given their history and nature, cities can only grow or decline (Weber 1958; Tilly 1976). Receiving internal and international migrants is not a zero-sum game where locals lose. On the contrary, migration is key for the well-being of city residents. The Romans had a saying: *Ubi bene, ibi patria* (where one prospers, there is one's homeland), and my interviewees agree with this. Therefore, the most effective way to integrate migrants, and have them enrich the receiving societies, is to provide a welcoming context and equal opportunities. Urban belonging results in a positive dynamic that creates wealth and enriches the culture of the destination cities. The analysis of the many factors that make cities more or less hospitable for newcomers shows how complex the process is. The process of segregation and exclusion that makes immigrants feel less invested in the community's success and more alienated can lead to unemployment, violent policing, sporadic rioting, and generalized discontent and distrust. In contrast, the creation of cities that all residents can call "home" is good for newcomers and natives alike.

APPENDIX
Interview Instrument

Below is the New York questionnaire, which was translated and adapted to each of the field sites.

Nickname/alias	_____	Highest education	_____	
Gender	M F	Profession	_____	
Age	_____	Place of interview	_____	
Race/ethnicity	_____	Date	__ / __ / __	
Migrant generation	1st 2nd 3rd	[*Interviewer: Fill box after interview.*]		

1. Where were you born? (city, country)_____ ,
2. What year did you come to the United States?_____ / US-born
3. Where were your parents born? (city, country)
   Father _____ Mother _____
4. What year did your parents come to the United States? _____
   Father: _____ / US-born   Mother: _____ / US-born
5. Why did you [and/or them] migrate?
   Them _____   You _____
6. Did you [your parents] achieve this or see achieving it in the near future?
7. How did you [and/or them] come to the United States?
8. Why New York City?
9. Did you have family members or friends in New York City before coming?
   1) Yes   2) No
10. Would you like to live in another city? _____ Which city and why?

11. Would you like to live in another country? _____ Which country and why?

12. Do you think your life is better as a result of living in the United States?

13. Do you plan to move back to your country of birth [or that of your parents]? Why?

    1) Yes   2) No

14. Do you go back to visit?   Yes __ No __ How often? __ (times per year)
    How about your parents?   Yes __ No __ How often? __ (times per year)
    How about your siblings? Yes __ No __ How often? __ (times per year)

15. Do you send money back? Yes __ No __ How often? __ (times per year)

16. How much? _____US$ For what purpose? (education, medical) _____

17. How often do you talk to people in your country of origin?

Solving Everyday Problems

18. What do you do on a typical weekday?
    What did you do last weekend?

19. Are you employed (or unemployed)? For how long?

    1) Yes   2) No

20. How did you get your job?

21. Looking back over the past six months, who are the people with whom you discussed matters important to you? (List their relation to you, ethnicity, how often you see each other.)

Name/pseudonym	1 _____	2 _____	3 _____	4 _____	5 _____
Relation	1 _____	2 _____	3 _____	4 _____	5 _____
Ethnicity/race/origin	1 _____	2 _____	3 _____	4 _____	5 _____
How often	1 _____	2 _____	3 _____	4 _____	5 _____

22. Whom do you trust the most?

23. Whom do you go to for help/advice/support?

24. Whom do you ask for money when in need? Where? Bank Loan office Pawn Other

25. Whom are you closest to in your family? _____ In your life? _____

26. How often do you visit your family members?

27. Approximately how many friends would you say you have?

28. Do you practice a religion? What is your religion? _____
    1) Catholicism   2) Judaism   3) Islam   4) Buddhism   5) Protestant denomination _____ Other: _____   6) None

29. Are you an active practicing believer? (Please circle one)
    Yes   No   Somewhat
30. How often do go to your church/synagogue/mosque/temple? Is it in your neighborhood?
31. In which language is the service?
32. What do you think of your religious leader?
33. Do you belong to a religious/service group? [Bible group, catechism, evangelical, charity]
    1) Yes   2) No
34. Are you a part of any other social club (community organization, NGO, union, etc.)?
    1) Yes   2) No
35. What do you consider is your biggest concern about the future?
36. What is your opinion of the police in NYC?
37. Have you ever been helped by a social worker? Please elaborate.
38. Are you familiar with what social workers do?   Yes   No
39. Do you know where you could find one if you wanted to?"   Yes   No
40. Have you ever been helped by a teacher/professor?   Yes ___   No ___
    Please elaborate.

Intergroup Relations and Boundary Making

41. How would you describe yourself?
42. How would you classify yourself? 1) American 2) Foreigner 3) Binational
    4) Other _____
43. Do you feel like you belong to a community? Which one?
44. What do you think brings this community together?
45. With whom do you have nothing in common?
46. What is your rapport with these other people?
47. Do you have friends who are different from you (race, class, religion, nationality)?
    1) Yes   2) No
    What categorical group(s)? _____
48. Do you think different groups of people can get along?   Yes   No
    Give an example of: peaceful cohabitation _____
    conflict _____
49. In which neighborhood do you live? _____ How long have you lived there?
50. Do you own or rent (please circle one)? With whom do you live?

51. What do you think of living in your neighborhood?
52. How would you describe your neighborhood (ghetto, middle-class, enclave, etc.)? Why?
53. Who are your neighbors?
54. What do you think about your housing?
55. How safe do you feel in your neighborhood?
56. How often do you travel out of your neighborhood? Where do you go?
57. Have there been any riots or disturbances in your neighborhood lately?
58. Is there anything else about your neighborhood that you would want to mention?
59. Do you think the place where you were born affects your daily life? If so, how, and if not, why?
60. Do you think the color of your skin affects your daily life? If so, how, and if not, why?
61. Have you ever been a victim of discrimination?
    1) Yes 2) No Elaborate _____
62. Has the government ever helped you? If so, how?
63. Has the government ever hurt you or affected you negatively? If so, how?
64. Can you think of a change in the law that had a direct and immediate effect on you? If so, which one?
65. Have you had any encounters or problems with the law (criminal, civil, migration court)?
    1) Yes 2) No
66. Have you ever been unjustly stopped (detained) by the police?   Yes   No
67. Do you think there is anyone in the government on your side?
68. What do you think of the U.S. president?
69. What do you think is good about living in this country and what is bad?
    Good   Bad
70. Where do you get your news from? (circle all that apply)
    Newspaper (host country/   TV news (host/country)
    country of origin)
    Radio (host/country)   Internet (home/cybercafé)
71. Do you generally vote?   Did you vote in the last election?
    1) Yes 2) No   1) Yes 2) No
72. Have you ever participated in street protests? Please elaborate.
73. What is the (humanitarian) cause that you care the most about?

Family structure information					
	Age	Race/ ethnicity	Highest education	Profession	Country of residence
Self					
Partner (specify type)					
Father					
Mother					
Sons					
Daughters					
Others					

Family budget			
	Monthly costs ("host" country)	Monthly cost ("home" country)	Notes
Rent			
Food			
Entertainment			
Other			

74. How has the current economic crisis affected your job/business/household economy?
75. What did you think about this survey? Does it represent the main aspects of your experience?
76. What do you think about your social position in the United States/place in American society?
77. What did you use to do back home? Did you have a job/profession? Which one? _____
78. Would like to add anything else?

Thank you very much for your help!

References

Abdelhady, Dalia. 2008. "Representing the Homeland: Lebanese Diasporic Notions of Home and Return in a Global Context." *Cultural Dynamics* 20(1): 53–72.

———. 2011. *The Lebanese Diaspora: The Arab Immigrant Experience in Montreal, New York, and Paris.* New York: New York University Press.

Adams, William James. 2006. "Review of *France in Crisis: Welfare, Inequality and Globalization since 1980* by Timothy B. Smith." *Journal of Economic Literature* 44(2): 458–459.

Adida, Claire L., David D. Laitin, and Marie-Anne Valfort. 2016. *Why Muslim Integration Fails in Christian-Heritage Societies.* Cambridge, MA: Harvard University Press.

Ajuntament de Barcelona, 2017. "La Població Estrangera a Barcelona Gener 2017." *Informed Estadístics.* Barcelona: Departament d'Estadística.

Alba, Richard D. 2009. *Blurring the Color Line: The New Chance for a More Integrated America.* Cambridge, MA: Harvard University Press.

Alba, Richard D., and Nancy Foner. 2009. "Entering the Precincts of Power: Do National Differences Matter for Immigrant Minority Political Representation?" In *Bringing Outsiders In: Transatlantic Perspectives on Immigrant Political Incorporation*, edited by Jennifer L. Hochschild and John H. Mollenkopf. Ithaca, NY: Cornell University Press.

———. 2014. "Comparing Immigrant Integration in North America and Western Europe: How Much Do the Grand Narratives Tell Us?" *International Migration Review* 48: S263–S291.

———. 2015. *Strangers No More: Immigration and the Challenges of Integration in North America and Western Europe.* Princeton, NJ: Princeton University Press.

——. 2016a. "Integration's Challenges and Opportunities in the Wealthy West." *Journal of Ethnic and Migration Studies* 42(1): 3–22.

——. 2016b. "Strangers No More: A Rejoinder." *Ethnic and Racial Studies*: 1–9.

Alba, Richard D., and Victor Nee. 2003. *Remaking the American Mainstream: Assimilation and Contemporary Immigration*. Cambridge, MA: Harvard University Press.

Almaguer, Tomás. 1994. *Racial Fault Lines: The Historical Origins of White Supremacy in California*. Berkeley, CA: University of California Press.

Amara, Fadela, and Sylvia Zappi. 2006. *Breaking the Silence: French Women's Voices from the Ghetto*. Berkeley: University of California Press.

Amrani, Younes, and Stéphane Beaud. 2004. *Pays de Malheur! Un jeune de cité écrit à un sociologue, Cahiers libres*. Paris: La Découverte.

Anderson, Benedict. 1983. *Imagined Communities: Reflections on the Origin and Spread of Nationalism*. London and New York: Verso.

Anyangwe, Eliza. 2017. "Brand New Macron, Same Old Colonialism." *The Guardian*. Available at www.theguardian.com/commentisfree/2017/jul/11/slur-africans -macron-radical-pretence-over?CMP=fb_gu.

Aparicio, Rosa, Carolien Van Ham, Mercedes Fernández, and Andrés Tornos. 2005. *Marroquíes en España, Colección Sociedad, Cultura, Migraciones*. Madrid: Universidad Pontificia Comillas.

Appiah, Anthony. 2006. *Cosmopolitanism: Ethics in a World of Strangers: Issues of Our Time*. New York: W. W. Norton & Co.

Aragón Medina, Jorge, Alba Artiaga Leiras, Mohammed A. Haidour, Alicia Martínez Poza, and Fernando Rocha Sánchez. 2009. *Las Políticas Locales para la Integración de los Inmigrantes y la Participación de los Agentes Sociales*. Madrid: Catarata.

Aranda, Elizabeth M. 2008. "Class Backgrounds, Modes of Incorporation, and Puerto Ricans' Pathways into the Transnational Professional Workforce." *American Behavioral Scientist* 52(3): 426–456.

Armenta, Amada. 2015. "Between Public Service and Social Control: Policing Dilemmas in the Era of Immigration Enforcement." *Social Problems*: 16.

Astor, Avi. 2009. "'¡Mezquita No!': The Origins of Mosque Opposition in Spain." *Grup de Recerca Interdisciplinari en Immigració: UPF Working Paper* Series 3. Barcelona: Universitat Pompeu Fabra.

——. 2016. "Social Position and Place-Protective Action in a New Immigration Context: Understanding Anti-Mosque Campaigns in Catalonia." *International Migration Review* 50(1): 95–132.

Astor, Avi, and Mar Griera. 2016. La Gestión de la Diversidad Religiosa en la España Contemporánea. In *Anuario CIDOB de la Inmigración 2015–2016*. Barcelona: CIDOB.

Bail, Christopher. 2014. *Terrified: How Anti-Muslim Fringe Organizations Became Mainstream*. Princeton, NJ: Princeton University Press.

———. 2008. "The Configuration of Symbolic Boundaries against Immigrants in Europe." *American Sociological Review* 73(1): 37–59.

Bakkach El Aamrani, Mostafa. 2009. "Somos españoles," edited by La Ruta: La Voz del Partido Renacimiento y Unión de España (PRUNE). Ceuta, España.

Baldwin, Peter. 2009. *The Narcissism of Minor Differences: How America and Europe Are Alike*. Oxford, UK: Oxford University Press.

Balibar, Etienne. 2004. *We, the People of Europe? Reflections on Transnational Citizenship*. Princeton, NJ: Princeton University Press.

Barsali, Nora, François-Xavier Freland, and Anne-Marie Vincent. 2003. *Générations Beurs: Français à Part Entière, Série Monde/Français d'ailleurs, peuple d'ici*. Paris: Autrement.

Bawer, Bruce. 2006. *While Europe Slept: How Radical Islam Is Destroying the West from Within*. New York: Doubleday.

BBC. 2009. "The Moorish Conquest of Spain." Retrieved in April 2010 from www.bbc.co.uk/dna/h2g2/A30481652.

Beaman, Jean. 2017. *Citizen Outsider: Children of North African Immigrants in France*. Oakland: University of California Press.

Bean, Frank D., Susan K. Brown, and James D. Bachmeier. 2015. *Parents without Papers: The Progress and Pitfalls of Mexican American Integration*. New York: Russell Sage Foundation.

Bean, Frank D., Susan K. Brown, James D. Bachmeier, Tineke Fokkema, and Laurence Lessard-Phillips. 2012. "The Dimensions and Degree of Second-Generation Incorporation in US and European Cities: A Comparative Study of Inclusion and Exclusion." *International Journal of Comparative Sociology* 53(3): 181–209.

Beaud, Stéphane, and Michel Pialoux. 2006. "Racisme Ouvrier ou Mépris de Classe? Retour sur une Enquete de Terrain." In *De la question sociale à la question raciale? représenter la société française*, edited by Didier Fassin and Eric Fassin. Paris: La Découverte.

Bellah, Robert Neelly, and Phillip E. Hammond. 1980. *Varieties of Civil Religion*. Eugene, OR: Wipf & Stock.

Ben Jelloun, Tahar. 1977. *La plus haute des solitudes*. Paris: Seuil.

Benson, Rodney. 2013. *Shaping Immigration News: A French–American Comparison*. New York: Cambridge University Press.

Bergad, Laird W. 2013. Demographic, Economic and Social Transformations in the Mexican-Origin Population of the New York City Metropolitan Area, 1990–2010. In *Latino Data Project: Report 49*. New York: Center for Latin American, Caribbean & Latino Studies, Graduate Center, City University of New York.

Bernstein, Nina. 2007. "A Mexican Baby Boom in New York Shows the Strength of a New Immigrant Group." *The New York Times*, June 4.

Berry, John W., Jean S Phinney, David L Sam, and Paul Vedder. 2006. "Immigrant Youth: Acculturation, Identity, and Adaptation." *Applied Psychology* 55(3): 303–332.

Bertossi, Christophe, Jan Willem Duyvendak, and Peter Scholten. 2015. "The Coproduction of National Models of Integration: A View from France and the Netherlands." In *Integrating Immigrants in Europe: Research-Policy Dialogues*, edited by Peter Scholten, Han Entzinger, Rinus Penninx, and Stijn Verbeek, 59–76. Cham, Switzerland: Springer International Publishing.

Besserer, Federico. 2004. *Topografías Transnacionales: Hacia una Geografía de la Vida Transnacional*. México DF, México: Universidad Autónoma Metropolitana, Iztapalapa; Plaza y Valdez Editores.

Bezunartea, Patricia, José Manuel López, and Laura Tedesco. 2009. "Muslims in Spain and Islamic Religious Radicalism." Policy Working Paper 8, MICROCON. Brighton, UK: University of Sussex.

Bloemraad, Irene. 2006a. "Becoming a Citizen in the United States and Canada: Structured Mobilization and Immigrant Political Incorporation." *Social Forces* 85(2): 667–695.

———. 2006b. *Becoming a Citizen: Incorporating Immigrants and Refugees in the United States and Canada*. Berkeley: University of California Press.

Boccagni, Paolo. 2016. Migration and the Search for Home: Mapping Domestic Space in Migrants' Everyday Lives. New York: Palgrave Macmillan.

Bohrt, Marcelo A., and José Itzigsohn. 2015. "Class, Race, and the Incorporation of Latinos/as: Testing the Stratified Ethnoracial Incorporation Approach." *Sociology of Race and Ethnicity* 1(3): 360–377.

Bonilla-Silva, Eduardo. 2006. *Racism without Racists: Color-Blind Racism and the Persistence of Racial Inequality in the United States*, 2nd ed. Lanham, MD: Rowman & Littlefield Publishers.

Bordes-Benayoun, Chantal, and Dominique Schnapper. 2006. *Diasporas et Nations*: Paris: Editions Odile Jacob.

Boubekeur, Amel. 2007. "Islam militant et nouvelles formes de mobilisation culturelle." *Archives en Sciences Sociales des Religions* (139): 119–138.

———. 2008. "Time to Deradicalise? The European Roots of Muslim Radicalisation." *The International Spectator* 43(3): 85–99.

Boubekeur, Amel, and Olivier Roy, eds. 2010. *Whatever Happened to the Islamists? Salafis, Heavy Metal Muslims and the Lure of Consumerist Islam*. New York: Columbia.

Bourdieu, Pierre. 1984 [1979]. *Distinction: A Social Critique of the Judgement of Taste*. Cambridge, MA: Harvard University Press.

————. 1991. *Language and Symbolic Power.* Cambridge, MA: Harvard University Press.

————. 1996 [1989]. *The State Nobility: Elite Schools in the Field of Power.* Oxford, UK: Polity Press.

————. 1998. *Practical Reason: On the Theory of Action.* Stanford, CA: Stanford University Press.

Bourdieu, Pierre, and Jean Claude Passeron. 1990. *Reproduction in Education, Society, and Culture.* London: Sage Publications.

Bourgois, Philippe. 1989. "In Search of Horatio Alger: Culture and Ideology in the Crack Economy." *Contemporary Durg Problems* 16(4): 691–649.

————. 2003. *In Search of Respect: Selling Crack in El Barrio,* 2nd ed., *Structural Analysis in the Social Sciences.* Cambridge, UK: Cambridge University Press.

Bouteldja, Naima. 2011. "Unveiling the Truth: Why 32 Muslim Women Wear the Full-Face Veil in France." In *At Home in Europe.* New York: Open Society Foundations.

Bowden, Brett. 2013. "'Poisons Disguised with Honey': European Expansion and the Sacred Trust of Civilization." *The European Legacy* 18(2): 151–169.

Bréchon, Pierre, and Jean-François Tchernia, eds. 2009. *La France à travers ses Valeurs.* Paris: Armand Colin.

Brown, Evrick, and Timothy Shortell. 2015. *Walking in Cities: Quotidian Mobility as Urban Theory, Method, and Practice.* Philadelphia: Temple University Press.

Brubaker, Rogers. 2004. *Ethnicity without Groups.* Cambridge, MA: Harvard University Press.

Bucerius, Sandra. 2014. *Unwanted: Muslim Immigrants, Dignity, and Drug Dealing.* New York: Oxford University Press.

Buchanan, Patrick. 2006. *State of Emergency: The Third World Invasion and Conquest of America.* New York: St. Martin's Press.

Burawoy, Michael. 2003. "Revisits: An Outline of a Theory of Reflexive Ethnography." *American Sociological Review* 68(5): 645–679.

Calavita, Kitty. 2005. *Immigrants at the Margins: Law, Race, and Exclusion in Southern Europe, Cambridge Studies in Law and Society.* Cambridge, UK: Cambridge University Press.

Caldwell, Christopher. 2009. *Reflections on the Revolution in Europe: Immigration, Islam, and the West.* New York: Doubleday.

Calhoun, Craig J. 1997. *Nationalism: Concepts in Social Thought.* Minneapolis: University of Minnesota Press.

————. 2002. "The Class Consciousness of Frequent Travelers: Toward a Critique of Actually Existing Cosmopolitanism." In *Conceiving Cosmopolitanism: Theory, Context and Practice,* edited by S. Vertovec and R. Cohen. Oxford, UK: Oxford University Press.

————. 2010. "Rethinking Secularism." *The Hedgehog Review,* 35–48.

Carpentier, Alejo, Benito Pérez Galdós, and José Ma. Blanco White, eds. 2008. *El Dos de Mayo, Tres Miradas*. Madrid: Fundación Dos de Mayo, Nación y Libertad.

Carter, Elizabeth A., and Monica McGoldrick. 1999. *The Expanded Family Life Cycle: Individual, Family, and Social Perspectives*, 3rd ed. Boston, MA: Allyn and Bacon.

Castañeda, Ernesto. 2006. "Los Minutemen en la universidad: el debate migratorio actual y los debates ideológicos pasados." *Estudios de Política y Sociedad* 2(3): 29–40.

———. 2009. "The Great Sleep-In: Demonstrating for Public Housing in Paris." *Progressive Planning* 178(Winter): 31–33.

———. 2012a. "The Indignados of Spain: A Precedent to Occupy Wall Street." *Social Movement Studies* 11(3–4): 309–319.

———. 2012b. "Places of Stigma: Ghettos, Barrios and Banlieues." In *The Ghetto: Contemporary Global Issues and Controversies*, edited by Ray Hutchison and Bruce D. Haynes, 159–190. Boulder, CO: Westview Press.

———. 2012c. "Urban Citizenship in New York, Paris, and Barcelona: Immigrant Organizations and the Right to Inhabit the City " In *Remaking Urban Citizenship: Organizations, Institutions, and the Right to the City*, edited by Michael Peter Smith and Michael McQuarrie, 57–78. New Brunswick, NJ: Transaction Publishers.

———. 2013a. "Living in Limbo: Transnational Households, Remittances and Development." *International Migration* 51(s1): 13–35.

———. 2013b. Waiting for Real Reform: How Half-Way Measures Leave Immigrants in Limbo and Deprive America of Their Talents. Cambridge, MA: Scholars Strategy Network.

———. 2014a. "The *Indignados* and Occupy Movements as Political Challenges to Representative Democracy: A Reply to Eklundh." *Global Discourse* 4 (2–3): 223–235.

———. 2014b. "The Socially Polysemantic Border: Positionality and the Meaning of the Fence." *The Middle Ground Journal: World History and Global Studies* 8.

———. 2015. "The *Indignados* and the Global Diffusion of Forms of Protest against Authoritarianism and Structural Adjustment Programs." In *Waves of Social Movement Mobilizations in the Twenty-First Century: Challenges to the Neo-Liberal World Order and Democracy*, edited by Nahide Konak and Rasim Dönmez, 11–28. Lanham, MD: Lexington Books.

———. 2017. "Transnationalism in the Lives of Migrants: The Relevance of Znaniecki's Work to Understand Contemporary Migrant Life." In *Contemporary Migrations in the Humanistic Coefficient Perspective: Florian Znaniecki's Thought in Today's Science*, edited by Jacek Kubera and Lukasz Skoczylas. Poland: The Florian Znaniecki Scientific Foundation.

———, ed. 2018. *Immigration and Categorical Inequality: Migration to the City and the Birth of Race and Ethnicity*. New York: Routledge.

Castañeda, Ernesto, and Kevin Beck. 2018. "Stigmatizing Immigrant Day Labor: Boundary-Making and the Built-Environment in Long Island, New York." In *Im-*

migration and Categorical Inequality: Migration to the City and the Birth of Race and Ethnicity, edited by Ernesto Castañeda. New York: Routledge.

Castañeda, Ernesto, Kevin Beck, and Josue Lachica. 2015. "Walking through Contemporary North American Barrios: Hispanic Neighborhoods in New York, San Diego, and El Paso." In *Walking in Cities: Quotidian Mobility as Urban Theory, Method, and Practice*, edited by Evrick Brown and Timothy Shortell. Philadelphia: Temple University Press.

Castañeda, Ernesto, and Lesley Buck. 2011. "Remittances, Transnational Parenting, and the Children Left Behind: Economic and Psychological Implications." *The Latin Americanist* 55(4): 85–110.

———. 2014. "A Family of Strangers: Transnational Parenting and the Consequences of Family Separation Due to Undocumented Migration." In *Hidden Lives and Human Rights in America: Understanding the Controversies and Tragedies of Undocumented Immigration*, edited by Lois Ann Lorentzen. Santa Barbara, CA: Praeger.

Castañeda, Ernesto, Cristina Morales, and Olga Ochoa. 2014. "Transnational Behavior in Comparative Perspective: The Relationship between Immigrant Integration and Transnationalism in New York, El Paso, and Paris." *Comparative Migration Studies* 2(3): 305–334.

Castañeda, Ernesto, and Cathy Lisa Schneider. 2017. *Collective Violence, Contentious Politics, and Social Change: A Charles Tilly Reader*. New York: Routledge.

Castells, Manuel. 2000. *The Rise of the Network Society*, 2nd ed. *The Information Age: Economy, Society and Culture*. Oxford, UK: Blackwell Publishers.

Castles, Stephen, and Alastair Davidson. 2000. *Citizenship and Migration: Globalization and the Politics of Belonging*: New York: Routledge.

Cea D'Ancona, Ma. Ángeles, and Miguel Valles. 2010. *Xenofobias y Xenofilias en Clave Biografica*. Madrid: Siglo XXI.

Centner, Ryan. 2012. "Microcitizenships: Fractious Forms of Urban Belonging after Argentine Neoliberalism." *International Journal of Urban and Regional Research* 36(2): 336–362.

Clare, Matthew, and Dalia Abdelhady. 2016. "No Longer a Waltz between Red Wine and Mint Tea: The Portrayal of the Children of Immigrants in French Newspapers (2003–2013)." *International Journal of Intercultural Relations* 50: 13–28.

Coll, Kathleen M. 2010. *Remaking Citizenship: Latina immigrants and New American Politics*. Stanford, CA: Stanford University Press.

Collins, Patricia Hill. 2010. "The New Politics of Community." *American Sociological Reviews* 75 (1): 7–30.

Cook-Martín, David, and Anahí Viladrich. 2009. "The Problem with Similarity: Ethnic-Affinity Migrants in Spain." *Journal of Ethnic and Migration Studies* 35(1): 151–170.

Coontz, Stephanie. 1997. *The Way We Really Are: Coming to Terms with America's Changing Families*. New York: BasicBooks.

Costes, André. 1988. "L'Eglise Catholique dans le Débat sur l'Immigration." *Revue européenne de migrations internationales* 4(1): 29–48.

Coulter, Ann. 2015. *Adios, America: The Left's Plan to Turn Our Country into a Third World Hellhole*. Washington, DC: Regnery Publishing.

Crettiez, Xavier, and Isabelle Sommier. 2002. *La France Rebelle: Tous les Mouvements et Acteurs de la Contestation*. Paris: Editions Michalon.

Crul, Maurice, Jens Scheider, and Frans Lelie. 2012. *The European Second Generation Compared: Does the Integration Context Matter? IMISCOE Research*. Amsterdam: Amsterdam University Press.

Daniels, Roger. 2004. *Guarding the Golden Door: American Immigration Policy and Immigrants since 1882*. New York: Hill and Wang.

D'Antonio, William V. 2007. *American Catholics Today: New Realities of Their Faith and Their Church*. Lanham, MD: Rowman & Littlefield Publishers.

Davies, William. 2017. *The Limits of Neoliberalism: Authority, Sovereignty and the Logic of Competition*. London: Sage Publications.

Dávila, Arlene M. 2004. *Barrio Dreams: Puerto Ricans, Latinos, and the Neoliberal City*. Berkeley: University of California Press.

De Genova, Nicholas. 2004. "The Legal Production of Mexican/Migrant 'Illegality.'" *Latino Studies* 2004(2): 160–185.

de Zayas, Rodrigo. 2006. *Los Moriscos y el Racismo de Estado: Creacón, Persecución y Deportación (1499–1612)*. Córdoba: Almuzara.

Dear, Michael J. 2013. *Why Walls Won't Work: Repairing the US–Mexico Divide*. New York: Oxford University Press.

Delhay, Cyril. 2006. *Promotion ZEP: Des Quartiers à Sciences Po*. Paris: Hachette Littératures.

Deltombe, Thomas. 2005. *L'Islam Imaginaire: la Construction Médiatique de l'Islamophobie en France, 1975–2005, Cahiers libres*. Paris: Découverte.

Demetriou, Chares. 2012. "Processual Comparative Sociology: Building on the Approach of Charles Tilly." *Sociological Theory* 30(1): 51–65.

Dendoune, Nadir. 2007. *Lettre Ouvert a un Fils d'Immigre: Cher Sarko*. Paris: Danger Public.

Descoings, Richard. 2007. *Sciences Po: De La Courneuve à Shanghai*. Paris: Presses de la Fondation Nationale des Sciences Politiques.

Díez Medrano, Juan. 1994. "Patterns of Development and Nationalism: Basque and Catalan Nationalism before the Spanish Civil War." *Theory and Society* 23(4): 541–569.

Dolgon, Corey. 2005. *The End of the Hamptons: Scenes from the Class Struggle in America's Paradise*. New York: New York University Press.

Doytcheva, Milena. 2007. *Une Discrimination Positive à la Française: Ethnicité et Territoire dans les Politiques de la Ville.* Paris: La Découverte.

Dreby, Joanna. 2010. *Divided by Borders: Mexican Migrants and Their Children.* Berkeley: University of California Press.

———. 2015. *Everyday Illegal: When Policies Undermine Immigrant Families.* Berkeley: University of California Press.

Durkheim, Émile. 1893. *De la Division du Travail Social: étude sur l'organisation des sociétés supérieures.* Paris: F. Alcan.

Düvell, Franck, Anna Triandafyllidou, and Bastian Vollmer. 2010. "Ethical Issues in Irregular Migration Research in Europe." *Population, Space and Place* 16(3): 227–239.

Duyvendak, Jan Willem. 2011. *The Politics of Home: Belonging and Nostalgia in Europe and the United States.* London: Springer.

Duyvendak, Jan Willem, Peter Geschiere, and Evelien Tonkens. 2016. *The Culturalization of Citizenship: Belonging and Polarization in a Globalizing World.* London: Palgrave Macmillan.

EFE. 2009. "Dos alcaldes y 85 concejales de los 8,112 ayuntamientos son extranjeros." *El Mundo,* August 7. Available at www.elmundo.es/elmundo/2009/08/07/espana /1249643521.html.

Ersanilli, Evelyn, and Ruud Koopmans. 2011. "Do Immigrant Integration Policies Matter? A Three-Country Comparison among Turkish Immigrants." *West European Politics* 34(2): 208–234.

Espiritu, Yen Le. 1992. *Asian American Panethnicity: Bridging institutions and identities.* Philadelphia, PA: Temple University Press.

Fassin, Didier, and Eric Fassin, eds. 2006. *De la Question Sociale à la Question Raciale? Représenter la Société Française.* Paris: La Découverte.

Favell, Adrian. 2016. *Philosophies of Integration: Immigration and the Idea of Citizenship in France and Britain.* London: Palgrave Macmillan.Springer.

Fernandez-Kelly, Patricia. 2008. "The Back Pocket Map: Social Class and Cultural Capital as Transferable Assets in the Advancement of Second-Generation Immigrants." *The Annals of the American Academy of Political and Social Science* 620(1): 116–137.

Fibbi, Rosita, and Philippe Wanner. 2008. "Labour Market TIES Project; Turkish and Autochthonous Ancestry Groups in Switzerland, Germany, France and the Netherlands." TIES Academic Conference, Amsterdam, Netherlands, December 13.

Filali, Abdellatif. 2008. *Le Maroc et le Monde Arabe.* Paris: Scali.

Fitzgerald, David. 2009a. *A Nation of Emigrants: How Mexico Manages Its Migration.* Berkeley: University of California Press.

———. 2009b. "Uncovering the Emigration Policies of the Catholic Church in Mexico." Migration Policy Institute; retrieved on June 12,from www.migration information.org/Feature/display.cfm?ID=729.

FitzGerald, David, and David Cook-Martin. 2014. *Culling the Masses: The Democratic Origins of Racist Immigration Policy in the Americas*. Cambridge, MA: Harvard University Press.

Flesler, Daniela. 2010. *The Return of the Moor: Spanish Responses to Contemporary Moroccan Immigration*. West Lafayette, IN: Purdue University Press.

Flores-Yeffal, Nadia Y. 2018. "Migration-Trust Networks: Unveiling the Social Networks of International Migration." in *Immigration and Categorical Inequality: Migration to the City and the Birth of Race and Ethnicity*, edited by E. Castañeda. New York: Routledge.

Foner, Nancy. 2013. *One out of Three: Immigrant New York in the Twenty-First Century*. New York: Columbia University Press.

Foner, Nancy, Jan Rath, Jan Willem Duyvendak, and Rogier van Reekum. 2014. *New York and Amsterdam: Immigration and the New Urban Landscape*. New York: New York University Press.

Fourcaut, Annie, Emmanuel Bellanger, and Mathieu Flonneau. 2007. *Paris/Banlieues: Conflits et solidarités*. Paris: Creaphis.

Fox, Cybelle. 2004. "The Changing Color of Welfare? How Whites' Attitudes toward Latinos Influence Support for Welfare." *American Journal of Sociology* 110(3): 580–625.

———. 2012. *Three Worlds of Relief: Race, Immigration, and the American Welfare State from the Progressive Era to the New Deal*: Princeton, NJ: Princeton University Press.

Fuentes, Norma. 2007. "The Immigrant Experiences of Dominican and Mexican Women in the 1990s: Crossing Boundaries or Temporary Work Spaces?" In *Crossing Borders and Constructing Boundaries: Immigration Race and Ethnicity*, edited by Caroline Brettell, 94–119. New York: Lexington Books Press.

Gabaccia, Donna R. 2010. "Nations of Immigrants: Do Words Matter?" *The Pluralist* 5(3): 5–31.

Gaïd, Mouloud. 2008. *Les Berbers dans l'Histoire: en Espagne Musulmane*. Alger: Editions Mimouni.

Gálvez, Alyshia. 2009. *Guadalupe in New York: Devotion and the Struggle for Citizenship Rights among Mexican Immigrants*. New York: New York University.

Gans, Herbert J. 2017. *The Levittowners: Ways of Life and Politics in a New Suburban Community*. New York: Columbia University Press.

García, Paola, and Jéssica Retis. 2011. "Jeunes et minorités ethniques dans la presse européenne: Les médias et les émeutes parisiennes de 2005." *Global Media Journal* 4(1): 77–92.

García de Cortázar, Fernando. 2007. *Los Perdedores de la Historia de España*. Barcelona: Editorial Planeta.

Gebhardt, Dirk. 2016. "Re-thinking Urban Citizenship for Immigrants from a Policy Perspective: the Case of Barcelona." *Citizenship Studies* 20(6–7): 846–866.

Geisser, Vincent, and El Yamine Soum. 2008. *Discriminer pour Mieux Régner: Enquête sur la Diversité dans les Partis Politiques*. Ivry-sur-Seine: Éditions de l'Atelier.

Gerstle, Gary, and John H. Mollenkopf. 2001. *E pluribus unum? Contemporary and Historical Perspectives on Immigrant Political Incorporation*. New York: Russell Sage Foundation.

Golash-Boza, Tanya Maria. 2015. *Deported: Immigrant Policing, Disposable Labor, and Global Capitalism, Latina/o sociology series*. New York: New York University Press.

Gómez, Laura E. 2007. *Manifest Destinies: The Making of the Mexican American Race*. New York: New York University.

Gonzales, Roberto G. 2015. *Lives in Limbo: Undocumented and Coming of Age in America*. Oakland: University of California Press.

González Alcantud, José Antonio. 2002. *Lo Moro: Las Lógicas de la Derrota y la Formación del Estereotipo Islámico. Pensamiento crítico/pensamiento utópico*. Rubí, Barcelona: Anthropos Editorial del Hombre.

González Enríquez, Carmen. 2014. The Price of Spanish and European Citizenship. Madrid: Real Instituto Elcano.

Goss, Stephen, Alice Wade, J. Patrick Skirvin, Michael Morris, K. Mark Bye, and Danielle Huston. 2013. "Effects of Unauthorized Immigration on the Actuarial Status of the Social Security Trust Funds." In *Actuarial Note*, edited by the Office of the Chief Actuary. Baltimore, MD: Social Security Administration.

Griffith, Robert. 2017. "Behind the Headline: Why Is Catalonia Vying for Independence?" *Cat Flag*. Retrieved in 2017 from https://catflag.wordpress.com/2017/10/22/behind-the-headline-why-is-catalonia-vying-for-independence/.

Guzman, Ralph. 1971. "The Function of Anglo-American Racism in the Political Development of 'Chicanos.'" *California Historical Quarterly* 50(3): 321–337.

Hackett, Conrad. 2015. *5 Facts about the Muslim Population in Europe*. Washington, DC: Pew Research Center.

Haenni, Patrick, and Stéphane Lathion, eds. 2009. *Les minarets de la discorde: éclairages sur un débat suisse et européen*. Crausaz, Switzerland: Infolio.

Hagan, Jacqueline Maria. 2009. *Migration Miracle: Faith, Hope, and Meaning on the Undocumented Journey*. Cambridge, MA: Harvard University Press.

Hajjat, Abdellali, and Marwan Mohammed. 2016. *Islamophobie: Comment Les Élites Françaises Fabriquent Le "Problème Musulman."* Paris: La Découverte.

Hellman, Judith Adler. 2008. *The World of Mexican Migrants: The Rock and the Hard Place*. New York: New Press.

Hoerder, Dirk, and Leslie Page Moch, eds. 1996. *European Migrants: Global and Local Perspectives*. Boston, MA: Northeastern University Press.

Hondagneu-Sotelo, Pierrette. 1994. *Gendered Transitions: Mexican Experiences of Immigration*. Berkeley: University of California Press.

———. 2008. *God's Heart Has No Borders: How Religious Activists Are Working for Immigrant Rights*. Berkeley: University of California Press.

Hondagneu-Sotelo, Pierrette, and Ernestine Avila. 1997. "'I'm Here but I'm There': The Meanings of Transnational Motherhood." *Gender & Society* 11(5): 548–571.

Houllebecq, Michel. 2015. *Submission: A Novel*. New York: Farrar, Strauss and Giroux.

Huntington, Samuel P. 1996. *The Clash of Civilizations and the Remaking of World Order*. New York: Simon & Schuster.

———. 2004. *Who Are We? The Challenges to America's Identity*. New York: Simon & Schuster.

INE. 2007. *Encuesta Nacional de Inmigrantes 2007*. Madrid: Instituto Nacional de Estadística.

Inequality Watch. 2015. "Poverty according to the Origin in European Union." InequalityWatch.eu, retrieved on April 15 from http://inequalitywatch.eu/spip.php?article158&id_groupe=19&id_mot=84.

L'Information Citoyenne. 2006. "Qu'est-ce que SOS Racisme?" Edited by Claude Perrotin. Paris: L'Archipel.

INSEE. 2012. *Immigrés en 2012 : Comparaisons régionales et départementales*. Paris: Institute National de la Statistique et des Études Économiques.

———. 2017a. "Département de Paris (75)." Paris: Institut National de la Statistique et des Etudes Economiques. Retrieved on October 12, 2017, from www.insee.fr/fr/statistiques/1405599?geo=DEP-75.

———. 2017b. "Population par Sexe, Âge et Situation Quant à l'immigration en 2014: Unité Urbaine de Paris (00851)." Paris: Institut National de la Statistique et des Etudes Economiques. Retrieved on October 12, 2017, from www.insee.fr/fr/statistiques/2874034?sommaire=2874056&geo=UU2010-00851.

Institut d'Estadística de Catalunya. 2017. "Població per Sexe Barcelona." Barcelona: Generalitat de Catalunya. Retrieved on October 12, 2017, from www.idescat.cat/pub/?id=ep&n=9122&geo=prov:08#Plegable=geo.

Jackson, Pamela I., and Peter Doerschler. 2012. *Benchmarking Muslim Well-Being in Europe: Reducing Disparities and Polarizations*. Bristol, UK: Policy Press.

Jiménez, Tomás R. 2010. *Replenished Ethnicity: Mexican Americans, Immigration, and Identity*. Berkeley: University of California Press.

Jiménez, Tomás R., and David Fitzgerald. 2007. "Mexican Assimilation: A Temporal and Spatial Reorientation." *Du Bois Review: Social Science Research on Race* 4(2): 337–354.

Jones-Correa, Michael. 1998. *Between Two Nations: The Political Predicament of Latinos in New York City*. Ithaca, NY: Cornell University Press.

Kasinitz, Philip, John H. Mollenkopf, and Mary C. Waters, eds. 2004. *Becoming New Yorkers: Ethnographies of the New Second Generation*. New York: Russell Sage.

Kasinitz, Philip, John H. Mollenkopf, Mary C. Waters, and Jennifer Holdaway. 2008. *Inheriting the City: The Children of Immigrants Come of Age*. New York and Cambridge, MA: Russell Sage Foundation and Harvard University Press.

Kastoryano, Riva. 2002. *Negotiating identities: States and Immigrants in France and Germany. Princeton Studies in Cultural Sociology*. Princeton, NJ: Princeton University Press.

Katz, Michael B. 1996. *In the Shadow of the Poorhouse: A Social History of Welfare in America*. 10th anniversary ed. New York: BasicBooks.

———. 2008. "Why Don't American Cities Burn Very Often?" *Journal of Urban History* 34(2): 185–208.

———. 2012. *Why Don't American Cities Burn?* Philadelphia: University of Pennsylvania Press.

Katznelson, Ira. 2005. *When Affirmative Action Was White: An Untold History of Racial Inequality in Twentieth-Century America*. New York: W. W. Norton.

Kaufmann, Jean-Claude. 2017. *Burkini: Autopsie d'un fait divers*. Paris: Les Liens qui libèrent.

Keating, Michael. 2007. *Federalism and the Balance of Power in European States*. Paris: OECD.

Kennedy, John F. 1959. *A Nation of Immigrants: The One Nation Library*. New York: The Anti-Defamation League.

Kennedy, Marie, and Chris Tilly. 2008. "They work here, they live here, they stay here!" *Dollars&Sense* (277).

Kepel, Gilles. 1987. *Les Banlieues de l'Islam: Naissance d'une religion en France*. Paris: Seuil.

Koopmans, Ruud. 2009. "Trade-offs between Equality and Difference: Immigrant Integration, Multiculturalism and the Welfare State in Cross-National Perspective." *Journal of Ethnic and Migration Studies* 36(1): 1–26.

Koopmans, Ruud, Paul Statham, Marco Giugni, and Florence Passy. 2005. *Contested Citizenship: Immigration and Cultural Diversity in Europe*. Minneapolis: University of Minnesota Press.

Kuru, Ahmet T. 2008. "Secularism, State Policies, and Muslims in Europe: Analyzing French Exceptionalism." *Comparative Politics* 41(1): 1–19.

Kurzman, Charles. 2010. *The Ummah and Transnational Islam*. San Francisco, CA: American Sociological Association.

Lacomba, Cristina. 2016. "The Role of Language and the Presence of Previous Immigration Cohorts in Immigrant Political Engagement: Ecuadorian Collective Action in New York City and Madrid." *Ethnic and Racial Studies*: 1–19.

Lacorne, Denis. 2003. *La crise de l'identité américaine : du melting-pot au multiculturalisme, Tel.* Paris: Galimard.

Lagrange, Hugues, and Marco Oberti. 2006. *Émeutes Urbaines et Protestations: Une Singularité Française.* Paris: Presses de la Fondation Nationale des Sciences Politiques.

Lainer-Vos, Dan. 2006. "Social Movements and Citizenship: Conscientious Objection in France, the United States, and Israel." *Mobilization: An International Journal* 11(3): 277–295.

Lamont, Michèle. 2000. *The Dignity of Working Men: Morality and the Boundaries of Race, Class, and Immigration.* New York and Cambridge, MA: Russell Sage Foundation and Harvard University Press.

Laurence, Jonathan, and Justin Vaisse. 2006. *Integrating Islam: Political and Religious Chanllenges in Contemporary France.* Washington, DC: Brookings Institution.

Le Cour Grandmaison, Olivier. 2008. "Colonisés-immigrés et « périls migratoires »: origines et permanence du racisme et d'une xénophobie d'Etat (1924–2007)." *Cultures & Conflits* (69).

Levitt, Peggy. 2001. *The Transnational Villagers.* Berkeley: University of California Press.

———. 2007. *God Needs No Passport: Immigrants and the Changing American Religious Landscape.* New York: New Press.

Lobo, Arun Peter, and Joseph J. Salvo. 2013. *The Newest New Yorkers: Characteristics of the City's Foreign-Born Population.* New York: New York City Department of City Planning.

Loch, Dietmar. 2009. "Immigrant Youth and Urban Riots: A Comparison of France and Germany." *Journal of Ethnic and Migration Studies* 35(5): 791–814.

Lucassen, Leo. 2005. *The Immigrant Threat: The Integration of Old and New Migrants in Western Europe since 1850, Studies of World Migrations.* Urbana: University of Illinois Press.

Mahé, Alain. 2006. *Histoire de la Grande Kabylie: XIXe–XXe siècles: anthropologie historique du lien social dans les communautés villageoises,* 2. éd. Saint-Denis: Bouchène.

Marshall, T. H. 1950. *Citizenship and Social Class.* Cambridge, UK: Cambridge University Press.

Martineau, Harriet. 1856. *A History of the American Compromises.* London: J. Chapman.

Martinez, Isabel. 2016. "Supporting Two Households: Unaccompanied Mexican Minors and Their Absences from U.S. Schools." *Journal of Latinos and Education* 15(3): 229–243.

Marwell, Nicole P. 2007. *Bargaining for Brooklyn: Community Organizations in the Entrepreneurial City.* Chicago, IL: University of Chicago Press.

Masclet, Olivier. 2001. "Une Municipalité communiste face à l'Immigration Algérienne et Marocaine Gennevilliers, 1950–1972 " *Genèses* 4(45): 150–163.

———. 2005. "Du « bastion » au « ghetto ». Le communisme municipal en butte à l'immigration." *Actes de la recherche en sciences sociales* 4(159): 10–25.

Massa, Mark S. 2003. *Anti-Catholicism: The Last Acceptable Prejudice?* New York: Crossroad Press.

Massey, Douglas S. 1987. "The Ethnosurvey in Theory and Practice." *International Migration Review* 21(4): 1498–1522.

———. 2007. *Categorically Unequal: The American Stratification System.* New York: Russell Sage Foundation.

———. 2008. *New Faces in New Places: The Changing Geography of American Immigration.* New York: Russell Sage Foundation.

———. 2012. "The Great Decline in American Immigration?" *Pathways* 9–13.

———. 2018. "Migration and Categorical Inequality." In *Immigration and Categorical Inequality: Migration to the City and the Birth of Race and Ethnicity,* edited by Ernesto Castañeda. New York: Routledge.

Massey, Douglas S., Jacob S. Rugh, and Karen A. Pren. 2010. "The Geography of Undocumented Mexican Migration." *Mexican Studies* 26(1): 129–152.

Massey, Douglas S., and Rene Zenteno. 2000. "A Validation of the Ethnosurvey: The Case of Mexico–U.S. Migration." *International Migration Review* 34(3): 766–793.

Mateo Dieste, Josep Lluís. 2003. *La "Hermandad" Hispano-Marroquí: Política y Religión bajo el Protectorado Español en Marruecos 1912–1956, Colección Alborán.* Barcelona: Edicions Bellaterra.

McMurray, David A. 2001. *In & Out of Morocco: Smuggling and Migration in a Frontier Boomtown.* Minneapolis: University of Minnesota Press.

Menjívar, Cecilia. 2000. *Fragmented Ties: Salvadoran Immigrant Networks in America.* Berkeley: University of California Press.

Metroscopia. 2010. *La Comunidad Musulmana de Origen Inmigrante en España.* Madrid: Gobierno de España.

MIPEX. 2014. "Migrant Integration Policy Index." CIDOB. Available at www.mipex .eu/.

Misra, Tanvi. 2017. "The Othered Paris." The Atlantic Monthly Group. *CityLab.* Available at www.citylab.com/equity/2017/11/the-othered-paris/543597/.

Mitchell, Timothy. 2002. "Orientalism and the Exhibitionary Order." In *The Visual Culture Reader,* edited by Nicholas Mirzoeff, 495–505. London: Routledge.

Le Monde. 2009. "Villiers-le-Bel: non-lieu requis pour les policiers." December 10. Available at www.lemonde.fr/web/recherche_breve/1,13-0,37-1102289,0.html.

Montague, Dena. 2013. "Communitarianism, Discourse and Political Opportunity in Republican France." *French Cultural Studies* 24(2): 219–230.

Mooney, Margarita A. 2009. *Faith Makes Us Live: Surviving and Thriving in the Haitian Diaspora.* Berkeley: University of California Press.

Moore, Barrington. 1966. *Social Origins of Dictatorship and Democracy: Lord and Peasant in the Making of the Modern World.* Boston, MA: Beacon Press.

Mora, G. Cristina. 2014. "Cross-Field Effects and Ethnic Classification: The Institutionalization of Hispanic Panethnicity, 1965 to 1990." *American Sociological Review* 79(2): 183–210.

Morán, C., and Quico Chirino. 2009. "Musulmanes de Granada impulsan la creación de un partido político nacional." Available at www.ideal.es/granada/20090216/granada/musulmanes-granada-impulsan-creacion-20090216.html.

Moran, Mattew. 2012. *The Republic and the Riots: Exploring Urban Violence in French Suburbs, 2005–2007.* Oxford, UK: Peter Lang.

Moya, Jose C. 2005. "Immigrants and Associations: A Global and Historical Perspective." *Journal of Ethnic and Migration Studies* 31(5): 833–864.

Nail, Thomas. 2015. "Migrant Cosmopolitanism." *Public Affairs Quarterly* 29(2): 187–199.

National Association of Latino Elected and Appointed Officials (NALEO). 2007. A Profile of Latino Elected Officials in the United States and Their Progress since 1996. Washington, DC: NALEO Educational Fund.

———. 2010. A Profile of Latino Elected Officials in the United States and Their Progress since 1996. Washington, DC: NALEO Educational Fund.

———. 2015. National Directory of Latino Elected Officials. Washington, DC: NALEO Educational Fund.

Nevins, Joseph. 2010. *Operation Gatekeeper and Beyond: The War on Illegals and the Remaking of the U.S.–Mexico Boundary,* 2nd ed. New York: Routledge.

New York Times. 2005. "While Paris Burns " November 8. Available at www.nytimes.com/2005/11/08/opinion/08tue2.html?sq=French%20riots%20November%208,%202005&st=cse&scp=5&pagewanted=print.

———. 2017. "In Their Own Words: Marine Le Pen and Emmanuel Macron." *The New York Times.* May 5.

Ngai, Mae M. 2004. *Impossible Subjects: Illegal Aliens and the Making of Modern America: Politics and Society in Twentieth-Century America.* Princeton, NJ: Princeton University Press.

Noiriel, Gérard. 2001. *Etat, Nation et Immigration: vers une Histoire du Pouvoir.* Paris: Belin.

Norris, Michele. 2006. "Coordinating Flags at Immigration Marches." NPR, April 11. Available at www.npr.org/templates/story/story.php?storyId=5336799.

Nuño, Luis F. 2013. "Mexicans in New York City." *Societies without Borders* 8(1): 80–101.

Nyers, Peter. 2016. "Incipient Cosmopolitanisms." In *Negative Cosmopolitanism*, edited by Terri Tomsky. Montreal-Kingston: McGill-Queen's University Press.

L'Observatoire National de la Pauvreté et de l'Exclusion Sociale. 2008. *Le Rapport de l'Observatoire National de la Pauvreté et de l'Exclusion Sociale 2007–2008*. Paris: La Documentation Française.

Observatorio Andalusí. 2010. El Islam en España. Madrid: Unión de Comunidades Islámicas de España.

Okamoto, Dina G. 2003. "Toward a Theory of Panethnicity: Explaining Asian American Collective Action." *American Sociological Review* 68(6): 811–842.

Organisation for Economic Co-Operation and Development (OECD). 2015. Indicators of Immigrant Integration 2015 Settling In. Paris: OECD.

Orsi, Robert Anthony. 2002. *The Madonna of 115th Street: Faith and Community in Italian Harlem, 1880–1950*, 2nd ed. New Haven, CT: Yale University Press.

Ospino, Hosffman. 2014. *Hispanic Ministry in Catholic Parishes: A Summary Report of Findings from the National Study of Catholic Parishes with Hispanic Ministry*. Boston: Boston College & CARA.

El País. 2009. "Condenado a ocho meses de cárcel el autor de la agresión racista en un tren de Barcelona." March 18, 2009. Available at www.elpais.com/articulo/espana /Condenado/meses/carcel/autor/agresion/racista/tren/Barcelona/elpepuesp /20090318elpepunac_11/Tes.

Parrado, Emilio A. 2012. "Immigration Enforcement Policies, the Economic Recession, and the Size of Local Mexican Immigrant Populations." *The Annals of the American Academy of Political and Social Science* 641(16): 16–37.

Passel, Jeffrey S., and D'Vera Cohn. 2009. A Portrait of Unauthorized Immigrants in the United States. Washington, DC: Pew Hispanic Center.

Passel, Jeffrey, D'Vera Cohn, and Ana Gonzalez-Barrera. 2012. Net Migration from Mexico Falls to Zero—and Perhaps Less. In *Pew Hispanic Center*. Washington, DC: Pew Research Center.

Paul VI. 1965. *De Ecclesia in Mundo Huius Temporis Gadium et Spes*. Vatican City: The Holy See.

Pedraza-Bailey, Silvia. 1985. *Political and Economic Migrants in America: Cubans and Mexicans*. Austin: University of Texas Press.

Pedraza, Silvia. 1996. "American Paradox." In *Origins and Destinies: Immigration, Race, and Ethnicity in America*, edited by Silvia Pedraza and Rubén G. Rumbaut. Belmont, CA: Wadsworth.

——. 2007. *Political Disaffection in Cuba's Revolution and Exodus.* New York: Cambridge University Press.

Pedraza, Silvia, and Rubén G. Rumbaut. 1996. *Origins and Destinies: Immigration, Race, and Ethnicity in America.* Belmont, CA: Wadsworth.

Peled, Yoav. 1992. "Ethnic Democracy and the Legal Construction of Citizenship: Arab Citizens of the Jewish State." *American Political Science Review* 86(2): 432–442.

Però, Davide. 2007. "Migrants and the Politics of Governance. The Case of Barcelona." *Social Anthropology* 15(3): 271–286.

Pew Research Center. 2007. Muslim Americans: Middle Class and Mostly Mainstream. Washington, DC: Pew Research Center.

Pew Research Center. 2014. *Religious Landscape Study.* Washington, DC: Pew Research Center.

Piore, Michael J. 1979. *Birds of Passage: Migrant Labor and Industrial Societies.* Cambridge, UK: Cambridge University Press.

Pineau, Marisa Gerstein, Mary C. Waters, et al. 2016. *The Integration of Immigrants into American Society.* Washington, DC: National Academies Press.

Pontecorvo, Gillo. 1967. *The Battle of Algiers* (film). Italy/Algeria.

Portes, A. 2007. "Migration, Development, and Segmented Assimilation: A Conceptual Review of the Evidence." *Annals of the American Academy of Political and Social Science* 610: 73–97.

Portes, Alejandro, Rosa Aparicio, and William Haller. 2016. *Spanish Legacies: The Coming of Age of the Second Generation.* Oakland: University of California Press.

Portes, Alejandro, and Ruben G. Rumbaut. 2001. *Legacies: The Story of the Immigrant Second Generation.* Berkeley: University of California Press.

——. 2006. *Immigrant America: A Portrait.* 3rd ed. Berkeley: University of California Press.

Portes, Alejandro, and Alex Stepick. 1993. *City on the Edge: The Transformation of Miami.* Berkeley: University of California Press.

Portes, Alejandro, Erik Vickstrom, and Rosa Aparicio. 2011. "Coming of Age in Spain: The Self-Identification, Beliefs and Self-Esteem of the Second Generation." *The British Journal of Sociology* 62(3): 387–417.

Portes, Alejandro, and Min Zhou. 2003. "The New Second Generation: Segmented Assimilation and Its Variants." *Annals of the American Academy of Political and Social Sciences* 530: 74–96.

Pulido, Laura. 2007. "A Day without Immigrants: The Racial and Class Politics of Immigrant Exclusion." *Antipode* 39(1): 1–7.

Quinones, Sam. 2001. *True Tales from Another Mexico: The Lynch Mob, the Popsicle Kings, Chalino, and the Bronx.* Albuquerque: University of New Mexico Press.

Rabben, Linda. 2011. *Give Refuge to the Stranger: The Past, Present, and Future of Sanctuary.* Walnut Creek, CA: Left Coast Press.

Reitz, Jeffrey G., ed. 2003. *Host societies and the reception of immigrants, CCIS anthologies; 2.* La Jolla, CA: Center for Comparative Immigration Studies University of California San Diego.

Ribert, Évelyne. 2006. *Liberté, égalité, carte d'identité.* Paris: La Découverte.

Rius Sant, Xavier. 2007. *El Libro de la Inmigración en España.* Córdoba: Almuzara.

Rosenberg, Clifford D. 2006. *Policing Paris: The Origins of Modern Immigration Control between the Wars.* Ithaca, NY: Cornell University Press.

Rousseau, Jean Jacques. 1913. *The Social Contract & Discourses.* Woodstock, Ontario: Dent.

Saada, Emmanuelle. 2000. "Abdelmalek Sayad and the Double Absence: Toward a Total Sociology of Immigration." *French Politics, Culture & Society* 18(1).

Saada, Emmanuelle. 2005. "Entre « Assimilation » et « Décivilisation »: l'Imitation et le Projet Colonial Républicain." *Terrain Imitation et Anthropologie* (44): 19–38.

Sabbagh, Daniel. 2002. "Affirmative Action at Sciences Po." *French Politics, Culture, and Society* 20(3): 53.

Sahlins, Peter. 1989. *Boundaries: The Making of France and Spain in the Pyrenees.* Berkeley: University of California Press.

Sainsbury, Diane. 2012. *Welfare States and Immigrant Rights: The Politics of Inclusion and Exclusion.* Oxford, UK: Oxford University Press.

Salas, Antonio. 2003. *Diario de un Skin: un Topo en el Movimiento Neonazi Español, En Primera Persona.* Madrid: Ediciones Temas de Hoy.

Sarkozy, Nicolas. 2004. "French Finance Minister Sarkozy Stresses Importance of Diversity." Columbia University Available at www.columbia.edu/cu/news/media /04/312_nicolasSarkozy/index.html.

Sassen, Saskia. 2001. *The Global City: New York, London, Tokyo,* 2nd ed. Princeton, NJ: Princeton University Press.

Sayad, Abdelmalek. 2004. *The Suffering of the Immigrant.* Cambridge, UK: Polity Press.

———. 2006. *L'immigration ou les Paradoxes de l'Altérité: L'illusion du Provisoire.* 3 vols. Vol. 1. Paris: Editions Liber.

Sayad, Abdelmalek, and Eliane Dupuy. 1995. *Un Nanterre algérien, terre de bidonvilles.* Paris: Ed. Autrement.

Schmalzbauer, Leah. 2014. *The Last Best Place? Gender, Family, and Migration in the New West.* Stanford, CA: Stanford University Press.

Schnapper, Dominique. 1991. *La France de l'intégration: Sociologie de la nation 1990.* Paris: Gallimard.

Schneider, Cathy Lisa. 2008. "Police Power and Race Riots in Paris." *Politics & Society* 36(1): 133–159.

———. 2014. *Police Power and Race Riots: Urban Unrest in Paris and New York*. Philadelphia: University of Pennsylvania Press.

Schult, Anne. 2017. *A Common Sense of National Decline: Populist Pundits and the Immigration Debate in Germany and France*. New York: Association for the Study of Nationalities, Columbia University.

Seidman, Michael. 2004. *The Imaginary Revolution: Parisian Students and Workers in 1968*. New York: Berghahn Books.

Semple, Kirk. 2010. "Immigrant in Run for Mayor, Back Home in Mexico." *The New York Times*, NY Region, June 1; available at www.nytimes.com/2010/06/02 /nyregion/02mexican.html?pagewanted=all.

Sennett, Richard. 1994. *Flesh and Stones: The Body and the City in Western Civilization*. New York: W. W. Norton & Co.

Serra del Pozo, Pau. 2006. *El Comercio Etnico en el Distrito de Ciutat Vella de Barcelona*. Barcelona: Fundación "la Caixa."

Shapira, Harel. 2013. *Waiting for José: The Minutemen's Pursuit of America*. Princeton, NJ: Princeton University Press.

Shepard, Todd. 2006. *The Invention of Decolonization: The Algerian War and the Remaking of France*. Ithaca, NY: Cornell University Press.

Shorter, Edward, and Charles Tilly. 1974. *Strikes in France, 1830–1968*. New York: Cambridge University Press.

Silberman, Roxane, Richard Alba, and Irène Fournier. 2007. "Segmented Assimilation in France? Discrimination in the Labour Market against the Second Generation." *Ethnic and Racial Studies* 30(1): 1–27.

Silverstein, Paul A. 2002. "The Kabyle Myth: Colonization and the Production of Ethnicity." In *From the Margins: Historical Anthropology and Its Futures*, edited by Brian Keith Axel. Durham, NC: Duke University Press.

———. 2004. *Algeria in France: Transpolitics, Race, and Nation, New Anthropologies of Europe*. Bloomington: Indiana University Press.

Siméant, Johanna. 1998. *La Cause des Sans-papiers*. Paris: Presses de Sciences Po.

Simmel, Georg. 1908. "The Stranger." In *Soziologie*. Munich: Dunker & Humblot.

———. 1971. "The Metropolis and Mental Life." In *Georg Simmel on Individuality and Social Forms*, edited by Donald N. Levine. Chicago: The University of Chicago Press.

Simon, Patrick. 2004. "Le rôle des statistiques dans latransformation du système de discrimination." *Confluences Méditerranée* 48: 25–38.

Simon, Patrick, and Vicent Tiberj. 2013. Sécularisation ou regain religieux : la religiosité des immigrés et de leurs descendants. In *Documents de travail*. Paris: INED.

Siri, Florent-Emilio. 2007. *L'Ennemi Intime* (film). Paris.

Skocpol, Theda. 1979. *States and Social Revolutions: A Comparative Analysis of France, Russia, and China*. Cambridge, UK: Cambridge University Press.

Smith, Andrea L. 2006. *Colonial Memory and Postcolonial Europe: Maltese Settlers in Algeria and France, New anthropologies of Europe*. Bloomington: Indiana University Press.

Smith, Christian. 1996. *Resisting Reagan: The U.S. Central America Peace Movement*. Chicago: University of Chicago Press.

Smith, Michael P., and Michael McQuarrie. 2012. *Remaking Urban Citizenship: Organizations, Institutions, and the Right to the City, Comparative Urban and Community Research*. New Brunswick, NJ: Transaction Publishers.

Smith, Robert C. 2006. *Mexican New York: Transnational Lives of New Immigrants*. Berkeley: University of California Press.

———. 2013. "Mexicans: Civic Engagement, Education, and Progress Achieved and Inhibited." In *One out of Three: Immigrant New York in the Twenty-First Century*, edited by Nancy Foner. New York: Columbia University Press.

———. 2014. "Black Mexicans, Conjunctural Ethnicity, and Operating Identities: Long-Term Ethnographic Analysis." *American Sociological Review* 79(3): 517–548.

Smith, Timothy B. 2006. *La France Injuste 1975–2006: Pourquoi le Modèle Social Français ne Fonctionne Plus*. Paris: Autrement.

Somers, Margaret. 2008. *Genealogies of Citizenship: Markets, Statelessness, and the Right to Have Rights*. Cambridge, UK: Cambridge University Press.

Spire, Alexis. 2005. *Etrangers à la Carte: l'Administration de l'Immigration en France 1945–1975*. Paris: Grasset.

Stepick, Alex, and Carol Dutton Stepick. 2009. "Diverse Contexts of Reception and Feelings of Belonging." *Forum Qualitative Sozialforschung / Forum: Qualitative Social Research* 10(3).

Stora, Benjamin. 2004. *Algérie: Histoire Contemporaine 1830–1988*. Alger Casbah Editions.

Suro, Roberto. 2005. *Survey of Mexican Migrants: Part One. Attitudes about Immigration and Major Demographic Characteristics*. Washington, DC: Pew Hispanic Center.

Telles, Edward Eric, and Vilma Ortiz. 2008. *Generations of Exclusion: Mexican Americans, Assimilation, and Race*. New York: Russell Sage Foundation.

Terrio, Susan J. 2009. *Judging Mohammed: Juvenile Deliquency, Immigration, and Exclusion at the Paris Palace of Justice*. Stanford, CA: Stanford University Press.

Thompson, Gabriel. 2007. *There's No José Here: Following the Hidden Lives of Mexican Immigrants*. New York: Nation Books.

Ticktin, Miriam Iris. 2011. *Casualties of Care: Immigration and the Politics of Humanitarianism in France*. Berkeley: University of California Press.

Tilly, Charles. 1976. "Cities and Migration." Center for Research on Social Organization Working Paper/I147, Ann Arbor, MI.

———. 1984. *Big Structures, Large Processes, Huge Comparisons, Russell Sage Foundation 75th anniversary series.* New York: Russell Sage Foundation.

———. 1986. *The Contentious French.* Cambridge, MA: Belknap Press.

———. 1998. *Durable Inequality.* Berkeley: University of California Press.

———. 2005. *Identities, Boundaries, and Social Ties.* Boulder, CO: Paradigm Publishers.

———. 2008. *Contentious Performances.* Cambridge, UK: Cambridge University Press.

Tilly, Charles, Lesley J. Wood, and Ernesto Castañeda. 2018. *Social Movements, 1768–2018.* New York: Routledge.

Torpey, John C. 2000. *The Invention of the Passport: Surveillance, Citizenship, and the State, Cambridge Studies in Law and Society.* Cambridge. UK: Cambridge University Press.

Torre, Wilbert. 2006. "Nueva York Recibe la Antorcha Guadalupana." *El Universal,* December 13.

Traugott, Mark 1993. "Barricades as Repertoire: Continuities and Discontinuities in the History of French Contention." *Social Science History* 17(2): 309–323

Tribalat, Michèle. 1995. *Faire France: une Grande Enquête sur les Immigrés et leurs Enfants, Cahiers libres. Essais.* Paris: La Découverte.

———. 2015. "Une estimation des populations d'origine étrangère en France en 2011." *Espace populations sociétés* 17(1–2): 1–26.

US Census Bureau. 2010. DP-1-Geography-New York City, New York: Profile of General Population and Housing Characteristics: 2010. In *US Census 2010.* Washington, DC: US Census Bureau.

———. 2017a. American Factfinder: Annual Estimates of the Resident Population April 1, 2010 to July 1, 2016. United States—Metropolitan and Micropolitan Statistical Area; and for Puerto Rico. *2016 Population Estimates.* Washington, DC: US Census Bureau. Retrieved on October 12, 2017, from https://factfinder.census.gov /faces/tableservices/jsf/pages/productview.xhtml?src=CF.

———. 2017b. "Quickfacts New York City." Retrieved on October 12, from www .census.gov/quickfacts/fact/table/newyorkcitynewyork,US/PST045216.

Van Hook, Jennifer, and Frank D. Bean. 2009. "Explaining Mexican Immigrant Welfare Behaviors: The Importance of Employment-Related Cultural Repertoires." *American Sociological Review* 74(3): 423–444.

Varela Huerta, Amarela. 2007. "Diez años de movimiento de migrantes sin papeles en Barcelona. Balance y perspectivas." In *Las luchas de los sin papeles y la extensión de la ciudadanía,* edited by Liliana Suarez, Macia Raquel, and Moreno Angela. Madrid: Traficantes de Sueños.

Venel, Nancy. 2004. *Musulmans et Citoyens, Partage de Savoir.* Paris: Presses Universitaires de France.

Vertovec, Steven, and Robin Cohen. 2002. *Conceiving Cosmopolitanism: Theory, Context and Practice.* Oxford, UK: Oxford University Press.

Volscho, Thomas W., and Nathan J. Kelly. 2012. "The Rise of the Super-Rich: Power Resources, Taxes, Financial Markets, and the Dynamics of the Top 1 Percent, 1949 to 2008." *American Sociological Review* 77(5): 679_699.

Wacquant, Loïc J. D. 2008. *Urban Outcasts: A Comparative Sociology of Advanced Marginality.* Cambridge, MA: Polity.

Waldinger, Roger David. 2015. *The Cross-Border Connection: Immigrants, Emigrants, and Their Homelands.* Cambridge, MA: Harvard University.

Waldrauch, Harald, and Christoph Hofinger. 1997. "An Index to Measure the Legal Obstacles to the Integration of Migrants." *Journal of Ethnic and Migration Studies* 23(2): 271–285.

Ward, David. 1989. *Poverty, Ethnicity, and the American City, 1840–1925: Changing Conceptions of the Slum and the Ghetto.* Cambridge, UK: Cambridge University Press.

Weber, Eugene Joseph. 1976. *Peasants into Frenchmen: The Modernization of Rural France, 1870–1914.* Stanford, CA: Stanford University Press.

Weber, Max. 1958. *The City.* Glencoe, IL: Free Press.

Weil, Patrick. 2002. *Qu'est-ce qu'un Français? Histoire de la Nationalité Française depuis la Révolution.* Paris: Grasset.

———. 2003. "Races at the Gate: Racial Distinctions in Immigration Policy: A Comparison between France and the United States " In *In From Europe to North America, Migration Control in the Nineteenth Century, The Evolution of States Practices in Europe and the United States from the French Revolution to the Inter-War Period*, edited by Patrick Weil, Randall Hansen, and Olivier Faron, 368–402. New York: Berghahn Books.

Willis, Paul E. 1981. *Learning to Labor: How Working Class Kids Get Working Class Jobs.* New York: Columbia University Press.

Yukich, Grace. 2013. *One Family under God: Immigration Politics and Progressive Religion in America.* New York: Oxford University Press.

Zolberg, Aristide R. 2006. *A Nation by Design: Immigration Policy in the Fashioning of America.* New York and Cambridge, MA: Russell Sage Foundation and Harvard University Press.

Notes

Chapter 1

1. The state is not a monolith; for example, some state agencies may help immigrants with food stamps, housing, education, and health, whereas simultaneously other governmental bodies may be more interested in surveillance and deportation. The state is a collection of ministries, institutions, and departments employing different bureaucrats, technocrats, and appointed and elected politicians—all with certain legal constraints and historical inertias. "The state" also faces internal pressure from self-appointed critics, opposition leaders and parties, interest groups, unions, and so on, as well as outside pressures and a growing discursive international human rights regime (Castañeda and Schneider, 2017: 71). Thus, a purely state-centric approach to immigrant integration will indeed overstate its influence on integration outcomes.

Chapter 2

1. I use only first names, nicknames, initials, or pseudonyms to protect the anonymity of interviewees, especially those undocumented. No identifying information was collected; therefore, respondents cannot be traced back for deportation.

2. But once the thirteen colonies gained independence from England in 1784 after the ratification of the Treaty of Paris, the new country did venture in aggressive territorial expansion. The borders between the United States and Mexico and other former British, French, Dutch, and Spanish colonies have been greatly redrawn many times, among them by the Louisiana Purchase of 1803, the Spanish Cession of 1819, the Annexation of Texas in 1845, the Guadalupe Hidalgo Treaty 1848, and the Gadsden Purchase of 1853 (see Gómez 2007).

3. Undocumented migrants can use an Individual Taxpayer Identification Number (ITIN) to pay taxes. Other undocumented workers use fake or third-person Social

Security Numbers (SSN); in these cases, the government withholds Social Security contributions from reported paychecks that undocumented workers are unlikely to collect. Government officials estimate that undocumented workers and their employers make a net contribution of over $12 billion annually to the Social Security Trust Fund (see Goss et al. 2013).

Chapter 3

1. They often prefer the term Imazighen (Amazigh in singular) instead of the commonly used term "Berber" because the latter derives from the word *barbarian*, used by the Romans to refer to all the people who did not speak Latin.

2. Contrary to the peace agreements in the 1962 Evian Accords, after the French left Algeria, many of the *harkis* who were not allowed to move to France and who could not find other ways to escape were killed. Estimates of the numbers of victims range from 50,000 to 150,000.

3. Although some people see Durkheim as sometimes emphasizing mental states and methodological individualism, which could be seen in his use of the word *anomie*, the origins and implications of the term are actually largely relational because an individual does not decide to be anomic but happens to be in that state due to fast social change in his or her surroundings and also due to a drastic break with previous relationships and familiar practices.

Chapter 4

1. Ships were rarely allowed to depart from Barcelona or other Catalan ports to the Americas during the colonial period. Therefore, few Catalans went to the Spanish colonies in Latin America and the Caribbean. Yet after the Spanish Civil War (1936–1939) many Catalan refugees, including influential Catalan nationalists, settled in Mexico and Latin America (Sobrequés i Callicó 2010).

Chapter 5

1. While I was in France some French would often say that they were Latino, too, classifying themselves as Latinos specially vis-à-vis Anglo-Saxon peoples. It is said that Napoleon was the one to first use the term *Latin America* in an overt attempt to curtail the influence and "the manifest destiny" of the United States in the Americas and the Caribbean –for which imperial France also had colonial designs and supposedly cultural claims going back to the Roman Empire expanding from Latium (Lazio, Italy), the original Latins. I use the term *Latino* because that was the preferred term used by my interviewees at the time in the United States, Spain, France, and Mexico. Thus, Latino here does not refer only to those individuals of Latin American origin living in the United States.

2. Some Moroccans participated in the bombing of the Madrid Metro station on March 11, 2004, but these events could be related more to the Spanish participation in the Iraq War than anything else. Most of the Spanish public opinion opposed Aznar's participation in the coalition forces, and President Zapatero announced the removal of troops after taking power. Despite widespread publicity of these events, this kind of participation in terrorist acts is very rare.

Index